T0284820

Women in the Valley of the Kings

Women
in the
Valley
of the Kings

*The Untold Story of
Women Egyptologists in
the Gilded Age*

Kathleen Sheppard

ST. MARTIN'S PRESS
NEW YORK

First published in the United States by St. Martin's Press, an
imprint of St. Martin's Publishing Group

WOMEN IN THE VALLEY OF THE KINGS. Copyright © 2024 by
Kathleen Sheppard. All rights reserved. Printed in the United
States of America. For information, address St. Martin's
Publishing Group, 120 Broadway, New York, NY 10271.

www.stmartins.com

Designed by Donna Sinisgalli Noetzel

The Library of Congress Cataloging-in-Publication Data
is available upon request.

ISBN 978-1-250-28435-8 (hardcover)
ISBN 978-1-250-28436-5 (ebook)

Our books may be purchased in bulk for promotional,
educational, or business use. Please contact your local
bookseller or the Macmillan Corporate and Premium Sales
Department at 1-800-221-7945, extension 5442, or by email
at MacmillanSpecialMarkets@macmillan.com.

First Edition: 2024

10 9 8 7 6 5 4 3 2 1

To my husband and son,
on whose toil most of my work has depended

Contents

Notes on the Text

There are always issues with transliteration of languages from non-Latin texts into Latin text, even with the best of intentions. I have tried to make the Arabic transliterations of places, names, and concepts as up-to-date as possible.

There are two women in this book who got married, and they changed their names when they did so. Kate Bradbury became Kate Griffith in 1896; Caroline Ransom became Caroline Ransom Williams in 1916. I have called them by their given names until they changed upon their respective marriages.

Women in the Valley of the Kings

Prologue

In January 2023, I stood on the East Bank of the Nile in the bustling city of Luxor in Egypt. It was dusk, and the sun was setting behind the mountains on the West Bank, casting a glow over the river and temples that people in this place have marveled at for millennia. I was at what is now ground level, looking up at the roof of the Amun Sanctuary of Luxor Temple, one of two major temples on this side of the river. Some thirty feet above my head, where my gaze lay, were the stones that made up the roof of this part of the temple. These same stones were at ground level 160 years ago, and they formed the foundation of the *Maison de France*, or the French House. Back then, the temple was full of mud, dirt, and sand that had been left behind from centuries of Nile floods. These remnants formed a hill that was about fifty feet higher than the ground at the river's edge, and almost completely buried Luxor Temple.

Before the Aswan High Dam was built in the 1960s, the Nile flooded once a year, bringing a predictable rhythm to life in the Nile Valley for millennia. This rhythm was so predictable, ancient Egyptians were able to reliably measure three distinct seasons: *akhet* (inundation), *peret* (winter), and *shemu* (summer). The inundation also brought fertile soil, which allowed for generally reliable agricultural products to feed animals and a flourishing civilization in an almost impossible desert. The flood would lay down layers of mud, making the landscape a palimpsest, creating a terrain that was constantly changing but also carried clear traces of its former self. The Luxor Temple is like the landscape—a constantly changing space that has retained the evidence of its original purpose. As the earth accumulated among the colonnades and courts over the centuries, a town grew up in the temple. A Roman fort had been built in and around the temple sometime in the third century CE. Later, a church was built on the ancient columns of the first court in the fourth century CE, then the Abu Haggag Mosque was built on top of that 250 years later. During the Middle Ages, villagers built pigeon houses inside the temple, so they had ready food, and their town remained for several centuries. The homes from the village were torn down and completely destroyed in the 1880s as part of some archaeological restoration projects that displaced hundreds of Egyptians.

I was looking up, trying to find any evidence that might remain of the French House. Built within the walls and on top of the roof of the ancient Luxor Temple, the French House was there by at least 1826 and was later enlarged by the French in the 1830s. The house was finally torn down in the 1880s, after half of it had been swept away in one inundation season years earlier. Between its building and destruction, the French House had been a temporary home to Egyptologists, military attachés, and travelers.

In January 1864, Lady Duff Gordon—Lucie—woke each morning to the sunrise peeking over Luxor Temple's ancient columns. She would hear the donkeys braying, dogs barking, and camels lowing. She wrote home to her husband about how she loved to sit out on her balcony and "drink the air" in the morning hours, until the sun's intense rays forced her inside.[1] The seating area had a broken veranda and latticework that sat above the mud-brick walls, and it was here that she wrote hundreds of letters back home to her family in London about her time in Egypt. In the evenings, on that same balcony, she sat watching the boats on the river as the sun set over the Libyan mountains.

She had watched from this exact spot. Separated by 160 years, and about thirty feet of elevation, I was standing right where Lucie Duff Gordon had lived her final years. Today, Lucie would still be considered young; she was only forty-one when she arrived in Egypt. Leaving behind her husband and three children, she moved there to nurse her own tuberculosis—the dry desert air should do the trick, her doctor said—and meanwhile she treated the maladies of the villagers, learned to speak Arabic, and taught the children

English. She became so immersed in the life and rhythms of Luxor that she constantly lost track of the days.

Her letters home were first published in 1865, and, in a time when women usually wrote fiction, the collection provided a glimpse into life on the Nile. In those days, when it was almost unheard of for a woman to travel alone, these letters opened up the idea of travel to Egypt for more Europeans and Americans—especially women.

In 1894, Maggie Benson took her first trip up the Nile. Not quite thirty years old, the serious Maggie was trying the same "change of air cure" to relieve breathing issues that Lucie Duff Gordon had tried, which had become all the rage at the end of the eighteenth century. Patients could be revitalized by focusing on new experiences in new places, which "cured" them of anxiety or listlessness. Also, if damp, cold, diseased air was the problem, as it frequently was at home in England, patients would be cured by a trip to the desert to breathe in new, fresh, dry air.

Maggie was the first woman to be given permission to excavate in Egypt. She had fallen in love with the country. Leaving the stress of her parents and life in England, Maggie and her younger brother, the novelist and archaeologist Fred Benson, convalesced in the Luxor Hotel, located just two hundred yards behind the Luxor Temple. The hotel's verdant garden was a restful place for Maggie, especially. It was a place where she could breathe in the sweet scent of flowers after she had wandered about the town. She wanted to learn more about the ancient inhabitants while living alongside the current ones. Maggie had to apply—twice—for permission to excavate at the Temple of Mut in the Karnak Temple complex, near the town of Luxor, but she finally got it.

A year later, Janet Gourlay, known as Nettie to her friends and family, captured Maggie's heart and joined the excavation, too. Nettie was slight, shy, and quiet, but kind, caring, and fiercely loyal to her Maggie. While most of what we know about Nettie comes from her time with Maggie, we know that these women unearthed hundreds of pieces of statues, cleared much of the temple of fill and debris, repaired broken statues, and replaced them in the temple.

Their publication, *The Temple of Mut in Asher* (1899), was and still is a crucial piece of scholarship about the site for archaeologists and general readers alike. Their travel to Luxor and their work there inspired more women to enter the field of archaeology in the twentieth century, and they came in droves.

Today, hardly anyone who marvels at the massive hypostyle hall in the Amun precinct of the complex takes the time to wander over to the Temple of Mut, a kind of way station on the Avenue of Sphinxes between the Luxor and Karnak Temple complexes. It is still a desolate place, surrounded by palm trees and mounds of detritus from the centuries. It is not easy to get to the Mut temple from the main precincts of Karnak. The signs aren't clear, and you have to buy an extra ticket as you enter the complex.

I made my way to the Mut complex, where the temple's inspectors were happy to see anyone come their way. They offered me a warm welcome with tea and biscuits. I sat in the shade with them to rest, then they showed me all of the Sekhmet statues—many of which had been put back in place by the crew Maggie had hired more than 120 years ago. The goddesses in black diorite (a type of granite) were surprisingly stark against the brown sandstone of the temple. I could see why Maggie was drawn to this place.

Myrtle Broome was also drawn to Egypt. From 1911 to 1913, she had trained in the top Egyptology program in Britain, at University College London, by UCL's top instructor, Margaret Murray. But with the Great War making work in Egypt difficult, and the fact that she stayed home to help her mother and father (not to mention that she was already thirty years old), Myrtle never thought she would actually get to travel to Egypt to work. In November of 1927, she and another Murray student, Olga Tufnell, were invited to work on a Middle Kingdom site called Qau el-Kebir. The tombs that had been opened there in previous seasons were deteriorating quickly, and talented, hardworking copyists were needed to record the art on the tomb walls. The work only lasted a few weeks, until late December, but Myrtle was hooked. By the autumn of 1929, she was back in Egypt, happy as could be to begin work with another woman artist, Amice Calverley, at Abydos.

The two women were supposed to spend a couple of seasons

copying the walls of the Temple of Seti I so they could be published. When they started the work, it seemed like it might go quickly, but it soon turned out they would be there for a while. Two seasons turned into a decade, then more and more time, until the final, fourth volume was published in 1958. There is a fifth volume that never got published. There is still more work to be done.

Each of these women, alone and together, has an amazing story to tell. Written over one another like a stratigraphy of heartache, happiness, struggle, and success, their accounts show how they overcame rules meant to keep them out of a discipline not built for them. Women played central roles in many major finds in Egypt, but their stories are rarely mentioned (if at all). Other histories tell us that men dug, explored, discovered, and theorized; women recorded, organized, catalogued, and corresponded. Men got dirty, had adventures, and excavated artifacts. Women, in fact, founded the institutions that would receive these artifacts and allow the rest of the world to see them.

The history of Egyptology should be told as the exhilarating chronicle of fascinating, passionate women who built crucial relationships with Egyptians and then wove together global connective networks. *Women in the Valley of the Kings* brings these women back into the spaces where they belong and tells their stories, often left out and, so, ultimately forgotten by time. They worked and explored and traveled. They dreamed and socialized and networked. Contemporary understandings of ancient Egypt would be radically different without them. These women made history.

The Grand Narrative and the Great Men

Egyptology seems to be manly men striving to seize the day—and the artifacts—for their competing homelands. They are remembered as conquerors of unknown lands and people, scholars who claim to understand a past that isn't their own.

The story of European Egyptology usually begins with Napoleon's heroic entry into Egypt in 1798 with his scientific and military expedition. The main purpose of the expedition was not only to capture Egypt from the Ottoman Empire so that the French could gain a new colony in their own growing empire, but also to collect information about the geography, politics, economics, and demographics of the area, as well as artifacts. This conquering army and their subsequent mission resulted in the sumptuous twenty-three-volume *Description de l'Egypte*, which was published over the course of thirteen years, from 1809 to 1822. This text introduced Europeans to Egypt and continues to be a foundational text in understanding the flora, fauna, and people of Egypt in the nineteenth century. *Description* was also an Enlightenment project: by recording and classifying people, places, and things, it allowed European powers to see just what was waiting for them if they could take control in Egypt.

Although British admiral Horatio Nelson fought the French Navy in Abukir Bay, Alexandria, almost from the day that Napoleon arrived in July of 1798, Napoleon took his fight, and his army, inland. After a deadly march across the desert, with few rations and no water, the French forces encountered the Egyptian military on land, at the village of Imbaba. Although called the Battle of the Pyramids, the engagement didn't happen on the Giza Plateau, but the armies could see the ancient monuments from where they fought. Napoleon encouraged his troops as they readied themselves, saying, "Soldiers, imagine how, from the heights of these pyramids, forty centuries look down on you!"[2] No scene or sentiment could be more exemplary of the next two hundred years in Egyptology: Western men fighting against Egyptians and one another, with trowels and guns, with publications and regulations, over excavation permissions, object ownership, and the right to continue digging in a country that wasn't their own.

In 1801, the French withdrew from Egypt through the Treaty of Amiens, and the British military left in 1803, leaving Egypt to Ottoman rule. Muhammad Ali Pasha (r. 1805–1848) wanted to modernize and Westernize Egypt, meaning he was somewhat friendly to European money, influence, and, of course, people coming in to excavate. The long legacy of Western exploitation that Ali's policies left behind has been like a new Battle of the Pyramids ever since. Reports on every new find were thrilling and mysterious. This allure of ancient Egypt held people in its grip. Who was this? A king? A queen? What was that object used for? Were those symbols really spells? Did tombs actually have curses on them? Where is the gold?

From 1816 to 1821, the British consul-general Henry Salt hired former circus strongman Giovanni Belzoni to locate as many large ancient artifacts as he could find, and then extricate in order to send back and sell to the British Museum in London. He got bonus points for anything made of gold. Belzoni was not trained in the science and fine methodology of excavation—no one was at this point—so he used dynamite to blow up anything that would stand in his way of retrieving his prizes. He used brute physical force to move Egyptians who would try to stop him. Belzoni proudly told tales of beating up local sheikhs in Luxor and threatening his Egyptian crew at gunpoint in order to get them to labor in the hot sun during Ramadan, when they could neither eat nor drink. He brought trophies back to England, like the alabaster sarcophagus of Seti I, now in Sir John Soane's Museum, London, and the massive Younger Memnon head, which was raised into place in the British Museum in 1819.

The excitement about the Younger Memnon statue sparked lyrical poetry from the likes of Percy Bysshe Shelley and Horace Smith the previous year. Even though the hieroglyphic script on the statue was largely unreadable at this point, some names were decipherable, leading Shelley to exclaim: "And on the pedestal these words appear / 'My name is Ozymandias, king of kings: / Look on my works, ye Mighty, and despair!'" In short, encountering ancient Egypt was like encountering an alien civilization that defied comprehension, but which at the same time was crying out to be understood. The exhilaration of its discoveries and its incomprehensible mystery are reasons why Egypt and its history have continued to capture the imaginations of young and old like almost no other area of historical study. In addition, the religious aspects of being in and controlling a land made famous in the Bible as the location of the Hebrew enslavement, the setting for the Exodus, and the refuge of the Holy Family meant that the nineteenth-century British and Continental European public clamored for more.[3]

Wealthier people were willing to pay for excavators or for entire institutions to dig up sites and bring home the treasures—more for their own glory than scientific value. Others would go to Egypt to train themselves in the practice of Egyptology and archaeology. From the start, the French and the British pitted themselves against each other in the race for more pharaonic materials. The Germans, Italians, Russians, and other Europeans were involved as well, but the British and French tended to dominate the field; Americans arrived a little later. Soon, understanding Egypt became a national pursuit on both sides of the Channel, and both sides of the Atlantic, to decode the mysterious history of ancient Egypt and control its present.

By the 1850s, the volley of control in excavation had landed squarely with the French as men such as Auguste Mariette, Gaston Maspero, and Victor Loret ruled the Department of Antiquities for the next seventy years. Making decisions about excavations and artifacts, these men controlled everything in Egyptology: who could excavate, where they would work, what they could take home, why the work was even done, and how much they shared with Egyptians themselves.

While Egyptian leaders like Muhammad Ali welcomed Western money and interest, by the end of 1882, Egyptian leadership fought to stop the European invasion. The nationalist 'Urabi Revolt, an uprising hoping to strengthen Egypt's political system and military against foreign interests and invasion, had failed. To the victor went the spoils, as well as the prestige and bragging rights—Britain moved in to assume control over the government, the economy, and most of all the archaeology.

Into the 1920s and beyond, Europeans and Americans continued to find and take pieces of Egypt's history back home for what they claimed was "safekeeping" and "protection" from destruction by "savage Arabs." From 1883, British Egyptologist William Matthew Flinders Petrie spent the next forty years excavating up and down the Nile, first exploring the Giza Plateau. He complained that the Egyptians didn't care properly for their own history, all the while sending entire site assemblages—meaning all the artifacts from a site—back to museums in the UK, Europe, and the United States. Scholars are still trying to track down everything he dispersed.

Petrie trained a number of his male university students in excavation techniques. He also trained both American James Breasted and Briton Howard Carter in excavation methods. Both men complained about life on-site, citing Petrie's habits of excavating quickly, cheaply, and efficiently, but not very safely or accurately. Neither Breasted, the founder of the first Egyptology department in the United States at the University of Chicago, nor Carter, the "discoverer" of King Tutankhamun's tomb, had the constitution for Petrie's pace of work or Spartan way of life. Few did. But it was a masculine way of living—camping in tombs or in the stark and bare desert, eating year-old tinned food, with hardly a scrap of fresh food, a comfortable bed, a pair of socks or shirt to be found.

Americans arrived relatively late to Egyptology, but when they did, they bounded onto the scene larger than life, bringing with them money and enthusiasm. Americans had access to more private donor money and more time to spend in Egypt than other Western nations, so once they showed up, they tended to lead the way. In the early 1870s, millionaire Charles Wilbour escaped prosecution in the United States for his involvement in the political and financial Tammany Hall scandal in New York by moving his family to Europe. Once in Paris, Wilbour began to train with top linguists and Egyptologists, such as Gaston Maspero, so that when he arrived in Egypt in 1880, he was already well-known and well-connected. For the next fifteen years, Wilbour traveled up and down the Nile, first on the museum steamer with Maspero and finally on his own boat, *The Seven Hathors,* collecting antiquities and excavating, but never publishing a word.

Theodore Davis was another millionaire from New York, arriving in Egypt a decade after Wilbour to escape the same scandal that had rocked Wilbour's life. His involvement in the Tammany Hall scandal, among other activities, spurred his escape first to Europe and then to Egypt. He made millions in the 1870s and 1880s and poured that money into building a mansion in Newport, Rhode Island, and funding excavations in Egypt. He also eventually had his own boat built, the *Bedauin,* and traveled up and down the Nile, collecting artifacts and funding excavations from 1889 to 1914. Unlike Wilbour, Davis had no training in Egyptology, but much like

Wilbour, he had money, so Egyptologist Gaston Maspero courted him, too.

Importantly, Davis uncovered and cleared over a dozen tombs in the Valley of the Kings and even chose to publish a few of his excavations. Both Wilbour and Davis were instrumental in populating the Brooklyn Museum and the Metropolitan Museum of Art in New York with their early Egyptian collections. Later on, wealthy American bankers and industrialists John Pierpont Morgan and John D. Rockefeller were benefactors for James Breasted's scholarly work in Egypt. The only one of these early Americans formally trained with a PhD in Egyptology (and who was not trying to escape a financial scandal), Breasted focused his work on copying inscriptions on temple walls and buying up antiquities after World War I.

There were dozens, if not hundreds, of other men from all over Europe and the United States, as well as Russia and later Asia, who came to Egypt looking for that Big Find that would bring them fame and fortune. Early on, the history of the discipline became a story told *by* men *about* men in Egypt. Early versions of this story, like John A. Wilson's *Signs and Wonders Upon Pharaoh* (1964) and Brian Fagan's *The Rape of the Nile* (1975), gave readers the same basic account as above. Even more recent versions, like Toby Wilkinson's 2020 *A World Beneath the Sands: The Golden Age of Egyptology*, run through the same timeline. Those names, sites, and stories tend to define Egyptology.

A New Golden Age

Our story begins not with Napoleon in 1798 but in 1873, with the earliest British women who ventured to Egypt as travelers. Amelia Edwards and Marianne Brocklehurst went to Egypt in search of something—health, sunshine, a life's purpose—and they found it. Both women, independently of each other, had been inspired to travel by Lucie Duff Gordon's *Letters from Egypt*. These letters from a lonely woman who had tried to find fresh, dry air for her tuberculosis-ridden lungs inspired countless women and men to travel to Egypt. Amelia and Marianne both established institutions that soon became centers of the burgeoning discipline of Egyptology in Britain. As we dig down into their stories, the timeline of activity and opportunity reveals itself like a new stratigraphic layer each time. As each won her own battles, she set up the women who came later. Because of Amelia and Marianne, women in Britain like Maggie Benson and Nettie Gourlay were able to be educated in Egyptology, and they worked together to do their own excavations while battling issues of oppression and exclusion. Emma Andrews's incredible success as a patron and archaeologist both depended on Maggie and Nettie's work and helped pave the way for Margaret Murray to teach women to go into the field. Margaret's work in the university department that Amelia Edwards created allowed the artists Myrtle Broome and Amice Calverley being on-site, where they used their abilities to create brilliant reproductions of the art on the walls of the Temple of Seti I at Abydos. Amelia Edwards's influence and money also resulted in Kate Bradbury and Emily Paterson, as well as Caroline Ransom, having leadership positions in central institutions, both small and large.

Women led the field of Egyptology in a number of ways *despite* and sometimes *because of* the obstacles men put in their way. Each new step, professionally, broke barriers for the next generation. Barred from education, they traveled, experienced, learned, and wrote about Egypt in ways they couldn't do in a classroom. Excluded from field training, they found opportunities to be present and excavate on their own. Prohibited from theorizing or imagining at the site, they re-created Egyptian art in astounding and wonderful ways. Forbidden from being allowed to find the artifacts, they acquired, organized, and maintained the world's largest and most important collections.

It is because of these women that we have the legacies of richly illustrated travelogues, of valuable excavation seasons on sites that had been deemed unimportant, of long-lost beautiful murals copied and presented in books for future scholars to learn from, of great collections in famous museums and foundational research institutions that survived and thrived during wartime and depression. Women were, in fact, the reason that any of the "Great Men" of Egyptology were able to be "Great" at all.

Frequently, these women worked in tandem with Egyptians, too. Both groups understood their usually subservient role to the Great Man on-site. But their work—excavating, training, guarding, funding, and selling pieces—made sure the European and American men were successful in the field. Egyptian workers appear alongside these women throughout the story of early Egyptology, likewise fighting for inclusion. Egyptians are not as well-known historically as Western women (which is really saying something), and their stories in the archives and published sources are virtually nonexistent, so their stories will be centered and significant, however small. As the story here unfolds, we will meet and follow men such as excavators, dahabeah captains, guides, *ru'asa* (excavation foremen), consuls, and dealers. Their accomplishments run through this history like a central thread that, if left out, would unravel the rich and varied tapestry of the story.

Women in the Valley of the Kings presents a new idea of a Golden Age, defined not by what men did politically but by the arrival of women on their own terms, beginning with Amelia Edwards's journey in 1873 and ending with Caroline Ransom Williams's death in 1952. These women and their professional and personal activities cause us to rethink the era and ask questions like: For whom was this age golden? What roles did women play in building and maintaining the colonial structures in Egypt? When, how, and by whom were Egyptians finally allowed to participate in the study of their own ancient remains? Make no mistake, these women still took artifacts during this so-called Golden Age, but their main disciplinary work was more constructive and sustainable, and less destructive, than men's work.

The women in this volume came to Egyptology because of a love for the ancient monuments, the people, and their history, not to mention the mystery of it all. For the most part, women's work in the field happened at different times and in different spaces than men's. Western women arrived in Egypt later than men did. Once they were in-country, their focus tended to be more on experience, travel, and preservation of material remains than discovery, although several women did uncover a number of important sites and artifacts. While they worked both on-site and off, women often used their money, influence, and expertise to create, support, and maintain institutions instead of spending most of their time excavating in the field. The discipline of Egyptology, therefore, looks different when women dominate the field. Based on their work as artists, diarists, and collectors, these women will be called Egyptologists. Based on their jobs in university classrooms, home museum collections, and disciplinary societies, Egyptology will be defined as building institutions and not deconstructing sites. Egyptology will finally be seen as women's work.

There are many different definitions of Egyptology, and even more that try to simultaneously carve out a definition of a "Golden Age" of the discipline. Egyptology could comprise the "wonderful things" to which the famous British archaeologist Howard Carter referred when he was asked what he saw as he first peered through the dark and dust into Tutankhamun's almost undisturbed tomb. Egyptology could include the wide public interest in Egypt's history that trailblazer Amelia Edwards said "never flags" in those who truly love Egypt. It could be the study and mastery of the ancient script of the people who walked, talked, lived, and loved in Egypt five thousand years ago. It could be the study of their remains, with the discerning mind put to solving the questions and problems that continually arise with new finds. It very well *is* all of these things.

The term ancient Egypt, usually designated as the period from around 3250 BCE to the arrival of Alexander the Great in 332 BCE at the end of the Late Period, commonly defines the general era studied by people who call themselves Egyptologists. The Greco-Roman period is a separate period, but is still considered Egyptology, beginning in 332 BCE and ending with the death of the final Ptolemaic ruler, Cleopatra VII, in 30 BCE. That does not mean that other periods and topics of Egyptian history do not matter—in fact, the geology, climate, economy, politics, and anthropology of Egypt matter a great deal. It is simply that those topics are not usually considered to be part of Egyptology, specifically. The study of many of the Egyptian scripts—at any point on the ancient timeline—is often understood as Egyptology. The search for, excavation of, and study of the material remains of ancient Egyptian civilization are usually understood as Egyptian archaeology, the discerning factor between the two being the focus on and comprehension of ancient scripts. Egyptian archaeologists can be Egyptologists and vice versa; it certainly helps to be both.

The term "Golden Age" of this discipline is also up for some debate. Typically, "Golden Age" refers to the period defined by the common Grand Narrative, from the coming of Napoleon and the French in 1798 to the finding of King Tutankhamun's tomb in 1922. It is a period in which wealthy, white Europeans and Americans ran rampant over the cultural heritage of a colonized country and its people, vandalizing and pillaging as they went. To be clear, the 130 or so years of European dominance in Egypt was a "Golden Age" for the Western study of Egyptology because neither the laws in place at the time nor the cultural norms put in place by the Western rulers stopped this looting behavior—in fact, the laws actually encouraged violence and oppression by allowing the men and women who came to Egypt to take what they wanted, with impunity, and reasonably expect to be safe and remain unmolested while doing it.

Writing mostly about Western women without acknowledging their role in the colonized history of Egyptology doesn't reflect the true story. These women *were* part of the colonizing institutions and were, therefore, colonizers themselves. The reality of the situation, however, is more complex because, for far too often, women and Egyptians were also the colonized. If one looks clearly at the accomplishments of the explorers in the following pages, one can see that they are the pillars on which the male heroes of Western Egyptology stood in order to rise to their lofty status. If we are to see the fascinating history of discoveries in Egypt clearly, we have to look at the women and prominent Egyptians who did the groundbreaking work among the pyramids and temples and place them where they really belong within the history of Egyptology—directly at the center. By finally acknowledging the accomplishments of these individuals, a more realistic picture of the history of the field and a truer, more inclusive definition of Egyptology emerge.

1

Amelia Edwards and Marianne Brocklehurst

It may be said of some very old places, as of some very old books, that they are destined to be forever new. The nearer we approach them, the more remote they seem: the more we study them, the more we have yet to learn. Time augments rather than diminishes their everlasting novelty; and to our descendants of a thousand years hence it may safely be predicted that they will be even more fascinating than to ourselves. This is true of many ancient lands, but of no place is it so true as of Egypt.

—Amelia B. Edwards,
Pharaohs, Fellahs and Explorers, 1891

The *Philae* arrived later to Luxor than the *Bagstones* did. The women aboard the dahabeah *Bagstones* had been waiting for their travel partners for several days, but they weren't in any rush to see the ancient sites. When the *Philae* finally sailed into view, Marianne Brocklehurst and her partner, Mary Booth, were lounging on the *Bagstones*. They gave each other a knowing look. Amelia Edwards and Lucy Renshaw were waving from the deck of the *Philae* as the crew prepared their boat for mooring. The ladies on the *Bagstones* knew in that moment that they would be sightseeing nonstop for the next week at least. As Amelia and Lucy slowly shuffled down the narrow wooden plank from the *Philae* to the riverbank, the plank bowed heavily under their feet. Amelia wasn't paying attention to

Fig. 1.1: "The French House, Luxor," G. Pearson (drawing published 1890).

that, though. She was staring at the Luxor Temple, larger than life, right before her eyes.

When Amelia finally set foot in the French House, on the roof of the southern end of the Luxor Temple, and stepped into the room from where Lucie Duff Gordon had written her letters that would call so many to Luxor, she was shocked at the way the house fit in so well with its surroundings. That is to say, it was almost in ruins. She couldn't safely climb to the balcony, washed away months ago by a strong Nile flood, but she sat in the dreary rooms with Lucie's couch, rug, and folding chair. Amelia breathed in Lucie's presence, inspired to impact people with her writing just as Lucie had done. In the more than four years after Lucie's death from tuberculosis in 1869, no one else had lived in the *Maison de France*. It simply wasn't safe enough to do so. The house would soon be completely destroyed when Maspero cleared the fifty feet of ancient dirt and rubble from Luxor Temple in 1885. But when Amelia and her traveling companions Lucy Renshaw, Jenny Lane, Marianne Brocklehurst, and Mary Booth were there in March 1874, they were still able to see the most valuable part of the home just as Lucie had seen it—the view. Amelia recorded in her journal for that day:

> *We were shocked at the dreariness of the place—till we went to the window. That window, which commanded the Nile and the*

*western plain of Thebes, furnished the room and made its pov-
erty splendid. The sun was near setting. We could distinguish the
mounds and pylons of Medinet Habu and the site of the Rames-
seum. The terraced cliffs, overtopped by the pyramidal mountain of
Bab-el-Molûk, burned crimson against a sky of stainless blue. The
footpath leading to the Valley of the Tombs of the Kings showed
like a hot white scar winding along the face of the rocks. The river
gave back the sapphire tones of the sky. I thought I could be well
content to spend many a winter in no matter how comfortless
a lodging, if only I had that wonderful view, with its infinite
beauty of light and colour and space, and its history, and its mystery, always before my windows.*[1]

This would be Amelia's only trip to Egypt, so her dreams of
spending many winters in this idyllic place were never to be. Much
more has been written about her than probably any other woman
traveler in Egypt. Amelia, the Godmother of Egyptology, is herself
an institution in the discipline she helped to create.

There was nothing particular about Amelia that marked her for
this role. She was a wealthy, independent British woman, and traveling to Egypt was what women like her did in those days, thanks
in big part to Lucie Duff Gordon having led the way. However, it
was what she did when she returned home to England that year
that made her different. Amelia began a concerted effort to "save"
Egypt and Egyptian monuments. To do so, she founded and helped
to subsidize the Egypt Exploration Fund (EEF) in 1882, now the
Egypt Exploration Society (EES). She trained women to take over
the administration of the Fund and found men to do the excavation
work. Her creation of the EEF solidified the colonial foundation of
Egyptology in the West. Along with the Fund, Amelia's journeying
in Egypt and her travelogue *A Thousand Miles Up the Nile* profes-
sionalized Egyptology in Britain. Her money, leadership, and popular work provided the foundations for the EEF and for the new
Egyptian archaeology department at University College London,
and both institutions continued to sponsor scholarship about the
place she loved.

Getting to Egypt

Amelia Edwards was born June 7, 1831, in London. On August 12, she was christened Amelia Anna Blanford Edwards at St. John the Baptist Parish in Hoxton, Middlesex. She was an only child. Her father, Thomas, was a former military officer and banker, and her Irish mother, Alicia, wanted her to have a good education and cultivated her early interest in art, music, and literature. Amelia had an education similar to Lucie Duff Gordon's in early Victorian Britain, which is to say she was educated at home in the subjects most girls weren't taught at the time, like philosophy and literature.

By the time she was twenty, at her core, Amelia was lonely and wanted companionship. To this end, she had accepted the proposal of a Mr. Bacon, who she knew loved her very much. She thought about his steady devotion to her as she readied herself to meet him on a cool spring day in 1851. Suddenly her stomach lurched. As she ran to the privy for the umpteenth time that morning, she realized that she wasn't physically ill. The problem with her nervous stomach was her. She appreciated, but could not bring herself to return, Mr. Bacon's feelings. Amelia respected him and liked him very much. She knew he was a good man with good prospects for a future, but she didn't think her level of esteem for him was enough to make a happy marriage, much less a happy engagement. She wanted something more than Mr. Bacon, someone different. It took her some time, but Amelia finally called off the engagement by the end of the year, ready to move on with her life and her writing.

In 1860, when Amelia was just twenty-nine, both of her parents died within a week of each other. It may have been illness, old age, or a combination of both. Her father was seventy-two; her mother was sixty-eight. She was close to both of her parents, and she now felt that she was alone in the world. As the only child and heir, she inherited the entire estate. It wasn't much money, but she had been very successful in her work up to that point, writing popular books such as *The Ladder of Life* (1856), *My Brother's Wife* (1857), *Hand and Glove* (1858), and *Barbara's History* (1864). So, in combination with her literary income, the inheritance was enough to make sure she could live comfortably. In her grief, she turned to a longtime family friend named Ellen Braysher. Ellen was thirty years older than Amelia, but the two were very close. Amelia had been staying intermittently with Ellen and her family in London for the previous five years, before her parents had died. By 1861, Amelia had moved in with them somewhat permanently, finding herself a home and companionship.

After the sudden and surprising deaths of Ellen's husband, John, in 1863 and her daughter, Sarah, in 1864, the grieving women moved out of their old London house and bought a home near Bristol, in Westbury-on-Trym, that they called the Larches. Here they lived, together, for the next twenty-eight years. The relationship between Ellen Braysher and Amelia was, to some, like mother and daughter, which may have been true. Others say they were lovers. Each of them, at the very least, had had intimate relationships with other women. Their devotion to each other lasted until their deaths. Ellen was often ill, and Amelia would race home to care for her. In letters she referred to Ellen as "my invalid," and, in 1865, Amelia dedicated a book of poems, entitled *Ballads,* to "my most beloved friend, Ellen Braysher." By this point, Amelia had fully embraced the fact that Ellen herself was Amelia's own place of refuge. Ellen's role as Amelia's love, support, and safety gave Amelia the unbounded freedom she had always wanted in her life but never had. She was free to travel, free to write and be professionally productive, and free to meet, woo, and love other like-minded women.

They settled into their new home at Westbury-on-Trym, and Amelia became acquainted, and fell in love, with several women. Amelia's main biographers, Joan Rees and Brenda Moon, each say that Amelia's passionate friendships hint at "the possibility of lesbianism" but that her "attachments to other women is not susceptible of easy labelling."[2] This is true, especially of women in this period. Amelia might not have called herself a lesbian, but she was physically affectionate in her relationships with women, and her writings were full of adoration.

In 1871, after reeling from two recent severe heartbreaks, Amelia was ready for a change of scene and a change of air. Leaving one's home in search of fresh air to cure any disease had been the practice of well-to-do Europeans since the Romans made their sea-voyage cure popular in the first centuries of the common era.[3] The idea was to leave the old, stale miasma (bad air) for new, fresh, good air either in the countryside, on the Continent, in the mountains, in the desert, or at sea. By the beginning of the nineteenth century, the sea-voyage cure was popular among tuberculosis sufferers in Britain who could afford the time and expense of being away from home. Later, the cure was deemed useful to anyone in need of relief from heartbreak, heartburn, and everything in between.

The change-of-air cure, Amelia knew, worked not just for lungs but also for hearts. She soon left for a trip to Rome on her own to meet friends, leaving Ellen safely at home. She traveled to Rome and remained there for the winter of 1871–72 to cure her broken heart, or at the very least find someone to help her mend it. By April of 1872, she had moved on to Salerno, a beautiful seaside town on the west coast of Italy, just southeast of Naples. There she met Lucy Renshaw for the first time.

Like that of many women in this period, Lucy's life is hidden from us, before her time in Egypt. She was born July 30, 1833, just two years after Amelia, and was equally as adventurous. Lucy was

Fig. 1.2: Amelia Edwards, c. 1890.

Fig. 1.3: Lucy Renshaw, c. 1874,
from Amelia's photo album.

from Hulme, within Greater Manchester, in northern England, and
was from a family even more financially well-to-do than Amelia.[4]
During the Industrial Revolution, the town of Hulme exploded
with cotton mills and textile manufacturing. Lucy's father, John,
was part of a wealthy area family; her mother, Maria Sarah Capes,
was ten years younger than her husband.[5] Lucy grew up in a large
house on Boundary Lane, with several servants in the household.[6]
By 1871, Lucy was thirty-seven, and, like Amelia, both her mother
and father had died. She continued living in the Oxford Street
house she and her father had moved to in Manchester at least ten
years before.[7] Lucy had four servants and her father's money; her
life was relatively comfortable.[8]

When they met in Salerno, Amelia felt a kinship with Lucy,
and she soon found that Lucy would travel with her to the most
untrodden and unfrequented places. Their first destination together
was the Dolomite region of Italy, where few British travelers had
ever gone. Both women had dreamed of going to the alpine region,
to get to know the mountains and people intimately, and to sketch,

draw, and climb to their hearts' content. They had men as guides and donkeys for riding, but otherwise it was Lucy and Amelia, and Lucy's maid, whom we only know by the letter S.[9] Amelia and Lucy, being of heartier stock (or so they thought), considered S too delicate for the path they would be taking. S had a tendency to complain and ended up holding them back, so she didn't last long on the journey.

The whole time they were in Italy, they only ran into three groups of English travelers. Being such outsiders, Lucy and Amelia were never allowed to forget that they were unmarried, pitied by all they met. Near the end of their journey, they approached the village of Selva. They had been traveling by donkey for over eight hours through rough terrain, and everyone was exhausted to their bones. The women who owned the village's inn watched the group on their approach. They sent the donkeys to be fed, their guides to eat and drink, and Lucy and Amelia to rest and wash. The innkeepers were shocked that two women, traveling alone in an isolated area, did so without husbands. They asked so many questions of Lucy and Amelia—were they sisters? No. Were they married? No, they laughed, neither of them were married. This answer received a chorus of *"Poverine! Poverine!"* Lucy and Amelia, for all of their adventure, were "poor little things," traveling all alone.[10] They didn't feel so alone with each other.

In the Dolomites, the two cemented their relationship as a couple just a few short months after they had met.[11] Amelia, it seemed, had recovered from her broken heart. In this period, it was easier for two women to travel together—much like Lucie Duff Gordon did with her maid Sally Naldrett—than it would have been for them to have adventures on their own. In July of 1872, possibly at the end of their Italian journey, Amelia gave a copy of *Ballads* to Lucy, the very book she had dedicated to Ellen. In it, the lovestruck poet had inscribed two poems in her own hand, addressed "To Lucy Renshaw." One was an older poem, possibly meant for a past lover. The second one was new and likely written just for Lucy, entitled "On the Rose She Gave Me."

I hold in my hand the rose you wore
Last night in your bosom—its perfume shed,
The faint, sweet blush of its beauty fled
Like the bloom from the lips of a maiden dead;—
—a rose no more!
Rock'd on thy heart as it rose & fell,
For thy sake forgetting the sun & the dew,
Breathing thy breath the long ev'ning through,
What it felt, what it saw, what it dream'd, what it knew,
Who shall tell?
Turn'd it pale, do you think, for the wild, brief bliss
Of loving those treasures near which it lay
(Twin blossoms that know not the light of day)
Which I would barter my soul away
But to kiss?
Oh, that the fate of the rose were mine!
Just for one night in thy bosom to lie—
For just that one night in thy bosom, to die,
Yielding life, love, song, in one long sigh
Were divine![12]

Broken relationships had pushed Amelia to Italy, but a loving partnership would spur her "most exciting and productive journeys." Those journeys were with Lucy, traveling around Italy, Egypt, and the Middle East in late 1873.[13]

After they returned to England, Amelia published her travelogue of the trip, *Untrodden Peaks and Unfrequented Valleys: A Midsummer Ramble in the Dolomites* (1873), her first travel book. Lucy appeared as a companion, known as L., "for briefness," but for the next fifteen years, she was a devoted partner to Amelia during numerous trips. Both women had proven their traveling prowess by riding into and through places where few British travelers had ever gone, and they lived to tell about it. *Untrodden Peaks* wasn't a trusty Baedeker's guidebook containing information about costs, exchange rates, and amenities along the way. It could be better compared to Lucie Duff Gordon's *Letters from Egypt* in both purpose and impact.

Fig. 1.4: Jenny Lane, c. 1876.

Untrodden Peaks was good for armchair travel and for showing women they could travel alone, unmarried, in the Italian country-side. Most importantly, it showed them how to do it. With Amelia's relaxed humor and practical, if vague, travel advice, the book was an instant success. And the process of writing it—romping with her dear friend and the freedom this afforded—gave Amelia such pleasure that she was prompted to start another one like it. And she wanted to do it with Lucy.

At the beginning of 1873, the women were back in England. Amelia was with Ellen at the Larches working on the proofs for *Untrodden Peaks.* Lucy was back home trying to find another maid—one hardier and sturdier than S, which wouldn't be hard to do. She hired a new maid, named Jane—later known by her nick-name Jenny—Lane. Jenny was the linchpin to their plans, as companions so often were for Amelia. By October, the women were back on the Continent for another winter abroad, leaving Ellen at home. They had begun, Amelia claimed, with just Europe in mind, but their plans quickly changed.

A Journey of a Thousand Miles

Jenny Lane was born in either April or May of 1833 or 1835, making her around the same age as Lucy and Amelia.[14] According to a note kept with her diaries, now in the Griffith Institute at Oxford, Jenny was the daughter of George Lane, a gardener in Sussex. She may have been part of the domestic staff at Lucy's father's home, and being young, single, and generally healthy, she would have made a good traveling maid.[15] After she returned from the trip with Amelia and Lucy in 1874, Jenny was married twice.[16] She didn't have children, but she had a niece, in whose possession her journals remained until they were purchased by the Griffith Institute in 2018. Jenny's diaries are the only record we have of her participation in this journey through France and up the Nile. The journals contain the only memories passed down to us about the women's time before the group arrived in Cairo as well as after they left Egypt, so they are a crucial record.

The three women started from England on September 4, 1873, crossing the Channel and making their way through France by train, on horse, and on foot. The farther south they went, the more the sun shone and the hotter they got. Jenny thought it was funny to see the local residents struck still like statues, gawking as the heavily dressed women walked by, clearly uncomfortable in their clothes in the heat. Jenny especially liked to get out of the hotels for some walking when the weather allowed it, but it took some time to get used to both the warmer temperatures and the exercise. But she did, quickly, and keeping up with Amelia and Lucy would be her goal for the rest of the trip.

It wasn't on a whim or by accident that they decided to go to Egypt, as Amelia so famously claimed in her bestselling *A Thousand Miles Up the Nile*. In fact, it took forethought and quite a bit of planning to get to Egypt, which Lucy had started to do while enjoying the nice weather in the South of France at the end of October. However, the weather was unpredictable at times, and when it turned again, the puddles and rain brought the mosquitoes. Jenny scratched the bites on her face as she looked in the mirror, turning this way and that. Her skin was spotted, red, and blotchy; it looked like a plum pudding. She was ready to leave the small southern French town of Nîmes, regardless of whether the sun came out again. She needed to escape the bugs. Amelia and Lucy, hoping to stay a little longer, had simply wanted to spend some time outside sketching the landscapes as they had done in the Dolomites the year before. Excepting that first week in Nîmes, when the weather was nice, the whole excursion had been a disaster. Washed out of the hills, nearly drowned on the plains, and soaked to the bone, these women of means set their plans in place and left for Egypt.[17]

They made their way from southern France to Brindisi, taking days to reach this port town on the north side of the Italian bootheel. There the women boarded a small steamer, the *Simla*, with about one hundred other passengers the night before it was due to leave. At 5:00 A.M., November 24, 1873, on what would be a bright morning with a calm sea, the boat left Brindisi. They looked forward to smooth sailing, but these winter trips across the Mediterranean were rarely calm. By the next day, it was obvious that the wind and rain would make for a rough passage. Each night the passengers had to struggle even to stay in bed due to the tossing and turning of the boat. During the day they were hardly able to roam about the decks for fear of falling overboard. Thanks to the rough waters, the *Simla* went off course by a hundred miles or so, so they had to readjust their route to make it to port. By the time they arrived at Alexandria, at noon on Thursday the twenty-seventh, the passengers were happy they could spend their mandatory forty-eight-hour quarantine in the calm waters of the harbor, their boat's mast marked with the familiar yellow flag.

During the quarantine, now that they were not battling the rolling sea, Jenny thought that life on the boat was wonderfully relaxing. All around her in the water she could see other boats with their yellow flags. She enjoyed the bright sun and warm breezes, and she could see Pompey's Pillar rising above its surroundings in town. Jenny compared the weather to a warm English summer—very different from France.

On the contrary, Marianne Brocklehurst, a fellow passenger on the *Simla*, was not looking forward to the boredom of quar-

Fig. 1.5: Marianne Brocklehurst, n.d.

antine. She had not fared well on the tossing boat and was happy her stomach was more relaxed, but she just wanted to get to Cairo. During quarantine, she passed the time with her lifelong partner Mary Booth, and the two quickly became acquainted with Amelia and Lucy, who they thought were "pleasant people."[18] We know them now as the MBs, thanks to Amelia including this shorthand for them in her travelogue, and they were about to embark on an exciting journey.

Marianne Brocklehurst was a daughter of John Brocklehurst, a Macclesfield silk manufacturer and one of its first members of Parliament, and his wife, Mary.[19] The family's legacy started in the button-making business, but by the late eighteenth and early nineteenth centuries, they were in the silk trade and textile manufacturing business, and they were wealthy. About the same age as Amelia, Lucy, and Jenny, Marianne was born in 1832 and had traveled widely with her sister Emma from when she was around twenty years old. She had an early interest in archaeology and photography. Like Amelia, Marianne had been engaged to a man when she was younger, but her father made her end the relationship because her fiancé didn't have enough money. Apparently his family was not the kind John wanted Marianne to marry into. She had other suitors but turned them all away, simply, said her sister Emma, because she was "not for marrying."[20] From then on, Marianne enjoyed quite a lot of freedom as an unmarried spinster, so it's hard to say she was disappointed at the end of the engagement. She became a photographer in the late 1860s and brought in Mary Booth as a business partner.

Mary herself was from an old, well-to-do Yorkshire family, and the two women were together for the rest of their lives, both personally and professionally. They were so happy together that when Emma met Mary for the first time in 1870, she wrote that she felt "quite cross and jealous" to see them together, because they "seemed so all in all to one another."[21] They lived in a home they called the Bagstones on Marianne's brother's estate, built with money Marianne inherited from her uncle. Jenny affectionately called them "the Bagstones ladies," and they appeared throughout both Amelia's and Jenny's journals.[22] Marianne kept her own journals, now in the Macclesfield Museum, complete with charcoal drawings and recollections that complement and supplement Amelia's and Jenny's memories. The MBs had brought with them to Egypt their manservant, George, and Marianne's nephew Alfred.

They were all passengers on the *Simla* and were cleared from quarantine on November 29 (according to Jenny's reckoning). As they waved goodbye to one another in the rush of moving baggage, finding porters, and getting to their trains, Amelia, Lucy, Jenny, and the MBs had already made plans to see each other again. They would travel up the Nile together—in separate boats, but as a group. But that first afternoon, after the two groups took their leave of one another, the women quickly toured Alexandria before they caught their train the following morning. They saw the sights prescribed in *Murray's* guidebook, which is to say they didn't see a lot, but Jenny enjoyed the drive around town. She wrote, "Of this Magnificent City [the] only two striking relics [that] remain [are] called Cleopatra's Needles one fallen & the other erect . . ."[23] These are now in New York and London, but they were still on the Alexandrian coast in 1873. They saw the tall Pompey's Pillar from a number of vantage points in the city. *Murray's* and Baedeker's *Egypt* advised that it was the only monument in town, so they drove to see it up close.

Most importantly, following the advice from the *Murray's* guidebook they were carrying, and much like Lucie Duff Gordon had
done ten years earlier, in Alexandria they hired their *dragoman*
(guide) for the rest of their trip. Jenny wrote in her journal that
it was "Mr. Talhamy a v[e]ry nice looking fellow."[24] We know the
most about him from Jenny's diaries. As a guide, negotiator, and
general fixer for their trip, Mr. Elias Talhamy would be invaluable
to Amelia, Lucy, and Jenny, as well as to the MBs, for the next six
months in Egypt as well as for their journey to Lebanon and other
places in the Middle East.

The morning of November 30 was hot, and the women, with
Mr. Talhamy, left Alexandria for Cairo early in the morning on
the seven o'clock train. Jenny sat by a window, disappointed in the
"wretched dusty ride and very uninteresting scenery."[25] The MBs
were on the same train, and the women used the time to get to
know each other a bit better. They talked over tea and breakfast,
through the sounds of the train and the anticipation of arrival in
Cairo.

Without letting on to each other, they were all uneasy about the
travel plans they had made in some haste on the decks of the *Simla*,
during that euphoric moment of seeing the coast of Egypt for the
first time and finally having calm waters and calm stomachs and
heads. They had jumped right into a vast plan of travel with people
they had just met—months up the Nile without a respite from one
another.

For years, guidebooks gave advice on everything from currency
to clothing. But the books also warned against traveling with people
they knew too well, or didn't know well enough. Baedeker's had
warned generations of travelers that

> greater care is required in the choice of companions for the
> dhahabîyeh-voyage, for the close and constant intercourse in
> rather narrow quarters and for perhaps two months at a time
> is apt to produce somewhat strained relations between those
> who are not originally sympathetic. The "dhahabîyeh devil,"
> indeed, is famous in Egypt for causing those who have em-
> barked as friends to disembark as foes.[26]

Speaking directly to travelers "with scientific aims," Baedeker's advised against "travelling with those who have no particular interest in the gigantic remains of antiquity, and who are thus constantly wishing to push on hurriedly from sheer ennui."[27] No doubt similar thoughts were running through the minds of everyone on the journey. Only time would tell.

As they got closer to Cairo and could see the pyramids from the window of the train, it seemed that the MBs and Amelia's group were well-suited as companions. Unlike so many other travelers, Jenny didn't mention the pyramids in her journal entry about the train ride. Amelia did, but certainly didn't find them very interesting at all. She thought they looked small against the vast desert and bright blue sky—nothing like the overwhelming monuments she had read about. Marianne glossed them over in her own journal, saying that they saw "the Pyramids afar" before they got to Cairo.[28]

The train arrived at Cairo's Principal Station just north of the Ismaliyah Canal a little after noon that Sunday, November 30, and they rushed to the famed Shepheard's Hotel. The Azbakiya Gardens, just off the edge of which Shepheard's was located, weren't that far from the train station, but they had to find porters and a cab, possibly the right hotel omnibus, and get checked in. Amelia, Lucy, and Jenny pulled up to an almost completely rebuilt Shepheard's Hotel. After a fire in 1869, which burned up the basement wine stores worth more than half of the cost of the building, Shepheard's was revamped to welcome guests for the opening of the Suez Canal that same year. When the women arrived at Shepheard's, it was large, bright, and almost brand-new. It had a courtyard into which the sun shone all day, which welcomed birds, featured palm trees, and allowed for green grass. Thomas Cook had just established his first office in Egypt at the hotel in 1872, making it easier for Western travelers to navigate in Egypt. Cook's offices would remain there until 1952.[29]

They must have made a spectacle walking into the most famous hotel in Africa. The women arrived before Mr. Talhamy and their luggage, just in time to take their seats in the new, large dining room already full of tourists.[30] Most everyone in the famous dining room would have been dressed in their finest clothes, ready to impress. Those already sipping their aperitifs and eating the first course of their luncheon were whispering about the three women in their dusty dresses, loose hair hanging out of their buns, and their sunburned faces. They were tired from the road, but still had the nerve to sit down and eat with everyone else. The guests would have asked the main travel questions of the day: Who were these women? How long would they be staying at the exclusive hotel? And, most important of all, would they be going up the Nile?

The Shepheard's guests would quickly learn who the women were, and that they were there because they wanted refuge from the rain in France. At least, that was the story they told. Amelia and Lucy had been planning to visit Egypt for a while, and Amelia wanted to write a new guidebook for women and the general public, with hopes it would be as popular as her *Untrodden Peaks*. The guests also learned, from discussion at dinner, that the women would be at the hotel for a couple of weeks, touring Cairo, seeing the monuments, meeting the people, and shopping. And, most decidedly, yes: they were planning to sail up the Nile.

Spurred on by Lucie Duff Gordon's *Letters from Egypt* and about to shift the world of Egyptology in Britain and Egypt forever, Amelia was on a mission, and she took Lucy and Jenny with her. Together with the MBs, they would form a woman-led British armada, invading Egypt for the sun, the sites, and the antiquities. Almost a decade later, the British would invade for military and economic gains, and women would march into Egyptology, ready to take over a man's world. In each of these there was money and glory at stake, and they were at the center of violent struggles for the next century.

Sailing Up the Nile

As they settled into Shepheard's Hotel, just off the green and fragrant, if busy, Azbakiya Gardens, Amelia and Lucy took in "scene after scene with its manifold combinations of light and shade, colour, costume, and architectural detail."[31] They relaxed on the terrace of Shepheard's—not yet the large and famous terrace that would become a staple of the European Cairo experience by 1892, but still an event that was practically a requirement. It was said that if you sat on the terrace long enough, drinking lemonade, tea, or brandy, you would see the whole world go by, and that's just what Amelia and Lucy did. They were excited, if a little nervous, to visit the sights in and around Cairo. None of them spoke Arabic, but they wandered through the narrow alleys that crisscrossed the Muski, a region of Cairo where locals lived, worked, and shopped. There were bazaars in Cairo for almost everything you needed: carpets, hardware, tobacco, sword-mounters, coppersmiths, clothes, leather goods, and more. There was also the English bazaar, but none of the women found it particularly interesting as they all tried, like others had done before them, to divest themselves of English influence while they were there.[32]

They found some comfort in fellow countrywomen, though. Jenny had met another English maid staying at the hotel, and they planned to go to hear a band playing in the gardens. As they walked to the pavilion, they passed by families having ice cream, people drinking tea at small tables near a kiosk, and the birds that seemed so exotic to them but were native to Egypt, like the hoopoe and the crane. They could almost believe they were in a European city like Paris, but something was just slightly different. Jenny couldn't put her finger on it. It wasn't the sunshine or the warm sun; she was used to those on delicious English summer days. It was just a feeling—the wind blowing by their faces smelled not of the green gardens but of the desert and the river, of the humanity that was just beyond the borders of the enclave. They enjoyed the band and their stroll through the gardens after it was over. But the sights she saw the following day brought her out of her dreamy state.

As she walked around the alleys of the city, running errands for Amelia and Lucy, Jenny saw strange sights that "quite bewildered" her English sensibilities. She was not used to seeing veiled women or men in robes walking on city streets in their bare feet. Jenny was astonished that the bread and other food she saw lying in neat rows on the ground were sold to people to be eaten.[33] Later, they went to the al-Azhar Mosque to see the dervishes and to an English church the first Sunday they were in town. The whole group loved to drive down the shady Shubra road, which was then an avenue of acacia trees about three miles long stretching north from central Cairo to the khedive's Shubra Palace.

Beyond the sightseeing and shopping, Amelia knew that the first business of the trip was to decide on a dahabeah to take the group up the Nile. She was a little nervous about the process. The MBs had found their boat on the first full day in Cairo, signing a contract for three months on the Nile, with the vice consul as a witness. Having a witness was a standard practice, mainly so tourists weren't taken advantage of and could have some recourse if their contracts weren't honored. But none of that mattered; the first deal fell apart and the vice consul was useless. In the end the MBs had to change their boat. On December 8, they finally decided on the *Lydn,* which they immediately renamed the *Bagstones* in honor of their home in England where they shared so many happy times. Amelia hoped that she could make her decision as quickly but with less trouble, so she counted on Mr. Talhamy to do the work.

The weather in Cairo, even in December, was "too hot to go out," the Englishwomen in multilayered cotton (and possibly wool) dresses kept remarking, and the place where they had to shop for boats, the Bulak, was such "a desolate place by the river" that instead of speeding through the process, Amelia claimed she had a dreadfully difficult time.[34] She wrote that "the first ten days or so, some three or four hours had to be devoted every morning to the business of the boats," with no end or resolution in sight.[35] The boats, she complained, were either too small, too large, or too dirty. All of them were too expensive. None of them were what she wanted. Amelia's account, however, while in line with most travel guides, did not match Jenny's own recollection. Jenny remembered that it was Lucy who was indeed "very busy settling about our trip up the Nile," and within six days of arrival in Cairo, with Mr. Talhamy's help, she had "engaged a charming boat called the Philae." The hard work of negotiating done, they left Mr. Talhamy to get the boat ready while they continued sightseeing.[36] Unlike the MBs, Amelia and Lucy didn't change the name of their boat.

Amelia, Lucy, and Jenny then had a few extra days to visit the pyramids. Thursday, December 11, turned out to be another hot, sunny day in Egypt. They left the hotel right after lunch and took a carriage to the Giza Plateau. In 1869, a road to the plateau had been paved for Empress Eugénie of France, who was visiting for the opening of the Suez Canal. Jenny wrote that they drove west across the Nile on what was then the El Gezira Bridge from the city, and then up the paved road, "a splendid Avenue of Palms 3 miles long." They then "had to alight from the carriage at the bottom of the hill and walk across a small portion of desert almost to our knees in sand."[37] The women struggled through the sand in their skirts, eyes squinted by the sun, but they could see the pyramids looming larger with every step they took. Amelia couldn't believe what she saw. These weren't the tiny, lackluster pyramids she remembered scoffing at through the train window.

They all gawked at the Great Pyramid, that of Khufu, hardly believing its size. Amelia wrote that "the Great Pyramid in all its unexpected bulk and majesty towers close above one's head, the effect is as sudden as it is overwhelming. It shuts out the sky and the horizon. It shuts out all the other Pyramids. It shuts out everything but the sense of awe and wonder."[38] They wandered the plateau, seeing the other, smaller pyramids of Khafre and Menkaure. The Great Sphinx, still mostly under the sand, with just his head and shoulders poking out, would have been hard to see from the plateau, but see it they did. Since this was their first trip to the plateau, the women did not have enough time to see the pyramids in as much detail as they had hoped. Amelia wrote that they hadn't yet "been up the Nile and back, and gone through months of training" that would give them the "practical understanding of the manifold phases through which the arts and architecture of Egypt had passed, since those far-off days of Cheops [Khufu] and Chephren [Khafre]. Then, only, we can be said to have seen the Pyramids."[39] After having looked at the pyramids, they returned to the hotel by 7:00 P.M., after a "delightful drive home in the cool of the Evening."[40]

For these traveling women, as for many other prospective Egyptologists, the journey up the Nile would prove to be not only a leisurely act but also an educational endeavor that would prepare them to return home to England and impact the discipline.

By Saturday, December 13, they were on board the *Philae* and ready to sail and begin their training. The MBs had been over for dinner the night before, and they were all in great spirits, excited to be off on their great adventure. On that Saturday, Amelia and Lucy made one more quick trip into town to get their mail and do a final shopping trip. They snapped up last-minute items they needed from their detailed and extensive travel list, including coffee, tea, lemonade syrup, linens, and medicines. In 1873, it was still difficult to get European necessities south of Cairo, so they would need to take with them many of their own supplies. They said goodbye to some of their new friends at the hotel and made their way to the *Philae*. Amelia and Lucy had agreed with the MBs to keep their dahabeahs together as much as possible as they sailed upriver. Staying together would be difficult to do: the Nile flows north, so the trip south to Aswan would depend on good winds and high water to go against the river's flow. The whole group left around 2:00 P.M., with favorable winds.[41] Amelia wrote, as their huge sail filled and each boat fired six gunshots each, "Happy are the Nile travelers who start thus with a fair breeze on a brilliant afternoon."[42] They were indeed happy travelers.

The whole group were reveling in the *esprit du Nil,* or the spirit and excitement of traveling on the Nile. Thomas Cook brought his first tour group to Egypt in 1869 and made it easier for people to visit the country on steamers and trains; this meant that fewer people traveled on dahabeahs. By 1873, when Amelia, Lucy, Jenny, and the MBs were there, Cook was taking two hundred people per year up the Nile on steamers rented for the purpose. Amelia recalled that "the people in dahabeeyahs despise Cook's tourists; those who are bound for the Second Cataract look down with lofty compassion upon those whose ambition extends only to the First; and travelers who engage their boat by the month hold their heads a trifle higher than those who contract for the trip."[43] The women on the *Philae* and *Bagstones* were the most fortunate of these groups, of course.

The story of their journey up and then back down the Nile is one of the most famous travelogues about Egypt, possibly one of the most famous travel stories ever written. There was much for these women to celebrate about being on the Nile: the independence, the adventure, the freedom, and the possibilities. The sights and activities rarely disappointed. The women painted and drew, knitted, wrote letters, rested, and took shore excursions as they chose. They bought antiquities, hunted, maybe did a little digging, and got to know people in various towns up and down the river. This one journey would impact Egyptology into the twenty-first century.

Leaving the Bulak, where all traveler boats were moored, they passed the Giza pyramids, but their first stop was Badrasheen (Bedreshayn), for the statue of Ramesses II at Memphis and the tombs at Saqqara, including Djoser's Step Pyramid. They continued to the Second Cataract and back, mooring for the night, or several days, at various places along the river and taking shore excursions along the way. Amelia's travel itinerary, in conjunction with the popularization of Thomas Cook's journeys, solidified travelers' plans for the next fifty years at least. Beni Hasan, Dendera, Abydos, Luxor (twice) for Thebes and Karnak, Edfu, Aswan, and Abu Simbel were all on the packed calendar.

The group were also very interested in buying antiquities. Purchasing antiquities was not illegal, if done through the proper channels. It had been common practice even for archaeologists to purchase objects from the Cairo Museum's own store until the early twentieth century, and from dealers until the start of World War II. Jenny bought some of her own, and Amelia bought so many she had to have multiple crates shipped to her home in London from Cairo once the trip was over. Likewise, the MBs bought a number of prized pieces on their first trip, as well as on subsequent trips in 1876, 1883, and 1890. Some of Amelia's antiquities were, reportedly, illicit. If the Nile didn't make her heart beat a little faster from excitement, illegally procuring antiquities certainly did. She loved the "the pleasures of the chase" because of the danger in getting caught.[44]

Early in their trip, when they were still aboard the *Simla*, the women had heard rumors of a mummy for sale down in Thebes. They all wanted to get to Luxor quickly so they might have a chance at buying the ancient human remains. From the time they landed in Alexandria, they couldn't stop talking about it.[45] The *Bagstones* ladies made it to Thebes first, and when they finally saw the outside of the sarcophagus, they were dejected. The coffin was short, only about five feet long, but it didn't have any gold on the outside, as they'd hoped.[46] It was still beautiful, though; the outside was skill-fully painted with hieroglyphs, but neither of the MBs could read them, so they didn't care about anything it might have said. Still, they were both excited at the thought of smuggling something this large past the alert Egyptian guards and getting it to their boat.[47] Smuggling the mummy aboard their boat was no small feat and took two nights, at least one failed attempt, and some spent gun-powder and lead.

Once they got it on the *Bagstones,* the MBs carefully hid the coffin and its human remains. The first chance they got, they opened the case and unwrapped the mummified person themselves in their tiny dahabeah rooms under the cover of night. They believed it was the mummified remains of a man, an "altogether . . . festive object and not at all a funereal old frump."[48] Tired from the effort they put into the late-night unrolling, they fell fast asleep, leaving the human remains, stripped of the wrappings, standing up in the middle of their room.[49] The MBs knew they had to keep his existence on the boat secret. If they were caught by the authorities, they would be subject to a fine and would have had to return the sarcophagus and its remains to the Cairo Museum. If the crew of the *Bagstones* found out about this, they'd surely abandon the women. They were certain their cook was "doubtless . . . acquainted with the peculiar mummy 'bouquet'" after his years of service to French Egyptologist Auguste Mariette.[50] The MBs were not familiar with the smell, but neither could they stand it all night. They weren't sure what to do with the remains. Amelia, on the other hand, was frustrated that they had gotten the mummy and she didn't. They had outbid her by quite a lot. Later Amelia reported that the MBs gave the remains a water burial in the dark of night, dumping them off the deck, but they didn't. In the end, the sarcophagus and its occupant somehow made it back to England. The women probably just wrapped it back up, covered it, and stored it in their boat.[51]

Usually the group traveled together, but sometimes they didn't. For example, the *Bagstones* arrived in Luxor almost a week before the *Philae* did, with the MBs enjoying some sites on the West Bank before Amelia and Lucy were able to join them. On March 22, 1874, everyone was reunited. They toured temples, sites, and tombs. They enjoyed relaxing on board their boats—the first hotel wouldn't be built in Luxor for another three years—and they relished the warm breezes and the sunsets over the western mountains. All of them made the pilgrimage to the French House, where they marveled at the view Lucie Duff Gordon had from her balcony. A week later, the *Bagstones* left Luxor, saying goodbye to the *Philae,* but the women of the *Philae* remained to see more sites and buy more antiquities from dealers.

In fact, the *Philae* adventurers outstayed almost every other European traveler in Egypt. They were the last dahabeah to return to Cairo that year.[52] Their final weeks on the Nile went by "like one long, lazy summer's day," Amelia wistfully recalled. They arrived back in Cairo, having completed their weeks of "training," so that they could make their second and final trip to Giza to see the Sphinx and the pyramids. They did not go in the pyramids to see the burial chambers, but climbed them instead.

Nothing, Amelia wrote, could be less fatiguing than climbing the pyramids if you had the help of three Egyptians.[53] With two to pull and one to push, the women made their way up the large blocks, level by level, finally seeing the striking view from the top of the pyramid. It was from this vantage point that Amelia bade goodbye to Egypt for the last time. Looking south from the top of the Great Pyramid, they could see the entire pyramid field down to Saqqara and Dahshur and Meydum. Farther south still, Amelia wrote, "it is in this direction that our eyes turn oftenest—to the measureless desert in its mystery of light and silence; to the Nile where it gleams out again and again, till it melts at last into that faint far distance beyond which lie Thebes, and Philæ, and Abou Simbel."[54]

It must have broken Amelia's heart to leave Cairo for the last time on Friday, May 1, 1874. She and her party returned to England by going east this time, through the Suez Canal to other cities and towns on the Arabian Peninsula and Mesopotamia, spending time in Joppa and Beirut. From Beirut they decided to take a camping trip, so they rode horses and mules for three days to reach Damascus.[55] After several days there, they rode back to Beirut. Their boat prepared to leave on May 19, and Jenny was "very sorry" to leave Mr. Talhamy. She recalled that "he has been with us 6 Months & he was a v[e]ry nice kind fellow."[56] The three women then traveled through a number of Greek islands to what was then Constantinople. Taking their time to see many of the sights on their way back to England, they arrived in London in the evening of June 29. Lucy and Jenny would in time return to Egypt, but Amelia never would.

Returning Home

After ten months of adventure in Europe, the Ottoman Empire, and Egypt, Amelia knew there was work to be done. By 1874, plenty of Western men and women had gone to Egypt to explore, excavate, and send home artifacts and objects. The British Museum was already packed with statues, coffins, papyri, and more. But with no educational support, no centralized institution outside of the British Museum to organize, fund, and promote the study of ancient Egypt, there was little that anyone could learn from the accumulation of curious objects. When people traveled abroad, they were expected to bring back objects, stories, and information to share with museums and scholars. The MBs, Amelia, Lucy, and Jenny did just that, eventually and in their own ways.

Jenny traveled again to Egypt with Lucy and possibly the MBs in 1876, then got married in 1879 to George Collins.[57] After she was widowed in 1885, she began going by Jane. She remarried, to a man fully twenty years older than she was, William Norton Western, who died by 1891. She never had children. She brought back a number of antiquities from her extensive trips, many of which she recorded in her journal. Jenny also had a photograph collection, containing over 130 photographs, bought during her two trips to Egypt with Lucy.[58]

Lucy continued to work, and sometimes live, with Amelia and Ellen at the Larches, and sometimes Amelia lived with Lucy. It is unclear what, if anything, Lucy brought home. Amelia was the only one of the three who had been inspired to continue learning about Egypt's history and to share this with as many people as she could. Although her work launched a thousand trips up the thousand miles of the Nile she had just traversed herself, Amelia never returned to her beloved Egypt. She certainly had the means to go back, but the work she was about to embark on with the help of the MBs, Lucy, Stuart Poole, Samuel Birch, Emily Paterson, and Kate Bradbury would be the cornerstone of British Egyptology and professional Egyptology in the West for decades. It would almost break her.

The MBs also impacted Northern England with their collections from numerous trips. By 1898, they donated money and much of what they had accumulated to the purpose-built West Park Museum in their hometown of Macclesfield.[59] Amelia had remarked in *A Thousand Miles* that due to the smell of the mummy in their dahabeah, Marianne and Mary had "drowned the dear departed at the end of a week." But Marianne recalled that she sent the mummified remains to the British Museum, where Samuel Birch, then Keeper of Oriental Antiquities, did some study on the writings on the coffin. He wrote a letter back to Marianne saying that this had not been a man, or even a boy, but the mummified remains of a young girl, "Sheb-nut singer of the interior room . . . of the palace."[60] Sheb-nut's coffin and her remains now reside in the museum in Macclesfield, a testament to the problematic but important journey the MBs made to Egypt in 1873.

In London, Amelia had dozens of drawings, rubbings, and paintings along with boxes of antiquities that she needed to sort through. Amelia's collection was a lot like Charles Darwin's when he returned from his voyage on the *Beagle*. She had seen a new world, brought back specimens that would help her form and support her ideas over the coming years, and now she settled into her home to begin the long route to publication. She set to work unpacking her collections, writing to scholars with questions, and sending them some of her pieces in exchange for information. Like the MBs had done, she wrote first to Samuel Birch, asking for help with script she had copied at Abu Simbel, and she continued to check facts and ideas with him throughout her research. She had begun work almost immediately on the travelogue *A Thousand Miles Up the Nile,* and by the middle of 1875 she was sending Birch questions about details in her manuscript.

At first, she thought she would be writing a travel book for people interested in going to Egypt. She hoped it would be like her 1873 *Untrodden Peaks* because relatively few Englishwomen had been up the Nile, so the Nile was an unfrequented place for many; however, she quickly knew she had a different mission. She wanted to guide people through Egypt, not just geographically but also across time. Where Lucie Duff Gordon had shown readers life in modern Egypt, Amelia wanted readers to watch the ancient Egyptian landscape unfold in her work, the way it would if they themselves were traveling up the Nile. She researched and passionately wrote incredible historical detail about each site along the way, coupling it with her own memories and travel tips. Egypt, she wrote, is "a Great Book—not very easy reading, perhaps, under any circumstances; but at all events quite difficult enough already without the added puzzlement of being read backwards."[61]

The three women had seen that there was a lot more to uncover throughout Egypt in order to better understand its history, but Amelia knew they would need a concerted and organized effort to recover many of its historical objects. One of her biographers wrote of her: "She saw that the preservation of ancient Egypt demanded not only enthusiasm and scholarship, but the power to change national attitudes and marshal national resources, and that would mean a campaign."[62] The start of this campaign was her book.

A Thousand Miles Up the Nile was published in 1877 and was immediately a bestseller. One of her goals in this "long, and sometimes laborious undertaking" was "to bring the Nile, its scenery, its people, its associations ancient and modern, before the mind's eye of those who have never visited Egypt or the East; to recall all these things, and perhaps sometimes to make them clearer, to those who already know the river and its banks."[63]

She wanted to reach general, interested readers and introduce them to the vastness and wonder of Egypt. At the same time, *A Thousand Miles Up the Nile* also gave in-depth scholarly citations to aid readers who wanted to learn more and become more involved in the study of Egyptian history. To help her in these aims, she also worked tirelessly to save monuments and history in Egypt. She expressed the belief that, in Egypt,

> [m]uch has been discovered; but much remains hidden. Thus the old mystery hangs over Egypt to the last, and it seems as if we should never pluck the heart out of it. . . . We are always learning, and there is always more to be learned; we are always seeking, and there is always more to find.[64]

Whatever there was, Amelia would have to find it at the Larches. She was happy there. When she was writing, she worked most of the day, stopping only for meals and exercise and to take her dear Ellen out for drives and walks. She would arrive back home and look around her library, which housed her growing collection of over three thousand books and some of her antiquities.[65] She felt like she had to keep writing. Amelia was certain that, if everyone knew about the state of Egypt, they would come running to its aid. In early 1880, she told Samuel Birch that the editor of the *Morning Post* had agreed to publish "correspondence on Egyptological subjects" in the paper.[66] She wrote and wrote—books, talks, articles, reviews, and letters.

Meanwhile *A Thousand Miles* was sailing off shelves. She hoped that this written appeal to the public would lead to money to start an excavation fund. In her enthusiasm and excitement, she wrote to some of the most unexcitable people about it—Birch, his then-student Ernest Budge, and Henry Villiers Stuart, a member of Parliament. None of them had any interest in trying to reach the public in a grand manner. They didn't see the point in doing so. Instead they wanted to write scholarship for British scholars and not for the public to read in newspapers. They crushed her hopes when they told her that no one had any money to give to such pursuits as excavation in Egypt, so she should just let it go. She refused.

Everything changed when she got a letter from Reginald Stuart Poole, the son of Sophia Lane Poole and the nephew of Edward Lane, two early English travelers to Egypt. Stuart was also the

Keeper of Coins and Medals at the British Museum. He had visited Egypt when he was young, traveling with his mother and twice sailing the Nile with his uncle, and had always had an interest in the history of Egypt. Amelia saw the return address and tore open the envelope, hoping against hope for some good news. Stuart wrote that he had read *A Thousand Miles Up the Nile* with great delight and enthusiastically supported the venture with the *Morning Post*. Stuart promised that, with Amelia's help and expertise, he would write letters about Egypt for publication in the *Post*, too.[67] He also reassured her in a later letter not to be discouraged by Birch. He knew how she felt, though, because, having known the man for years, he told her, he, too, had been consistently discouraged by Birch, "for 28 years come the 27th February."[68]

With Stuart on board, she started receiving support from other men in the field: Archibald Sayce, who was at Oxford at the time but who had worked in Egypt, wrote to her and agreed to help. So did Heinrich Brugsch. Auguste Mariette, the French Egyptologist in charge of the Department of Antiquities, wrote from Cairo that he supported her mission. He reminded her that funds were also needed for a new museum in Cairo. He had been asking everyone for money. His museum, then at the Bulak on the banks of the Nile, was constantly being flooded. It would eventually be moved to the Gezireh Palace, then to a more permanent, purpose-built location in Midan Mariette Pasha, now Tahrir Square, in 1902. Stuart Poole suggested to Amelia not to accept help from the French—likely a wise decision given the fact that the two countries were still at odds over control of Egypt and its antiquities.

After several years of writing and asking and agreeing and foot-dragging, on Wednesday, June 16, 1880, a small group of "ladies and gentlemen interested in Egyptology held a private meeting in the Council Room of University College London, to consider the desirability of promoting research in Egyptology."[69] The group deemed the endeavor to indeed be desirable, and although there was considerable, powerful, and wealthy interest in the establishment of a fund from that point on, the promised subscriptions had yet to be given.

So, Amelia did what she always knew to do—she busied herself with writing more and more articles for *The Academy*, the *Times*, and the *Morning Post*. She reported as many new finds in Egypt as she could handle writing up—and she wrote feverishly. She was also "flitting about the country" with Lucy, who was still a fixture at the Larches, and spending time with Ellen.[70] In January of 1882, Amelia had finally started to call for those promised subscriptions and donations to the new research group. By the end of February, she counted A. C. Tait—the archbishop of Canterbury—and Erasmus Wilson as donors, and March brought more support and more money.

Finally, on March 27, 1882, thirty-five men and two women (Amelia and historian Jane Harrison) attended the first meeting of what was then the Delta Exploration Fund in Stuart Poole's office at the British Museum. The purpose of this new Fund was to excavate "the ancient sites of the Egyptian Delta, and the scheme has started with a reasonable prospect of success." Amelia and Stuart Poole were named honorary secretaries.[71] The MBs were also enthusiastic early supporters of the Fund, with Mary taking on the position as honorary secretary up north in Macclesfield by 1896, and Marianne donating money and time.[72]

The formation of the fund in 1882 meant that it benefited from the British bombardment of Alexandria in July of that year, and the subsequent defeat of the nationalist 'Urabi Revolt. This gave Britain effective control of Egypt and made it possible for Europeans to continue to run roughshod over Egyptian sovereignty for the next seventy years with little repercussion.[73] From this point on, Amelia was single-minded in her work: promote Egyptology to the public in order to raise money for the Fund to support more work in Egypt. As the scope of work expanded, the Delta Exploration Fund quickly became known as the Egypt Exploration Fund (EEF, the Fund). Amelia was working closely with a number of well-known archaeologists who were stationed all over the Mediterranean world. Importantly, she had gone from having just a few subscribers for the Fund in England in 1882 to over 160 in the United States and the UK by the end of 1886. American millionaire Theodore Davis was a member of the board in the States, and his partner, millionaire Emma Andrews, was the honorary treasurer for the Newport, Rhode Island, branch.[74]

First Excavations for the Fund

Amelia was scrambling to find a digger for the first official excavation season for the Fund—*her* Fund. She had suggested Heinrich Schliemann, the man who in the 1860s–70s had destroyed several layers of archaeological remains in Turkey in his quest to find the city of Troy. She thought maybe the famous name would bring attention to their work. Gaston Maspero, now the director of the Department of Antiquities after Mariette's death in 1881, worried about Schliemann's tactics being used in Egypt. He categorically refused to allow Schliemann to excavate.[75] In fact, he wrote to her in April 1882 lamenting the lack of English Egyptologists: "I do not know by what mischance England has not yet produced a young Egyptologist: the school is dying out without renewing itself."[76] He was right. The last English "Egyptologist" Amelia could recall was John Gardner Wilkinson. Wilkinson had lived in Egypt from 1821 to 1833, and the last time he had been there was 1855. He was the author of *Murray's Handbook for Travellers in Egypt,* the travel guide edition that Amelia, Lucy, and Jenny had taken with them on their journey.[77] Wilkinson had died in 1875, and there was no one to replace him. Amelia carefully considered Maspero's words. In the end, she found someone worthy: the Swiss Egyptologist Edouard Naville was chosen to excavate for the Fund at Tell el-Maskhuta in the eastern Delta beginning in January of 1883.[78]

Naville was unavailable for the following season of 1883–84, so Poole suggested that the young, self-taught, and, most importantly, English William Matthew Flinders Petrie be chosen. Petrie, just thirty years old at the time, had recently finished measuring and surveying the pyramids on the Giza Plateau. His brand-new book, *The Pyramids and Temples of Gizeh,* was a significant and empirically based investigation into the architecture of the Giza Plateau.[79] Petrie wanted to excavate in Egypt and began his career for the Fund in 1883 doing so at Tanis (San el-Hagar) in the northeastern

Delta.[80] He performed so well that season that he was asked to excavate again the following year in the western Delta with the goal of finding the Greek site of Naukratis, which he did. That year he had a new assistant with him, the Oxford-educated classicist Francis Griffith. As there was no university training for Egyptology or Egyptian archaeology at this time in Britain, field excavators were men either trained in classics, like Griffith, self-taught, or not trained at all. This caused several problems in early Egyptology.

Even though Petrie had trained himself, he was different from others digging in Egypt. He was interested in the small finds—like potsherds, small statues, beads—as opposed to large statues and monuments, which made him a favorite of both Amelia and the Fund. He was also frugal—others might say cheap. On-site, Petrie often built his own shelter, ate straight out of tin cans, and used the desert as a toilet. He was frequently found in varying degrees of undress. The biggest surprise for most Europeans and Americans who saw Petrie working tended to be that he did not wear socks or shirtsleeves while on excavation.[81] His life on-site, and at home, was Spartan; he expected others working with him to follow his lead.

Despite, or more likely because of, his habits, Petrie quickly became Amelia's protégé and pet project at the Fund. As she did with people she was fond of, Amelia was soon writing to Flinders as a mother would to a dear son, and he saw her as a true mentor. They saw eye to eye on most issues. They were both mindful of the need to conserve money. They both understood the importance of timely publication of results—Amelia wrote for the public in the papers; Petrie wrote for subscribers and scholars in a site report. They were both excited to display their finds each year to the public, as well. They also had to keep recruiting new members.

To understand the place of the Fund in the early years, it is also crucial to understand the importance of excavating in the Delta. The Egyptian Nile Delta, in the northern part of the country, has been a rich agricultural area for thousands of years. Settlements have proliferated there over the millennia, but little evidence survives because of the wet conditions, constant flooding, and farming that take place there. The mud brick and other such material remains disappear quickly. So Amelia, Stuart, and the rest of the Fund knew they were working against time.

By the end of 1886, Petrie had left the Fund, having grown frustrated with how they made decisions on spending, chose excavation sites, and more. He was cutting costs everywhere he could, but the Fund overspent (according to Petrie) on publishing the plates for his *Tanis* excavation report.[82] He fumed to Amelia that they should spend more money on excavation than on the publications—without the first, you couldn't support the second. Stuart Poole, however, was tired of Petrie. He had wanted Petrie to bring home the large statues for display in the British Museum, not the small pieces that the public was not particularly interested in. He told Amelia that the Fund was wasting time on Petrie. Petrie needed the financial support, but he wanted the freedom to work where and how he wished, and to do with the objects what he wished.

Around the time Petrie was complaining to Amelia about the administration of the Fund, Amelia was either frequently ill or caring for Ellen Braysher, who was also ill. Amelia was worried about the Fund, too, and the future of it. Poole was resigning, Petrie had already resigned (he had left for Egypt to photograph depictions of different racial types on temple walls for eugenicist Francis Galton), and there was frequent infighting.[83] Petrie had even pushed Amelia to leave the Fund, but she refused. She did continue to support Petrie, though, and thought of him as a son. She had already written to him that she had promised UCL a "modest endowment" in her will and hinted that he might be the first beneficiary of it.[84] Amelia was only fifty-six, so that would be years down the road.

Despite her being "dead beat," Amelia continued working. She wooed excavators such as Frank Griffith and Edouard Naville, and wealthy supporters such as Lord Carnarvon and Manchester textile merchant Jesse Haworth. She traveled all over the UK, giving public lectures about the Fund's work in the Delta and elsewhere in Egypt. By this point, in late 1887, the Fund had at least partially subsidized over twenty-five excavations at sites like Tanis and Naukratis, as well as the pyramid sites of Abusir and Dahshur and as far south as Aswan.[85] Also by 1887, Lucy Renshaw and Amelia were not as close as they once were. Perhaps it was the business of the Fund that kept them apart. Perhaps it was the fact that much of Amelia's energies went to Flinders and Ellen. Letters from Amelia to Lucy don't exist, as far as we know, so what happened between them remains a mystery. Lucy, however, lived a long life, dying in a hospital in 1913 when she was eighty years old.

It was around the time of this upheaval in the Fund that Amelia met the wealthy Kate Bradbury, who was born in 1854 to a wealthy textile businessman and his wife near Manchester. She was over twenty years younger than Amelia, but the two connected quickly and intensely. They met in late 1887 or early 1888, and by February of 1888, Kate was staying with Amelia in Bristol and going with her to visit the Pooles in London. Amelia was instantly smitten, but without much reciprocation from Kate. Amelia had written to Stuart about her new acquaintance, and he responded to Amelia that he would be happy to meet Kate. He wrote to her that he did not think it was "hard to feel a deep interest in her after all you have told me and written me. Of course I have carefully burnt the private pages of your letter."[86] We do not know what she had written about Kate, but based on later evidence, we can guess that it was about her romantic feelings for her new friend. By May of 1888, Kate was regularly staying at the Larches with Amelia and Ellen. Despite their age difference, this relationship had a major impact on both of their lives. As Ellen became increasingly ill, Kate took on the role of companion and friend, and, in letters from Amelia, she became "my own love" and "my own darling one."[87] She came to understand the importance that Ellen held for Amelia, as well. And the three lived together for the last four years of Ellen's life.

Kate became Amelia's personal secretary, and Amelia trained her in the business and management of the Fund. Amelia also fired the Fund's secretary, Hellier Gosselin, and brought on Emily Paterson as a paid assistant secretary.[88] Emily was tasked with the daily administration duties that wore Amelia out, such as daily correspondence with excavators and subscribers. Kate was more of a personal aide and companion to Amelia, and she accompanied her on a lecture tour to the United States from 1889 to 1890 so Amelia could garner more support for the Fund. Kate continued to fill her role as Amelia's secretary, fielding correspondence and responding to it, revealing her private and privileged knowledge of Amelia's thoughts and plans. Neither the Egypt Exploration Fund itself nor Amelia's final lecture tour would have been "so great if Kate had not been at her side" as an assistant, maid, nurse, and partner.[89]

The grueling yet outrageously successful tour left both women exhausted. Amelia fell twice—once right before a talk and once on the boat home—first breaking her wrist and then her arm. Once they returned home, Amelia suffered further health issues. She continued to fall apart. Sometime in June or July of 1890, she had what was believed to be a precancerous tumor removed from her left breast.[90] With Emily's and Kate's help, she continued to work for the Fund, going against doctor's orders to rest. Toward the end of 1890, she began lecturing again in Edinburgh, then returned home to see her beloved invalid Ellen at the Larches, with Kate at her side.

Throughout 1890 and 1891, Amelia was not fully recovered from all of her travels, yet she was as busy as ever preparing her American lectures for publication in *Pharaohs, Fellahs and Explorers*.[91] It was an important book for promoting interest among the general public in Egypt, and it is still a main source for historians today. She substantially revised these lectures, giving them titles like "The Explorer in Egypt," "The Buried Cities of Ancient Egypt," and "The Hieroglyphic Writing of the Ancient Egyptians." In editing her talks, she "preserved the colloquial style—in the hope," she wrote, "of being better remembered by those who have heard them."[92] The book was successful in part because of her style of delivery. The Assyriologist Rev. Archibald Sayce, one of Amelia's acquaintances, wrote a review of *Pharaohs* in the periodical *The Academy* not long after the book was published. He expounded on Amelia's talents, writing that she was "more than an Egyptologist—she is an Egyptological enthusiast, and she knows how to communicate her enthusiasm to others."[93] She had clearly proven this in the United States, having given these lectures on more than one hundred occasions to tens of thousands of people in total. After a cursory summary of her work and a few corrections, Sayce ended by exhorting all readers to engage with it, saying, "It should be studied by everyone who desires to combine pleasure with profit."[94]

In order to take a little break after their US trip, Kate and Amelia traveled together to Monte Carlo, Monaco, in March of 1891. Amelia's weakness and continued lung illnesses brought coughing and congestion. Her doctors thought the change of air in southern Europe would help her. The women traveled all over the area, going to Italy as well. Amelia must have shown Kate some of her favorite places from almost twenty years earlier. Revived and rested, they returned to England by August. During this trip, Amelia's relationship with Kate had progressed, too. Amelia had taken to simply calling her "Baby" in all her letters to Flinders Petrie, and he knew whom she was referring to.

Despite life being very good for Amelia at this point, her wellness was short-lived, and by Christmas, she was ill again with bronchitis. Kate, who had been up north visiting her family, came immediately to her side. She became the main carer for both Amelia and Ellen. In the end, the influenza took over: Ellen Braysher died in January 1892 at the age of eighty-six; Amelia died six weeks later on April 15 at the age of sixty-two. Ellen and Amelia are buried in the same vault in the churchyard of St. Mary's in Bristol. The gravestone is an Egyptian obelisk with an ankh, and has been Grade II listed by English Heritage, which celebrates it as a landmark in LGBTQ+ history.

Lasting Legacies

Emily and Kate were left to mourn and then settle Amelia's affairs, which included helping to fund the initiatives for Egyptology set out in her will, written just six years earlier. One of the first things they had to take care of was the establishment of a department of academic Egyptology. Having been influenced by Maspero's warning about English Egyptology years before, Amelia wanted to support such a department for "'the teaching of Egyptology with a view to the wide extension of the knowledge of the history, antiquities, literature, philology, and art of Ancient Egypt.'"[95] She rarely spoke about it publicly, but Amelia fervently supported women's emancipation and was the vice president of the Society for Promoting Women's Suffrage, one of many suffrage societies that fought for women's right to vote in the UK.[96] So, one of the primary stipulations in the bequest was that the "classes, scholarships and exhibitions" at the newly founded department "were to be open to students of both sexes."[97] This meant that the only university that could accept her gift would be, at that time, the only university in England that allowed women to earn degrees: University College, London.

Petrie and all others who would hold the newly established professorship in Egyptology would have duties such as conducting annual excavations in Egypt, giving lectures about the excavations, and teaching classes in "the deciphering and reading of hieroglyphs and other ancient Egyptian scripts and writings."[98]

Other provisos in Amelia's will made it clear to everyone that Flinders was her first choice to hold the new position. For instance, she resolved that "no official of the British Museum shall be eligible for the chair" and surprisingly added: "Neither shall the first Professor occupying the Chair be a man above forty years of age."[99] If these requirements could not be met, the Ashmolean Museum at Oxford was to have the collections and money, and if they failed, the items would go to the Fitzwilliam at Cambridge.[100] So it passed that in November of 1892, just under two years shy of his fortieth birthday, Flinders Petrie was named the first Edwards Chair of Egyptology at UCL and, consequently, the first university chair holder of Egyptology in Britain. Amelia's collections of Egyptian objects, which she acquired primarily from her trip and the Fund's excavations, along with her large library were bequeathed to the university as well.

Amelia's personal relationships were central to her work. Her stable home life with Ellen gave her the freedom to travel, which she did with Lucy and Jenny. This meant that she was able to participate in a number of activities that, as a woman, she would not have normally been able to do without a man to supervise her. Later on, Kate became her partner in life and travel, allowing Amelia to continue to spread the good word of the Fund to audiences all over the United States and the UK and to raise money for it. In doing this work, she institutionalized Egyptology and Egyptian archaeology in Britain; everything after that stemmed from her foundation.

Amelia's *A Thousand Miles Up the Nile* is a bestselling travelogue, guidebook, and historical account of monuments of ancient and modern Egypt. It is also a book of dos and don'ts for traveling in Egypt, which was finally demystified for women and nonwealthy people. If a woman—or five—could successfully navigate the Nile and return safely, maybe anyone could. Amelia's books would have a wider impact than Lucie Duff Gordon's for getting people (especially women) to travel to and through Egypt.

Marianne Brocklehurst's legacy is less visible than Amelia's, making it a bit harder to trace. The MBs went back to Egypt together several times. They met influential Egyptologists and loved to compete to purchase items. In April of 1896, they were at the Mena House hotel, on the Giza Plateau, visiting with American dilettante Charles Wilbour, who, in the end, gave his own collection to the Brooklyn Museum, and Flinders Petrie, whom they must have known from his work with the Fund. They also visited with early women Egyptologists Mary Brodrick and Margaret Benson, who was at Mena House at the end of her penultimate excavation season at the Temple of Mut in 1897. They all appear in Marianne's letter to Percy Newberry, an Egyptologist from Liverpool, apologizing for buying a scarab out from under him for five pounds. To add insult to injury, she told Newberry that Petrie could have the piece if he liked.[101]

After years of traveling together, the MBs returned home for good in the late 1890s. They had amassed quite a collection of antiquities, with Marianne's being so important that her sister, Emma Dent, wanted to buy it for display in her home, Sudeley Castle, for £1,000 (the equivalent of about £80,000 today). But Marianne wanted to build a museum in her hometown of Macclesfield. Her goal was "the education, refinement and pleasure of the people for all time to come," and by 1897, she and her brother Peter had accomplished that goal. They founded the West Park Museum in West Park, Macclesfield, and her collection remains there today. The museum holds other pieces, but the ancient objects are the centerpiece. She also founded and was the secretary of a branch of the Fund in her hometown.

Marianne fell and broke her collarbone in October of 1898. She died later that month, her death possibly being self-inflicted. She never saw the museum opened. Mary Booth was left the Bagstones, and she lived there until she died in 1912 at the age of eighty-two, alone and without Marianne. She chose to be buried in the same grave as her companion.

Amelia, Lucy, Jenny, Marianne, and Mary all laid the groundwork for women to come to Egypt. They first showed that women *could* travel on their own, without the help of men. Then, they told women that they *should* travel to Egypt and wrote about how and why to do it. The next group of women veered off that well-trodden path and began to dig.

2

Maggie Benson and Nettie Gourlay

Mistress of peace and of the war cry. Lady of heaven, queen of the gods—Great Mut. Creator. Protector. Lady of joy. Cobra of dread. The vigilant mistress of Karnak. Mighty ruler in her Theban Temple. She whose spirit exists because her temple endures. She whose temple and city will exist for millions of years.

—Hymn praising Mut, consort of Amun, mother of Khonsu

It was a bright, clear day in January 1894, and Margaret Benson, better known as Maggie to her friends and family, squinted her eyes against the sunlight reflecting off the deep blue water of the Mediterranean. She and her brother, Fred, had just made the crossing from the Greek port of Piraeus on a steamer, bound for Alexandria, Egypt. The crossing was rough, the boat tossed and turned by the turbulent waters of the ancient Roman lake. Maggie didn't really get sick, but her stomach was only just starting to settle as she scanned the horizon for the Thomas Cook tourist boat that should have been nearby, ready to take her and the other tourists to shore. All she could see was the flat coast of Alexandria, punctuated by the lighthouse, near Ras el-Tin Palace, and Pompey's Pillar.

Her excitement was only slightly diminished by her brother's distress. Fred, who had not fared as well on the boat as his older sister, was watching the Egyptian health officials look over the steamer's passenger papers. He was fretting that the whole boat would be quarantined in port for forty-eight hours, as many boats were upon arrival from European ports. But, all of a sudden, it seemed, the health officials were gone—they wouldn't be in quarantine. Tourist boats overwhelmed the steamer, with smaller vessels of all shapes, sizes, and colors closing in. It was the best water show Maggie had ever seen. All at once, on board the ship, porters began offering hotels, carriages, luggage services, river tours, and more. There was whistling, waving, and shouting in half a dozen languages. Maggie relished the excitement of arrival in Egypt.

In the melee, Fred kept saying to anyone who asked, almost as a calming mantra in the chaos of landing: "I want Cook. I want Cook." After some time, an agent dressed in the famous scarlet sweater with a bright yellow "COOK" emblazoned on the front found Fred and Maggie, and they were flooded with relief to be in good hands. For the rest of their trip that year, if anyone bothered them, they simply said, "I've got Cook," and they were left alone.

Their relief in finding Cook's agent was equal in measure to their exhaustion. They had been traveling for weeks through southern France, Italy, and Greece, chasing the same miraculous change-of-air cure that Amelia Edwards and countless others had tried before. Jean-François Champollion, largely credited with deciphering hieroglyphs in 1822, wrote home on his first and only trip up the Nile

Fig. 2.1: Maggie Benson, c. 1893.

Fig. 2.2: Fred Benson, c. 1894.

in 1827 that he had never felt better in his life than in the desert. In 1849–50, Florence Nightingale obviously knew about the benefits of the desert air, as she wrote home from Egypt that she felt in much better health there. The fact that Maggie knew to go there for her own health was not out of the ordinary.

The Bensons had finally come to Egypt hoping to relieve Maggie's rheumatism, which, in the nineteenth century, was a vague diagnosis for a number of illnesses, including pulmonary inflammation and painful joints, the symptoms that plagued her. Having suffered from stress, anxiety, and depression—and the physical ailments that accompanied them—she told her mother that she could "feel the weather" of cold and damp Kent, in southern England, in her body and needed to go to warmer climes to heal.

At home, she was frequently laid up in bed for days, unable to breathe well, or her joints hurt so badly that she could hardly move. Often, Maggie was not only physically ill but also emotionally unwell. Her depression, like her joints, made it impossible for her to get out of bed, much less walk around. Like so many others before her, she sought the sun, sand, and dry air of Egypt as a cure and to make her happy—and for a while, it did. So, Maggie and Fred, siblings and longtime travel partners, began their first trip through Egypt on a Thomas Cook cruise up the Nile to Aswan.

Even though Fred and Maggie were new to the Nile, Thomas

Cook & Son were not. They had been taking people on river cruises for over twenty years by the time the Bensons joined them. Cook's influence had changed tourism in Egypt to favor Western visitors, which meant that the Bensons' trip would be relaxing and enjoyable. Their cabins on board were relatively spacious, and they were well-fed with fresh fruit, fresh dairy, and fresh meat every day. Maggie and Fred were also offered excursions to important sites almost every day. While he enjoyed the cruise, Fred didn't want to see everything—he wanted to relax; however, Maggie took advantage of all the amenities Cook offered. She went on every excursion she could, happily sitting astride a donkey to venture to the tombs at Saqqara, just south of Cairo. She climbed the cliffs at Beni Hasan to see the rock-cut tombs and their beautiful painted walls. She shopped at the bazaars in most of the towns on the way up the Nile, especially in Asyut, a large town just to the south of Abydos.

The steamer passed through Luxor for a couple of days on the way up to the temple of Edfu. The siblings had a few excursions to the major temples and tombs on the East and West Banks, and Maggie enjoyed every one of them. She went to tomb 17, known at the time as Belzoni's tomb, and tomb 11, known then as Bruce's tomb, named after the men who had found them. These were two of the most beautiful and well-preserved tombs at the time, and travelers who went to the Valley of the Kings had to stop and see them. Then they moved on to the town of Gebel el-Silsila. Maggie wouldn't have gone ashore there, though, because she could see most of it from the steamer. Once they reached Aswan, early in the morning as the rising sun was hitting the cliffs on the West Bank, they were surrounded by the villagers who knew that Cook's tourists were ready to shop. They offered ostrich feathers, eggs, clothing, antiquities, birds, and other animals for sale. Maggie didn't say that she bought anything, but it wouldn't have been a surprise if she did. Heading farther south, both Bensons enjoyed an exciting ride on a smaller boat traversing the First Cataract, just south of Aswan. Maggie assuaged her mother's worry by telling her that the ride was "not at all dangerous," despite the fact that over the years many boats had capsized and their passengers had died. Then, they turned around, beginning the journey back down the Nile. By late January of that first trip, they reached sunny Luxor for a second time and decided to settle themselves there for several weeks.

In 1894, there were few hotels they could stay in, and the best ones were owned and run by Thomas Cook, including the Luxor Hotel. As Maggie had hoped, thanks to the dry desert air and warm sunshine, her breathing had grown much better over the weeks they had been traveling. The pain in her joints dissipated, and she reveled in the luxuries of the Luxor Hotel as her health improved. No longer bedridden as she had been at home, she enjoyed sitting on the wide terrace for meals and tea, lounging in the gardens with the fragrant flowers and opportunities for people-watching, and sleeping in her comfortable rooms. She was able to go on a "lovely little expedition" nearly every day. Having engaged a "nice little donkey and boy" of her own, she was able to take her time, following paths, going up to the top of the hills and back down into the Valley of the Kings, and some days visiting and studying up to five tombs. Fred had gone back to Greece for a time while Maggie stayed in Luxor, and she soon became so enamored of Egypt and Egyptians—both ancient and modern—that by the time Fred returned, he found that she had already arranged to return the following year to excavate.

Like Amelia Edwards and Marianne Brocklehurst just twenty years before her, Maggie was one in a long line of travelers who became an archaeologist or antiquities collector because of their experience among the monuments in Egypt. If one had the time to travel and the money to support excavations or purchasing artifacts, or both, that was enough to make you an archaeologist at this point in the history of archaeology in Egypt. Her first season in 1895 would extend to three very successful excavation seasons in the Asher (Isheru) district of Karnak Temple at the Temple of Mut. In fact, by the late 1890s, women were so firmly entrenched in travel narratives that hundreds of women were inspired to travel to Egypt for enjoyment, health, and study. Maggie Benson was one of these women. Soon, she would meet another woman like her, Janet Gourlay, known as Nettie, who would become her friend, lover, and excavation partner. Together, they would find hundreds of artifacts in the Temple of Mut, clear and remap the temple, and return many statues and other pieces to their original places. The resulting publication, *The Temple of Mut in Asher*, was published in 1899 by Victorian giant John Murray. It was written for both the interested general public and archaeologists, and would become both a best-seller and a substantial contribution to the discipline of Egyptology.[1] Together, the women would return for a final season in 1900. Maggie and Nettie were more successful and powerful together than they would have been apart, and their partnership was crucial to the work they did in Luxor at the end of the nineteenth century.

Margaret Benson, the Minister's Daughter

Margaret Benson was the fourth of six children born to preoccu-pied parents Edward White Benson and his wife, Mary (Minnie) Sidgwick, on a warm June day in 1865. Her Victorian home life was generally stable (if sometimes stressful) but marked with tragedy. Her brother Martin died in 1878 when he was just eighteen years old, probably from meningitis, but the family put it down to the stress of his genius. In 1890, Maggie's older sister and closest con-fidant, Nellie, died after a short but brutal battle with diphtheria, a highly contagious bacterial infection that affects mucous mem-branes. One day, Maggie saw Nellie happily collecting a few books to read while she was isolating with the infection, sure she would come out of it just fine in a week or so. They said brief goodbyes, knowing they would see each other again. A few days later, however, the infection proved too strong for Nellie, and with no real treat-ment available for diphtheria at the time, she died quickly. Nellie was just twenty-seven years old, two years older than Maggie, and the shock of Nellie's death seemed to taint all her memories of her childhood confidant with grief.[2]

It wasn't until later in life that the Benson siblings really began to reflect on those days. Maggie's older brother Arthur and her younger brother Fred both wrote a number of autobiographical accounts, which provide insight into their home life growing up. They tell of tensions between their parents, the disappointment Ed-ward felt toward all of his children, and the way Minnie, married to a boorish religious bully, struggled spiritually and emotionally.

We know so much about Maggie and her family because of these accounts, as well as the letters and diaries that her family preserved. All of these memories told a love story between their parents that began with a kiss, which sounds endlessly romantic. It wasn't.[3]

Their first kiss happened when Minnie was an obedient twelve-year-old girl sitting on the knee of twenty-three-year-old Edward, a theology student bound for greatness in the Victorian Anglican Church. Immediately after she accepted his proposal of marriage that day, she sobbed in his arms. For the next six years, Edward courted his young cousin while she worried about the affair, knowing she didn't love him the way he thought she did, the way she thought she should, but couldn't. Her own mother, Mary, didn't want the two to get married, either, worrying that Minnie was too young to agree to such a commitment (and Mary had some strong romantic feelings for Edward herself). Alas, they were joined in holy matrimony when Minnie turned eighteen, and they spent the rest of Edward's life together—sort of.

Minnie dutifully carried out her obligations as a Victorian wife and mother—supporting her husband's work, being the hostess to countless dignitaries, bearing and caring for several children, managing the household servants, and more—but even from a young age Minnie knew she simply wasn't attracted to men. This was apparent throughout their courtship. In his turn, Edward was endlessly disappointed that his betrothed didn't write him more passionate love letters, and he tried to instruct her on how to do so in a way that was pleasing to him. In fact, most of their courtship consisted of Edward trying to train Minnie to be his ideal wife, but it wasn't working. She was unhappy in the relationship before the wedding, and that unhappiness continued throughout her life thanks to Edward's constant dissatisfaction with her as a wife and lover, which wasn't helped by the fact that she loved women.

Throughout the years, Minnie had passionate relationships with several women, including Emily Edwardes, Charlotte Bassett, and Lucy Tait. When her relationships got serious enough, Edward would frequently, almost frantically, call her back to him by revisiting the time he proposed—he would place Minnie on his knee and they would pray. Minnie would often feel the guilt and failure Edward wanted her to feel, and she would reluctantly return to his bed to resume her duties as his wife. But sometimes she would simply run away. Once, Minnie left her young children with Edward so she could go live in Germany for several months with a Miss Hall. She finally settled in at home, though, several years before Edward died in 1896. By the time of his death, Edward had been the archbishop of Canterbury for thirteen years and the family lived in Lambeth Palace, the archbishop's official residence. By then, Minnie had met the love of her life, Lucy Tait, the daughter of the previous archbishop of Canterbury (and Egypt Exploration Fund donor), and brought her to live in the palace and share her bed.

Minnie was treading a line between her demanding husband, her spiritual fervor, and the Victorian family she was raising.[4] But with divorce being impossible for her as the wife of the highest official in the Anglican Church, she did the only thing she could do— she adapted. As long as Minnie was discreet, she could maintain her relationships with women. Often, for women in marriages like Minnie's—and there were a lot of them—an intimate friend could give them a whole new life. During the Victorian period, same-sex relationships, especially for women, could also be empowering. In these loving and often long-term partnerships, women were able to live out their ideal marriage—including with the bonding of sexual intercourse if they chose, but they did not have to be completely defined by it. That's exactly what Minnie did. She taught her children, especially Maggie, to live how they wished.

Maggie was known to be a passionate and devoted friend whose relationships were rarely lighthearted and easy. Her brother Arthur described her as "profound, deliberate, untiring, slow in execution, thorough, and her charm, which was great, was not easily or lightly revealed. She was shy and retiring in manner, diffident and tentative; apt to consolidate her friendships by long and quiet companionship . . ."[5] Because of her deep and intense emotions, due, likely, to the emotions her mother expressed in her own life, Maggie "suffered greatly through" her own relationships, as Arthur wrote of her, yet she still "got great joy out of her affections."[6] Her relationship with her mother was fraught—Minnie was gone much of the time to visit her lovers or, as the children were told, to recuperate from an illness. Maggie's letters to her mother were full of news from home—Fred, "the baby," had begun walking, she and her father had gone on a side-saddle pony ride, and more—always emphatically begging for her mother to come home.

By the time Maggie was eighteen, she was attending Lady Margaret Hall at Oxford University, studying political economy. During this time, she became heavily involved in the numerous intellectual and social societies, she played cricket and field hockey and took up swimming. She found it easy to make friends and connect to others easily and deeply. One of her friends from her time in Oxford, a Miss Jourdain, recalled that "she was apt to be easily overdone, chiefly because she invariably put so much force and feeling into what she did."[7] She seemed to have been very like her mother in the emotional and physical energy she put into her personal connections.

She left Lady Margaret Hall in 1886. Oxford didn't allow women to earn degrees until 1921, so Maggie would have only earned a certificate of completion for all of her hard work. It is possible she missed some of the lectures in 1885 because she was recovering from scarlet fever in Switzerland. Her brothers' writings reveal that she was never particularly healthy, but this is the first record of any illness and the true beginning of a life of invalidism interspersed with bursts of health and energy.

After leaving Oxford, she went back to her family—her mother, father, and siblings who remained at home. She spent time with her cousins, Kitty and Stewart McDowall, who lived with the Bensons and for whom Maggie was appointed a guardian. Their mother, Maggie's aunt Ada, died in their infancy, and their father could not adequately care for them.[8] The family time helped to fulfill Maggie, but by the time she was twenty-five, in 1890, she had painful symptoms of rheumatism and arthritis, two related autoimmune inflammatory diseases she would battle for decades to come. Minnie's relationships, especially the one with Lucy Tait, however, made the already anxious Maggie even more so, as she worried her mother would love Lucy more than she loved Maggie. This caused even more heartache for Maggie, leading to more illness, and since she had to be free of it, she and Fred left home.

A Change of Scenery and a Change of Air

As the Benson siblings made their home at the Luxor Hotel in the spring of 1894, Maggie decided to fully immerse herself in the comforts it offered. The hotel was built in 1877, situated about two hundred meters back from the Nile's banks and behind the Luxor Temple, in the middle of luxurious gardens and surrounded by farmland. To enter the hotel, visitors walked through a veritable forest of trees that had "pretty little tufted yellow flowers making the air fragrant with their delicate perfume."[9] Fred thought that the gardens were fit for the gods, and Maggie wrote to her mother that "one thing that keeps attracting one's eyes is a red bougainvillea with sun on it against a background of pale blue sky and greyish palm-trees, it is wonderful—and the birds are distracting."[10] She was so distracted that it was hard for her to write letters home. These gardens became central to Maggie's sense of well-being in Luxor.[11]

For travelers like the Bensons who wished to make a long stay in Luxor, the hotel offered a discount along with a daily morning coffee, lunch, and "a substantial dinner." The rooms themselves were touted as "clean, but not luxurious."[12] Being a long-term resort hotel, the Luxor had a resident English physician, Dr. W. Longmore, who also worked at the local hospital. This medical connection continued to draw people to the hotel who needed health treatment and rest, like Maggie did. Fred wrote that his sister suffered not only from physical ailments like rheumatism that people could see on the outside but also from "an internal malady, depressing and deadly: a chill was a serious thing for her, fatigue must be avoided."[13] The Egyptian air helped to keep the chill away and to restore her energy.

Toward the end of their first trip to Egypt, in mid-March, Maggie had heard that there was a place where she could see granite statues with the heads of cats and wanted to investigate. She got on her trusted donkey, accompanied by her donkey boy and Fred, and rode from Luxor Temple to Karnak Temple. The temples are almost two miles apart, and Maggie took her donkey along the ancient route, an avenue of ram-headed sphinxes. In ancient times, this road went from the front pylon of Luxor Temple to the gateway that leads to the Temple of Khonsu at Karnak. This road has now been excavated and is walkable today, though two main roads span the ancient path as overhead bridges, yanking visitors back into the twenty-first century in a jarring way. But for Benson, she rode on a dirt track between the slow-flowing Nile River on her left, the avenue of sphinxes on her right, and the sun high above her head, until she entered the ancient palm grove that surrounded Karnak Temple. "The palms," she recalled, "cast interlacing shadows on the path, and the sphinxes . . . hold between their paws little figures of the king who erected them."[14] This road led (and still leads) to the northern gate of the Temple of Mut, in the Lake of Asher, which was the name of the precinct of this part of the temple complex.

The mother goddess Mut was the consort of the chief god, Amun, whose main temple in all of Egypt was at Karnak, so it was fitting that Mut's temple was connected to it. Together with their son, Khonsu, whose temple was also connected to his parents' temples at Karnak, they were known as the Theban triad and were regularly celebrated as such. The Temple of Mut had originally been built in the early eighteenth dynasty (c. 1550–1292 BCE), but it was later refurbished by Queen Hatshepsut. As the only known female pharaoh, Hatshepsut identified with the mother goddess Mut on a deep level, and, needing to strengthen the legitimacy of her rule, she tried to make a powerful and concrete connection to her in life.[15] Mut could be depicted as a vulture, a cow, or a woman in a red dress, but in many statues she was Sekhmet, the strong-willed lion-headed goddess; at other times, she appeared as the more relaxed, peaceful cat Bastet. It was these remnants of the Temple of Mut that were waiting to be found under the packed Nile mud.

When Maggie arrived, she saw that the temple itself was almost completely destroyed, but there were a few black granite statue heads jutting up from the brown, parched earth. The gates were filled almost to the top with dirt, making access to the inner temple difficult. The walls of the temple were so broken and buried that there was very little anyone could see of the temple upon visiting. The figures were scattered about, Maggie wrote,

> at one place a group, at another a single mutilated head, and again two figures close together leaned towards one another as if they were secretly lamenting the downfall of the great gods. . . . At the far end of the temple a lion-headed figure quaintly whitened by saltpetre from the soil stood out against the background of the lake.[16]

As she continued to look around, she could see all around her the old and the new. The homes in the small village of Karnak were built in and around the great ancient pylons of the temple complex, glowing in the sun. The shady palm groves broke enough so she could see the Libyan hills on the West Bank of the Nile that had watched over this sacred area for thousands of years. Girls were grazing their goats; women were leading cattle to the water for a drink; men were washing themselves nearby. As she inhaled the slightly sweet-smelling air, basking in the warmth of the setting sun as the wind danced on her cheeks, she wondered if she might be able to stay here. She soon found help from her brother and Amelia Edwards's friend Edouard Naville, who supported her plans of clearing the site to bring the ancient into the light of the present.

It wasn't that others didn't try to clear the temple before; it had just been a very long time. In the 1840s, French Egyptologist and founder of the Antiquities Department Augustus Mariette, with Prussian Egyptologist Karl Lepsius, had cleared part of the temple area and created a map of it, which appeared in Mariette's 1875 book about Karnak.[17] American millionaire Charles Wilbour improved on Mariette's map in the 1880s, but never published his work. So, there was hope for Maggie to do some original work. Her first application for permission was refused, but Naville promptly wrote to Jacques de Morgan, then head of the Department of Antiquities, to support Maggie's application; de Morgan granted the permission immediately. This was how Maggie Benson became the first woman given official permission to excavate in Egypt. She was warned, however, not to expect to find anything at the temple, which is likely why she was allowed to work there.[18] Fred helped, and the Bensons were also able to pay for their own project, which almost guaranteed their permission to dig. Despite having no archaeological training whatsoever, Maggie began to feel like a real Egyptologist as she made preparations for the first season.[19]

The Work Begins

The first season lasted about five weeks, starting in January of 1895. When Maggie and Fred arrived at the site that first morning, the scene couldn't have been more different than what Maggie had dreamed of in the previous year. They walked into a group of over thirty men and boys waiting to work, and, as was customary, all of them had brought their own baskets and picks. When they saw Maggie and Fred, the group began shouting, pushing, jumping, and begging to be hired. Maggie was horrified at the disorder of the scene, but took heart when another excavator working nearby told her that he routinely broke many sticks over the backs of the potential crew members while trying to maintain order on-site (Maggie didn't do this). In the end, they chose "four men and sixteen boys, an overseer, a night guardian, and a water-carrier."[20] After this harrowing feat, Maggie sat down on a ledge, still worn out from the journey to Egypt. She recovered quickly in the warm weather, showing what Fred wrote as "the most glorious contempt of bodily ailments which I have ever seen" when she took to leading the men and boys around the site to plan the season together.[21]

The men were the diggers; the boys took on the role of basket boys, hauling baskets of dirt from the excavation to a mound to be sifted and disposed of. The overseer, or reis, was generally in charge of the diggers, keeping order and reporting back to the archaeologist in charge, which was Maggie. Their first reis asked for higher wages than normal because he wished to be compensated for having to report to a woman (he didn't last long). The night guardian had the unenviable task of protecting the site from the possibility of plundering by his neighbors. Some subversive watchmen would allow their friends or family to trespass in the dark of night to take pieces to sell, and they would claim the following day to have accidentally fallen asleep. The water carrier, who filled a bucket of drinking water and carried it to all the workers, was a young, veiled girl. In the publication of their excavation, Maggie didn't really mention the names of her crew, even though the crew did all the heavy lifting. Many archaeologists at the time, including Maggie and Fred, didn't consider their names to be very important. While Maggie and Fred, and later their other British crew members, paid for the privilege to excavate in their chosen spot, they really did very little but watch the work being done before taking all the credit. The excavation crew, on the other hand, worked ten-hour days or longer in the sun, usually with breaks during the hottest parts of the day.

Maggie and Fred would arrive on-site in the morning to organize the workday for the crew. All the English archaeologists in Luxor that year were overcome by the "novelty of an English girl" conducting her own excavation. Maggie was able to get the help of Egyptologist Percy Newberry, who deciphered much of the script, and Fred, of course, was a strong back who had to find the best way to clear and arrange the heaps of dirt rapidly coming in from the excavation. After the morning, Maggie would go back to the hotel to eat lunch and rest. She would then return on her white donkey, hauling a tea basket for the afternoon, with her donkey boy behind her. They would have tea, watch the work, and then at sunset return to the hotel for dinner. Maggie would use this rest time at the hotel to think and talk to her brother, and the two would make notes about the work of the day. They would eat dinner and then play games, then repeat the schedule the following day if Maggie was feeling up to it. Often, they took days off due to Maggie's exhaustion and Fred's desire to have fun, leaving the excavation to the reis and the workers.

Maggie paid the workers every Saturday, and she thought she paid them well—around two piastres or five pence per day, which at the time was three days' worth of subsistence pay.[22] Generally, the money was not meant to sustain the workers for the whole year since the excavations were short, but it was meant to supplement the other work they did the rest of the year. Maggie and Fred also participated in the well-known custom of giving baksheesh, or extra money, like a tip, to the workers every time they found an object and turned it over to the director. It was meant to be an incentive for the diggers not to take pieces to sell to dealers, thus supplementing their income. Flinders Petrie was one of the most successful implementers of this practice, paying up to five Egyptian pounds to the worker who found the small head of a statuette of an early Egyptian king, Khufu, in 1903. Few of his sites were bothered because he paid his workers so well in this way. On Maggie's excavation, she was certain items were being stolen over the years, but she didn't know it for sure until the third and final season revealed the culprit.

Because Maggie was the one granted permission to run the excavation, she was considered to be the one in charge. It's hard to overstate how important Maggie's position was for women in archaeology in Egypt. For over one hundred years, European men had been coming to Egypt, excavating, collecting, and publishing work about the ancient Egyptian world, often with the help and hard work of their invisible, unpaid wives or female assistants, to say nothing of the hardworking Egyptian crew. Now, for the first time, a woman's name appeared as the lead archaeologist on a site. Maggie had the help of her brother Fred, who had previously excavated in Athens with David Hogarth, and Percy Newberry, who was working on a survey of the Theban necropolis across the river. Others who were nearby or who corresponded with her to give advice were Edouard Naville and Flinders Petrie. As her team got to work, Maggie assumed they would only find small pieces, foundation deposits, and remnants of walls and pillars; still, she held out hope for a cat statue or two.[23]

As the diggers got to work, they sang songs as they kept the pace; this practice continues on sites today. The basket boys sang to welcome Maggie and Fred to the site and to get the work started. One day, when Fred arrived, they sang a song about how the khedive (the ruler of Egypt) had arrived on-site. The crew members were quick to laugh and joke with one another, and the older men would sing a dirge when payday was taking too long. The Bensons judged this as their crew being "irresponsible and merry as children," but in reality they were likely trying to keep their spirits up on long, hot workdays.[24]

The first day, after the anxiety of selection, the diggers began to work in the gateway of the temple, that area that Maggie had seen the year before that was buried almost to the top. As the workers cleared the earth, the boys carried basket after basket of discarded dirt, creating a massive mound. It took them several days, but they found the ancient pavement ten or twelve feet down. As they dug, they found roofing blocks that had fallen long ago and were able to read a few names inscribed on the gate itself, including those of the kings Seti I, Ramesses IV, and Ramesses VI. They also uncovered a lion-headed statue lying across the path that they were able to raise up out of the dirt and replace, sitting it upright. As they continued to clear the dirt down to the original floor level, they uncovered a total of four pairs of pillars in the main court, not the five that Auguste Mariette had claimed almost fifty years earlier. Mariette had not been able to excavate down to the floor, nor had he excavated the whole court, so his map was not accurate. As they continued to work all around the court, they found eight lion-headed statues— five of which were complete, two with missing heads, and one, very large, of which they only found the upper half.[25]

Surprisingly for the Bensons, and probably for the Department of Antiquities, they found dozens of statues, pieces of statues, coins, and other small artifacts in that short season. Maggie wrote home to her father about the best find of the year in the last days of their season. As they rode out on their donkeys to the site one February morning, one of the boys ran up to meet them and announced that the crew had found a statue. Everyone on-site was celebrating— cheering, singing, and laughing—as Fred and Maggie arrived and saw the statue being washed of excess dirt. They could see it depicted a young man squatting with his arms crossed atop his knees, with a young face and inscriptions all over its black granite surface. It was a statue of the young scribe Amenemhat, from the reign of Amenhotep II (c. 1410 BCE), that Maggie described as "almost perfect."[26] She wrote immediately to Georges Daressy, then the Inspector of Upper Egypt, trying to decide where the statue should be temporarily kept.[27] After some discussion with the Egyptian subinspector, Daressy told Maggie and Fred that they could remove it to their rooms at the Luxor Hotel for safekeeping. First, it sat outside the hotel to be photographed, then, Maggie wrote to her father,

"I am going to have it in my room."[28] The statue eventually went to the museum at Giza, and Maggie got a cast of the statue to keep.[29]

Maggie gradually felt much better and physically stronger throughout this season in Luxor. Rather than fighting for breath as she struggled to walk, she found relief in the warm air and sunshine. She spent time outside, lounging in the hotel garden and on the veranda, reading and chatting with friends, and haggling with antiquities dealers. As much as she didn't want her own crew to steal from her excavation, Maggie believed that there was no way to stop the sale of antiquities to and from dealers, and so she happily bought pieces for herself from the same dealers she cursed. She enjoyed people-watching and found the animals that frequented the hotel grounds amusing. She had taken care of an injured bird the year before and was always ready to save another one. She felt immensely relieved now that her physical health was returning, and, as she wrote home to her mother, she loved having "pursuits and idles for pleasure" instead of having to be idle out of necessity because she was too ill to do anything else.[30] To beat the heat (there was no air-conditioning in those days), she and Fred made their way back home in March, meandering their way through France and on to London for the damp and mildewy English summer, excited to return the following year.

In London, they were greeted by their mother's palpable fear over their father's health. He had been experiencing breathlessness that wouldn't easily go away; he was overtired and overworked. But the archbishop himself didn't seem worried despite the fact his wife was frantic. Fred and Maggie spent their days in the unusually dry English summer of 1895 outside, riding horses with their siblings; writing to Newberry, who had also returned from Egypt; eagerly planning their next season; and trying to escape the web of their mother's worry. The winter couldn't come fast enough.

Meeting Nettie Gourlay

Fred and Maggie, who had dubbed themselves the "wandering children" of the Benson family for all of the traveling they did together, arrived back in Egypt in late December 1895. They started their

Mediterranean voyage from Marseilles that year, on the Messag-
eries line, and it was as rough a passage as their first. Maggie was
again glad she didn't get sick, but Fred, again, fared much worse,
having to stay in his cabin the whole time. They arrived in sunny
Alexandria much as they had in 1894 to the commotion of arrival in
port, finding their Cook man, and getting ready for another steamer
trip up the Nile. There were very few passengers on their Cook
steamer—maybe five on a boat meant for thirty—and Fred and
Maggie were relieved not to be forced to talk to anyone else. They
both loved the respite that cruising time gave them, and Maggie
did whatever she could to make the journey seem to last as long as
possible.

She went on all the excursions again while Fred, on the other
hand, wanted to be left so unaware of his surroundings that he
asked Maggie not to point out any objects of interest to him as
they cruised. One day Maggie looked up from her reading to see
eighteen massive vultures fighting over a huge animal carcass on the
shore. The birds were so loud and the fighting so brutal among them
that Maggie couldn't be sure what they were eating, but she wanted
Fred to see it. Suppressing all of her usual sibling habits, she avoided
telling him about the scene even though it was just feet away from
them. Maggie herself slept and read a lot, taking the time to learn
Arabic and read hieroglyphs. She was a fast learner, and by the time
they moored in Luxor a little over a week after arriving in Egypt,
she could speak a few words to the porters and was ready to try to
speak directly to her excavation crew.

They booked themselves at the Luxor Hotel again, which they
found in much the same glorious state as before. Before they began
to excavate, however, they decided to spend some time on the West
Bank to see temples and other remains. Needing the sure-footed
steps of a donkey for this, they hired their same donkey boys again.
As they rode through the sand and rock hills, blue and pink with
shadows, to the temples on the West Bank, they reveled in the scent
of the beanfields in bloom. They sat in the comfort of the shade
given by the imposing temple walls, with battle and offering scenes
as a backdrop to their drinking tea and buying antiquities from the
crowd of men usually gathered around them.

It was an idyllic month of January, and Maggie's health continued to improve after a depressing and difficult European summer
with her father, mother, and Lucy Tait. Fred kept writing to their
mother that Maggie wasn't tiring as easily as she had been at home,
and once wrote that she was "so lively the other night at dinner . . .
that you wouldn't have known your own daughter."[31] And her life
was about to get much more exciting: the excavation season would
be productive and she would also meet the love of her life.

Janet Agnes Gourlay, a Scottish student of Flinders Petrie, was
slightly nervous when her friend Lady Jane Lindsay said she wanted
to introduce her to someone. What was she like? Would they get
along with each other? The archbishop's daughter already had a reputation in Luxor as a recovering invalid with a strong personality
and her own excavation, not to mention the respect of Professor
Petrie and the other English excavators in town. Janet—Nettie to
her friends—wanted to excavate, and she knew Maggie could be
the key to her doing that in the Temple of Mut. But she also knew
Maggie would be a force to be reckoned with, and she wasn't sure
she was up to the task.

The day before the crew were set to go to work, Maggie was
lounging at the Luxor Hotel, relaxing and enjoying the fact that
she was feeling no pain. Lady Jane found Maggie in the lush garden setting and marveled at her well-being. This woman, who had
been so ill for so long, was smiling, writing, and talking with other
visitors. It was then that Lady Jane introduced Nettie to Maggie—
glowing with wellness and a golden touch of sunned skin. They saw
each other for the first time in the sweet, intoxicating air of the
Luxor Hotel gardens.

Not much is known about Nettie except for what we know from
Maggie's perspective and a few letters to Percy Newberry from Nettie in the Griffith Institute at Oxford University. The Nettie that
Maggie met in Luxor Hotel's gardens was a couple of years older
than she was, intelligent, and shy. Nettie's soft-spoken demeanor
drew Maggie in, but then she found out Nettie had some archaeological training that would surely come in handy on the excavation.
Nettie also had some of her father's money to help supplement
the excavation's budget. She had been to Egypt before this, pos-

sibly with her father, Henry, and some of her sisters on a January 1890 Thomas Cook cruise up the Nile on the steamer *Tewfik*.[32] Dr. Longmore had been the steamer physician on that boat.

Maggie and Nettie had an immediate and intense connection. Nettie was so different from the other women Maggie had known over the years—the outgoing, opinionated, Oxford women—that she jumped at the chance to befriend her. Both women suffered from disabling illnesses, so each understood the lifestyle the other needed to lead. It's difficult to say with certainty what Nettie's conditions were, but she was known to be a "great invalid" who "suffered much from disabling illnesses," according to Maggie's brother Arthur.[33] These possibly stemmed from a weakened immune system from a childhood illness, or clinical depression, or both. It was clear that Nettie had as deep a sense of love and devotion as Maggie did, which bound them to each other as partners for the rest of their lives.[34] Unlike Maggie, however, Nettie had clear judgment and a calmness that Maggie lacked. By all accounts they complemented each other well, which is why their bond was so strong and sure.

Maggie immediately wrote to her mother about Nettie as she had never written about anyone else. Maggie's friendships were known by all her family to be intense attachments, so Fred was not particularly surprised when Maggie fell head over heels in love. But Maggie insisted that Nettie was different, their connection was on a higher plane. Her fervent love for Nettie came through in letters home, and at the end of this second season, in May of 1896, Maggie wrote to her mother:

> . . . *How can I keep you up in this, for it changes so every day—oh, I hope you'll like her—you can't help it if you know her, but she is so horribly shy. She is only 33, but she makes me feel like a little girl sometimes—and you know I don't do that particularly easily. . . . She told me she hadn't ever talked so much to any one before. Oh, Mother, it's so odd to me to make a friendship like this—generally there has been something in the way—mostly I've not been sure of the other person, and generally I've had a radical element of distrust. But here one can't help trusting her absolutely,*

and it's only myself I distrust. She is so much bigger, and so much finer and more delicate in mind than most women. . . . There—I wanted you to know.[35]

Just a week after Maggie and Nettie met, Maggie wrote home that even she could see that there had been an "extraordinary change" in her health in the last few weeks. She was relieved that people she knew from home were no longer asking after her illnesses.[36] Yes, it was the sunny weather, the dry, fresh air, and the physical work on-site that were all helping her mental and physical state, but more than that it was Nettie and the true connection the two of them shared. Maggie's relationships and the emotions they brought out in her had always had an immense impact on how she felt. They were perfect for each other.

In same-sex relationships throughout history, women actually had a lot more power together than they would have had on their own. In most of the information we have about Maggie and Nettie, their lives are discussed as interwoven from the time they met until each of them died, unmarried. Unmarried—that dreaded state—describes their lives, in the end. But that was not the full story. Much like Maggie and Nettie, many other same-sex female couples, especially from before the mid-twentieth century, have been identified as constant companions or intimate friends in modern biographies. Often, we do not know many details about the couples' lives together, and in the end each partner dies after technically never having been married to the other. But we do know that they are perceived as a couple, and that in itself is powerful representation and recognition.

In the usually masculine and muscular history of Egyptology, there is a distinct erasure of queer partnerships in favor of discussing the importance of straight marriages (and even extramarital affairs) as factors in professional success. However, especially for women in field sciences like Egyptology, these long-term same-sex relationships were often necessary for women to participate in the field: women needed to travel, but if they were not married to men, they needed a traveling companion. To work in more isolated places like Egypt, women needed assistants and partners to help them.

These partnerships were expected of educated English women who traveled abroad, and for archaeologists, these relationships often operated very much like straight marriages by giving women the freedom to travel where they needed to go without judgment or hindrance, allowing them to take along the support they needed in remote locations, and, importantly, providing them the power to do their work. In the case of Maggie and Nettie, thanks to the women who came before them, these two wealthy, educated women could work without needing a man in a period when it was almost impossible for a woman to do so on her own.

Like with Amelia and the MBs, being in a same-sex scientific and domestic partnership also made women more productive professionally and more secure socially than they would have been as single women. For instance, because of Maggie, Nettie had the funds and permission to excavate in Luxor. By pairing with Maggie, she had the opportunity to put her university training to work and publish important scholarship. Because of Nettie, Maggie had a trained Egyptologist working on-site with her who would treat her as an equal and not as an assistant or subordinate. They were a true scientific couple in the field, and their productivity together shows that.[37]

Understanding both Maggie Benson and Nettie Gourlay as women who depended on being a scientific couple for their emotional and professional well-being is the crux of understanding their work in Egyptology. As we have come to recognize the integral role more women played in shaping science, especially archaeology, we know that this often came as part of a marriage to a man of science. Couples such as Flinders and Hilda Petrie have made their way into a growing pantheon of scientific couples, showing that mixed-sex couples are centered as a framework for understanding science. Ignoring or treating as secondary the relationship that was very much central to women's lives like Maggie's and Nettie's erases an important part of each of their stories, and in continuing to portray their relationship as secondary, we do them a disservice.

Their second season started strong at the end of January 1896, with more staff than the previous year so they'd be able to cover more ground, and even work simultaneously at two separate pits sometimes. The hiring process began in the same disarray as the previous year, with the prospective workers shouting, scrambling, and pushing to get a position. Not wanting to resort to violence (but being fully ready to), this year Maggie stood on a block in the middle of the fray, with her notebook in one hand and a whip in the other, trying to sort out who would dig for her that season. It was impossible to tell what was happening during the commotion, but suddenly the yelling stopped, and the men and boys dispersed and got to work. Fred and Maggie were able to hire between eight and twelve men to dig, up to twenty-four basket boys, a reis, night guardians, and a water girl.

During this highly productive season, Fred worked to update Mariette's map of the Mut precinct of the temple, and they found statuary quickly upon beginning their work at the end of January. The ground where they were digging was unusually tough. The men picked away, digging with their shovels and hands, but they hardly made any progress. When they finally broke through, they found some pots, which was always good, but the previous season they had gotten a taste for the bigger granite statues, and they wanted to find more. Nearby, as Maggie and Nettie drank their afternoon tea and relaxed in the shade, the excavators struck gold—well, granite. The crew unearthed a large black lion head that belonged to a statue they thought would be about sixteen feet high. They continued to uncover fragments of the statue and ultimately sent the fragments to the museum in Cairo for restoration.

Not long after finding the lion head, diggers spotted more polished black granite from another statue. What was it? Who was it? They knew they had to carefully clear the dirt out of the way. Basket after basket of painstakingly shifted earth was moved and dumped, slowly revealing the back of the upper part of a statue. They found that it was the statue of a king, whose arms were broken off at the elbow. When they were finally able to turn it over, they saw a slightly scarred but beautifully carved face. As they continued digging, they found the lower part of the statue, and after some skillful maneuvering, they were able to set up the base, place the top on it, and place it in the temple in the spot from which they believed it had fallen.

They were doing just what Maggie had dreamed of the first time she visited the space—bringing the ancient world into the light of the present day—and she was giddy with excitement. Nettie would have known more about what they had uncovered, and she shared Maggie's excitement over the find. Even though the cartouche (a small oval that usually contained a royal name) that bore the name of the owner of the statue had been chiseled out and the inscription erased, it turned out to be a seated statue of the enigmatic boy king, Tutankhamun.[38] This was some twenty-five years before his tomb would be found in the King's Valley on the West Bank in Luxor, and archaeologists didn't know much about him yet. At the time, this statue was appreciated for its beauty rather than the relatively unknown person it represented.

That season, they found so much stonework, statuary, and alabaster that the work moved slowly. They were able to uncover the bases of the walls so they could fix more of Mariette's mapping; they also cleared the second courtyard. One of their main finds, according to the site report from that year, was a rose-granite statue of Ramesses II (r. 1279–1213 BCE). It was large, and it broke in two pieces when they tried to upend it, but they had unearthed it basically where they believed it originally stood, so they were able to return it to its appropriate spot. They tried to move into the temple's hypostyle hall after that, but because so much stone from the columns had fallen, they decided to dig some foundation deposits instead. Nettie knew, and would have encouraged Maggie to direct the excavators, that foundation deposits are usually found near primary doorways and gateways of temples in a radius of about ten meters, and are often full of smaller amulets and other ritual objects meant to protect the building. These are the kinds of artifacts that are easily stolen on excavations. As this temple had multiple entry and exit points, and the crew would have had to sink a number of pits, they simply didn't have the staff for this task and weren't able to locate any deposits. They did, however, find a small chamber, built out of masonry, with a possible treasure chamber at one end. They didn't find anything in the space except for a few pieces of pottery and the head of a statue of the goddess Hathor, but they were sure it had contained other important offerings at one point.

Toward the end of the excavation that year, and a few days after finding almost a dozen more statues and pieces of statues in granite and alabaster, the crew got a visit from Georges LeGrain, who served as the Inspector at Luxor until 1917. He approached the crew, and, because they were led by a woman, he immediately demanded of Maggie and Nettie that they relinquish all the artifacts. He yelled at them and said he could not believe their stupidity in keeping their finds in their hotel rooms. Maggie was so despondent she was brought to tears trying to defend her actions. Nettie stood behind her strong, confident Maggie, utterly stunned into silence. No matter what the women tried to say, LeGrain wouldn't listen to them.

The director of the Department of Antiquities, Jacques de Morgan, the person who had given them permission to dig, was LeGrain's boss. De Morgan had told Maggie, Nettie, and Fred that they could and should store objects in the hotel for safekeeping. This was not an uncommon thing for archaeologists to do. In fact, Petrie was known to put pieces in boxes and then lay his mattress on top of those boxes to form a bedframe on which he would sleep. As LeGrain was berating the women, who were teary-eyed and at a complete loss for words, Fred walked up to see what the problem was. He defended his sister and her partner, arguing that de Morgan had given them permission to do what they did. After Fred made his case—no doubt the same case Maggie and Nettie had tried to make while being yelled at—LeGrain backed down. He relented and told them that if they would take complete responsibility for the safety of the objects, they could take them back to the hotel.[39] LeGrain's attack on Maggie and Nettie should be seen as an attack on what LeGrain thought was an expedition led by women who did not know what they were doing. Once Fred, a man, arrived on the scene, LeGrain's demeanor changed, and their course of work was allowed again. For LeGrain, women simply did not lead excavations. And up until Maggie, they hadn't.

In the end, after only about five weeks of digging in 1896, they had found dozens more pieces and two nearly complete statues— one of an eighteenth-dynasty architect known as Senenmut and one of Bak-en-Khonsu, a high priest of Amun during the nineteenth-

Fig. 2.3: Cutting down the southern slope. Maggie with the parasol. Photo by Henry Gourlay, in *The Temple of Mut*, plate V.

dynasty reign of the Pharaoh Ramesses II.[40] They were allowed to keep one statue of Ramesses II and heads of Ramesses III and an unnamed god. Regardless of the fact that Maggie had no training, she was a consummate professional thanks to the help of both Nettie and Fred.

As they made their way back home, Nettie traveled with Maggie and Fred. Fred went off to Capri, but Maggie and Nettie made their way to Aix-les Bains in France for a few weeks, and they spent most of their time there together. Nettie's father, Henry, was also with them, so some of the new couple's alone time was interrupted. Meanwhile, Maggie fretted terribly that her mother and father wouldn't like Nettie when they met her. Maggie told them that Nettie would usually speak to Maggie only when they were alone and would become much more reserved around other people. She was sure that Nettie would not speak around her father but was convinced she had to get her ready to meet him. As they both went back to their respective homes in England, Maggie's letters to her Dearest Nettie grew more and more passionate. Maggie wrote several to Nettie over the summer of 1896, but no responses to Maggie survive.

Maggie's missives were full of declarations of love and wanting and exhortations to meet up as soon as they could. Her parents were home, and her brothers came and went as their holidays allowed them to. But without Nettie being close to her that summer, Maggie began to experience waves of depression and anxiety, which she likened to "the way clouds grow and fade on a hot day." She missed Nettie so much that she physically felt the pain of separation from her. She fantasized about spending quiet nights with her again, writing, "I had been dreaming of you—as usual unsatisfactorily— namely that we had gone to Egypt for a week only, and nonsense of that kind."[41] Later, still lonely and wishing for Nettie's warm company, Maggie closed another letter, "Oh dearest, I wish I knew the Gaelic language, for I believe you are able to say all sorts of affectionate things in it which English can't express. I do want you in bodily presence very badly, my dearest, Yours, M. B."[42] It seemed she had finally fulfilled her dream of finding someone who she thought was "man enough to marry, and yet woman enough to love."[43]

They were able to meet a few times in the offseason, but it wasn't easy to do. Maggie was constantly worried about Nettie—how she was feeling, if she was getting enough or too much exercise, and how her new dresses were going to look on her, telling her, "I know you'll be beautiful."[44] Maggie wanted to touch and see and smell and be with Nettie in person, not at a distance. They frequently planned trips to London so they could steal away from their families to meet. Despite the distance, they were able to see one another with relative frequency. They were openly declaring their love for one another by early October, and of course making plans to go back to Egypt together in late November.

As the partner with formal training, Nettie was in charge of the correspondence with Percy Newberry as they prepared for the forthcoming season. She had hopes of excavating with Newberry on the West Bank once the women had completed excavations of the temple, and Newberry was overseeing the building of a home for them in the desert on the West Bank. The two women hoped it would be a private domicile for themselves, and Nettie specifically asked Newberry for a doorway between their two bedrooms, but, she continued, "we shan't be so extravagant as to think of a <u>wooden</u>

door! We can just [hang] up a curtain ourselves but the door space must be left just in case she should be ill. In such an unwelcome event it would make things so much more difficult if there were no communication."[45] Maggie was still having obvious issues with her debilitating rheumatism at home in England, and Nettie wished to do all she could to protect her. This request should also be read in the light of their love for one another. They dared not ask to share a bedroom, and definitely not a bed, but having an easy way of getting to one another in the middle of the night without having to step outdoors would be convenient. Nettie continued to be the point person during the construction of the house, and she was not shy in letting Newberry know what they desired. They were sure it would be a private respite for them in the winter.

Before they went back to Egypt that next winter, however, Maggie's father died of what is presumed to be heart failure, on the couch of the former prime minister William Gladstone on October 11. It wasn't that Maggie didn't love her father, or that Minnie didn't love her own husband, but their relationships could be better defined in terms of duty. Maggie often felt she didn't perform her duty as a good, Christian daughter to her archbishop father, which gave her lifelong feelings of inadequacy and failure, leading to anxious remorse. Minnie did her duty, publicly, as a Victorian wife and mother. But she knew that she didn't fulfill her own husband's desires, so for the seven years before he died, for her own happiness, she brought her lover, Lucy, in to live with them. Queen Victoria mourned personally with Minnie, likely not knowing the full story of their home life. Fred, Maggie, their brother Hugh, Minnie, and Lucy were tasked with moving the family and their belongings out of Lambeth and Addington Palaces, both houses being official residences of the archbishop. They moved into a house in Winchester, a large Georgian mansion with big rooms, and a shady garden with large trees and places to read, write, and rest. They counted on Nettie to make all the preparations to go to Egypt again. Needing the benefits of the weather and time away, Hugh, Minnie, Lucy, and Fred went with Maggie and Nettie.

Dirt in the Skirt and a Parasol for Shade

The whole Benson clan arrived in Egypt via Port Said, instead of Alexandria, in late December 1896, because it was easier to move Maggie to Cairo during the day from there. Nettie wrote to Newberry that "I do hope she will do well on our journey & that we shall arrive in good time."[46] They made the journey in time to see the new house and get settled into both it and the Luxor Hotel before their season began. The house was in the village of Gurna, under the shadow of the sacred ancient peak of El Qurn, near the Valley of the Kings and the ancient mortuary temples. They would have had a view of the desert, arable land, and the Nile, all the way to the East Bank and modern Luxor. That was the real desert air—away from tourists and crowded hotel dining rooms and verandas, away from people wondering who this group was and what they were excavating. Nettie loved their house and its location so much she told Newberry that "everybody in Egypt must want to go & live there!"[47] They probably stayed in their new house on days when they didn't go to the temple to supervise. The days they did excavate, they likely had rooms on hold at the Luxor Hotel; many archaeologists did this. Maggie needed recovery time in the house with Nettie; they needed each other.

Recovery time aside, the group kept working. Their final season began more auspiciously than the previous two. They started with more money than before—possibly due to some inheritance on Maggie's part, and Nettie's father gave them money again. In addition, when people would travel from European ports to Egypt, they met and became friends with other travelers on their boats. Sometimes these groups would become traveling companions, as Amelia Edwards and the MBs did, or professional contacts. We aren't sure whom the Bensons and Nettie met along the way, but Fred convinced some fellow travelers to donate money in support of their excavation. Thanks to their generosity, they had enough money to hire a huge crew: eight diggers and thirty to forty basket boys. With Hugh and Minnie having come to join the excavations following Edward's death, they also had a larger supervisory group.[48] Maggie's older brother Hugh was having some health issues, and he thought

the Egyptian weather would do him some good—it had worked
wonders for his sister, so why not try it? Minnie simply needed
to get away. Closing down their two homes after dealing with the
death of her husband had taken its physical and emotional toll.
Sure, she had the loving company of Lucy Tait, who joined them in
Egypt, but she also mourned her husband's death.

The previous season, the crew had left the site only partly cleared,
and there was a lot of dirt left to move. Maggie hired the workers,
with the usual confusion, on January 9, 1897, and they began work
the next day before Maggie, Nettie, and all arrived at the site. They
immediately found more statuary in the very place their 1896 dig
season ended.[49] The latecomers were summoned from their respite
at the Luxor Hotel by some of the crew. When they finally arrived
on-site, they found the crew working hard on their old mound.
As Maggie and Nettie peered into the pit that had been dug, they
saw two large masses of black granite peeking out from the brown
Nile dirt in startling contrast. One piece belonged to a statue frag-
ment that matched an incomplete squatting statue of a priest from
Thebes from the 1896 season. The other chunk of granite was the
head and shoulders of possibly the same priest, Mentuemhat.[50]

Once they fully uncovered the pieces, Nettie could see that
they were both beautifully worked. Maggie noted that head was
distinctly "un-Egyptian in type," with uncharacteristic wrinkles
around the eyes and a flattened forehead, making "a powerful ren-
dering of a powerful personality."[51] It was one of the main prizes
of the whole season, found on the very first day. Also, on that first
day, they found even more in their new trenches: fourteen pieces of
statues, some of them with heads and faces intact. They found pieces
of roofing and flooring stones, as well as a number of column bases
with which they traced a more accurate map than they had made
the year before.

Some of the pieces were stolen from the site over the years, and
especially during this final season, when the head of a statue went
missing and they had to figure out who took it. Instead of beating the truth out of members of the crew, as some archaeologists
did, Maggie instead offered money and work benefits to those who
might help figure out the mystery. The incentive worked. They fired

the boy who had been accused, but it turned out he had taken the fall for their reis, unnamed, who, they wrote, "was really responsible and at any rate incompetent."[52] They didn't get the head back, but they decided that their crew "were like naughty children" and continued to treat them as such.[53]

All in all, the season was extremely productive: they found pieces of fifteen inscribed statues, an alabaster arm, a sphinx, the statue head of a Saite woman, dozens of lion-headed Sekhmet statues (which began to be run-of-the-mill discoveries for the crew), and other small pieces. Many of these artifacts went to the Cairo Museum, some to the British Museum, and some Nettie and Maggie were allowed to take home, as was customary in excavating agreements at the time.

The last few days of the season, the crew worked on getting the temple back in order. They also continued to clear the temple down to the paving stones. LeGrain's reis helped the crew mend a number of the lion-headed statues, and they replaced about one hundred of them around the first court, but these accounted for only half the statues they had found. When they finally left the Temple of Mut, it had been returned to as much of its previous glory as was possible without much help from the Department of Antiquities. Nettie and Maggie had both hoped to return to the site again, but Maggie's difficult health issues meant they didn't return to Egypt until 1900, and even then it was only for a short season with Newberry and Americans Emma Andrews and Theodore Davis.

The lake in the Asher district still surrounded the temple on three sides and shone with the rising and setting sun, while a large statue of the goddess Sekhmet had been put back into her place, presiding over the open, sun-drenched courts. The large and imposing main pylons and columns of the Temple of Karnak lay to the north. Gazing to the west, visitors could see the Libyan mountains and watch the sun set over the ancient gods and goddesses who had ruled the lives and deaths of the people here for millennia. Maggie had longed to make the temple accessible to visitors so others could marvel at the work of ancient hands as she had done the first time she had ridden her donkey down the avenue of sphinxes to see the temple.

All the fresh air and work did little to relieve Maggie's health issues in this final season. She was weak when she arrived in Egypt, and Nettie knew it. As Maggie sat by the edge of the horseshoe-shaped lake near the temple she loved, she caught a chill and her lungs became congested. Already overtaxed from rheumatic inflammation, her lungs couldn't handle the stress. Maggie suffered a near fatal case of pleurisy. For those who develop pleurisy, the lining on the outside of the lungs can become so inflamed that it is almost impossible to breathe due to pain. Fluid can build up between the lungs and their lining, causing shortness of breath and sometimes partial or complete lung collapse. Maggie's condition was so serious that it was necessary to tap the fluid around her lungs so she could breathe, an operation likely performed by Dr. W. Longmore in a room at the Luxor Hotel.[54]

He would have had to be extremely able, and brave himself, to do the operation. The procedure today is invasive and usually done in a sterile operating room with anesthesia and an ultrasound to guide the large-gauge needle needed to properly drain the fluid. Dr. Longmore would have had the needle, but no ultrasound to guide him. It would have been extremely painful for Maggie, and difficult for the doctor, to say the least, but her room was a better option than the local hospital, meant only to treat Egyptian patients. After the procedure, her relief was immediate, and she could breathe again. A few days later, though, she suffered a heart attack, and no one thought she would survive it. Maggie wasn't afraid to die—she had made her peace with God and would have had relief from being sick all the time—but was more reluctant to leave her mother alone after her father's recent passing. She also thought of sweet, quiet Nettie, the woman who had brought so much stability and love into her life in such a short amount of time. Slowly but surely, her health and life returned.

After those stressful weeks at the end of the season, Fred and Maggie's youngest brother, Hugh, was tasked with heading north before everyone else. He was to return to the health resort town of Helwan, just a few miles south of Cairo (today fully engulfed in Cairo's urban sprawl), and book hotel rooms for the whole group there so Maggie could convalesce and recover enough to return to

England for the summer. Helwan would be breezy and dry, with fresh warm air coming off the Libyan desert, but it wouldn't be as hot as Luxor in the late spring. But when Hugh arrived, it was clear that he had come down with typhoid fever and needed to be taken to the hotel in an ambulance; Lucy Tait joined him with her own case of the illness a few days later after the entire group had arrived. They were all forced to stay in Helwan through June, paying the hotel extra to stay open for them. Everyone recovered. It was a tough final season at the Temple of Mut, tainted by illness and death, but the impact that Maggie and Nettie would have on the field of Egyptology, and on each other's lives, was carved in black granite.

Love and Archaeology

Once they were back in England, Maggie and Nettie continued to see each other frequently and for long periods of time, with Nettie sometimes staying with the Benson family for months. They jointly wrote and published *The Temple of Mut in Asher* in 1899, which became a groundbreaking report, revealing the temple as it had never been seen before. They also returned to Egypt in 1900, the year after *Temple of Mut* was published, for some fresh air and more restoration. Thanks to the French head of the Department of Antiquities, Gaston Maspero, who allowed Newberry to work further in the Valley of the Kings, and Emma Andrews's and Theodore Davis's patronage of the work, Nettie and Maggie were both permitted to help.

The two women arrived in Cairo on December 13, 1900, and could not wait to get to their house in Gurna. When they arrived, despite her own weakness during their travels, Nettie wrote to Newberry that "Miss Benson is very well I'm glad to say. The passage was a great rest to her. . . . If she has a couple of quiet days at Thebes, she will be as right as possible."[55] They made their way to Luxor and got to work almost right away. Maggie was doing better, as she usually did when she made it that far south. They worked on a tomb Newberry had cleared for his new American patrons, tracing and copying the scenes on the walls. Emma and Theo came over one day to see the work they were funding. It was their first time to be patrons of an excavation, so they were anxious to see the progress. When they arrived, they had to scramble over debris and crumbling stonework to get to the tomb, and they found Maggie and Nettie inside, hard at work. Emma noted the meeting in her diary with a tone of familiarity, so it is likely that they knew each other from earlier seasons when they may have run into one another at the Luxor Hotel. Nettie was occasionally invited to tea with the Americans that season, but Maggie didn't go, probably because she was ill. During this season and after, Nettie collaborated with Newberry on articles about the statue of Mentuemhat that the women had found earlier in the Temple of Mut. Their 1900–1901 season would be the last trip they would make together to Egypt, because Maggie's health was simply too unstable. But they remained as close as ever.

In 1906, the women had a portrait made of the two of them that has become famous. Nettie, delicate and reserved, dressed in a white lacy gown, sits behind Maggie, not looking at the photographer but instead gazing longingly down at Maggie. Maggie, strong, direct, and confident in a dark robe, sits in front with her back to Nettie, staring into the distance at something just off to the right of the viewer's shoulder. The portrait, with both women in their late thirties/early forties looking so vibrant and with a long, loving life seemingly ahead of them, has been described by none other than

Fig. 2.4: 1906 portrait of Nettie (left) and Maggie.

National Geographic as a picture of women who had become "fast friends" years before.

This portrait may have been made on their winter trip to Cornwall in that same year, after both women had recovered from the flu.[56] Maggie fell into another deep depression during this trip and at one point she must have thought she had gone crazy. She wrote to her brother that, while she was ill, she would look into the faces of people on the street and see their basest behaviors, evil, and malice reflected in their eyes. The whole world had become a psychedelic vision of brilliant colors and dizzying movement, and, she said, she sort of enjoyed it. But she quickly recovered from what may have been a schizophrenic or manic episode as part of her depression, and by the end of the year she was physically well, but her personality had changed.

The once-energetic woman now spoke in hushed tones of exhausted gloom. Her hallucinations and paranoia came back with a vengeance by 1910, and she wrote to Nettie sadly, wishing that she had been more worthy of her.[57] For the rest of her life, Maggie continued to suffer from heart and lung problems, probably exacerbated by her depression and anxiety. There was no medical treatment (outside of a change of air), or even diagnosis, for these illnesses in the early twentieth century, so she lived under the care of a private nurse.

Maggie's relationship with Nettie was fraught, but not for the reasons we may think. Sure, there was a strong nineteenth-century taboo and even laws against same-sex relationships, but these laws were more harshly enacted for men than for women. Men, it was believed, shouldn't be wasting their virility on other men and should instead be fathering strong, British families. For women, on the other hand, there were simply too many of them for each to have a husband. These "odd women" couldn't survive on their own, so women living with one another as constant companions and intimate friends was an acceptable solution, including for the women themselves.

Over the course of three seasons, Maggie, Nettie, Fred, and eventually much of the Benson family oversaw the excavation crew as they cleared much of the temple of landfill, exposing foundation deposits and finding remains and pieces of over two hundred statues and countless other pieces of sculpture. The pieces Maggie was able to keep ultimately ended up with her younger cousin, the eugenicist Rev. Stewart McDowall, who donated many of them to the Winchester College Museum, where they are still on display.[58] The group also reorganized the temple interior, attempting to restore items such as columns and statuary to their original locations.

Some historians write about Maggie herself as an amateur who came to Egypt on a whim and decided to dig for fun. Others are dismissive of her work as unprofessional and, while important, not *as* important as Auguste Mariette's or Georges LeGrain's work on the same areas. Fred had excavated with the British School at Athens from 1891 to 1895 and with David Hogarth in Alexandria in 1894, thus lending some authority to the women's work. But the organization and plan of the work, and the report that came from it, were efforts led by Maggie Benson, in conjunction with Nettie Gourlay. Their work on the site was and continues to be of use to Egyptologists working in Karnak, and it marked a shift in the normal gender roles in Egyptological excavations, especially in this period.

Not much is known about Nettie outside of her relationship with Maggie. She died in March of 1912 at the age of forty-nine, likely of the numerous, though unknown, illnesses that had plagued her during her entire life. One thing that is known about her death is that her beloved Maggie wasn't there. Nettie had always been the quiet strength behind Maggie's big personality, and Maggie always thought Nettie would be in her life. Maggie outlived Nettie by a few more years, dying from heart disease in 1916 at the age of fifty-one, but she continued to pine for her dearest Nettie. Their work together had paved the way for more excavation in the Isheru district of Karnak, which has been done by the Brooklyn Museum, Johns Hopkins University, and the American Research Center in Egypt since 1976.

As Maggie and Nettie left their adorable little house in Gurna for the last time in 1901, they bade goodbye to their American friends. At the same time, they watched as their successors came in. Emma Andrews, the patron whose generous donation to Percy

Newberry in 1900 allowed Nettie one more excavation season, had just begun making her own path in archaeology. Not as young as her two predecessors, Emma was nevertheless tenacious. She had personal and professional connections as well as the interest, intelligence, and money to do much more with her excavations than Maggie and Nettie were able to. Emma had money and time, but she was going to need every bit of it to keep up.

3

Emma Andrews

As a member of his family, Mrs. Andrews accompanied Mr. Davis on his annual visits to Egypt for a period of more than twenty years, and the charming description which she gives of their river-life on the "Bedawin," familiar to many of us who enjoyed their hospitality, is certainly worthy of a wider public and more permanent form in print,—though she could not be prevailed upon to consider this.

—Albert M. Lythgoe, Preface to the
Emma Andrews Diaries, February 1919

The morning of Friday, August 24, 1900, dawned cloudy and rainy on the rocky coast of Rhode Island. Emma Andrews was looking out the window of her bedroom, on the southernmost point of Aquidneck Island, at the gray ocean waves and fretting about the weather. It had been rainy for the last week or so, and her garden needed some work. Later that morning, during breakfast, her brow furrowed as she made some notes about the supplies she needed to care for her award-winning flowers. She was so proud, and she deserved to be. Designed by Frederick Law Olmsted, the architect of Central Park in New York City, her garden had marble statues, a sunken garden area, and a small Japanese tea room.[1] She wanted greenhouses, but Theo kept putting her off. Her partner of over twenty years, Theodore Davis, was quickly sorting through his mail at the other end of the breakfast table. Their large mansion, which Theo had built in 1885 and named the Reef, was about four miles from the town of Newport, where other Gilded Age millionaires, like the Cornelius Vanderbilts, had built their palatial homes. Because of the distance to town, Emma and Theo's servants didn't make it to the post office every day, so they each had piles of letters to read on that particular morning. One return address caught Theo's eye—that of Egyptologist Percy Newberry.

Emma and Theo had met Percy in early 1899, when he was digging at Thebes with support from the Marquess of Northampton. They immediately liked the quiet, hardworking Newberry, who was interested in botany and gardening, like Emma, and who enjoyed tea and food and talking all things Egypt, like Theo. When they first met Percy, he was a freelance excavator on the verge of losing his patron because the Lady Northampton was ill and needed care. He knew he might talk the American millionaires into donating money for an excavation, and he had a tried-and-true idea for how to win them over. Drawing on Emma's expertise in gardening and her love of ancient Egypt, Percy brought a box full of flowers to Emma at her hotel at the end of May. But these weren't just any flowers; they were three-thousand-year-old flowers from a tomb he had been excavating at Hawara, a site 250 miles north of Luxor. He delivered them in a tin box, and Emma was smitten at once. She took the box, marveling at the delicacy and beauty of the dried flowers. The whole trip home from England to Newport, she trusted no one else with her treasure and carried the box herself. Percy had just about won their support.

The following season of 1899–1900, Percy didn't make it to Egypt as he had no official institutional appointment and had indeed lost his patron, the marquess, just as he feared he would. Desperate to return to Egypt, he wrote a letter to Theo in August of 1900, and it was this letter that Theo had spotted in his stack of mail on the rainy morning of August 24. He opened it, getting Emma's attention in the process. In the letter, Percy appealed to Theo's offer from two years earlier to fund the clearing of a number of tombs on the West Bank of the Nile in Thebes. Along with the letter, he sent two of his books, *The Amherst Papyri* and *The Life of Rekhmara*, to remind the pair of Percy's scholarship and what they would be supporting with their money.[2] Theo was immediately interested, but he was busy. He finished his coffee, wiped his hands on his pants (a glimpse of the manners cultivated during his time surveying in the forests of Michigan), and directed Emma to respond to Percy, as quickly as she could, that the money would be his. She did so gladly, but with a twist.

Emma wrote to Percy that, as soon as they could possibly send the money, "we will gladly pay the costs of your work at Abd el Kurneh this winter, dividing the expense between us."[3] Percy received the response and was a little confused. Divide the expense? Between whom? He didn't have that kind of money. He was asking them for £250, the equivalent of $32,000 today, and if he had to cover some of that himself, he might as well not even go to Egypt. He thought of Nettie Gourlay and the house he had helped build for her and Maggie a few years before. Nettie was supposed to help him on this excavation, and Maggie was coming, too, for her health. He had also sent the two women *The Amherst Papyri*, and they were both looking forward to a final winter in Luxor in their new house on the West Bank. They would be so disappointed if they couldn't go.

On September 6, he wrote back to Emma, thanking her for the offer but telling her he couldn't afford to pay any of the expense. She received the letter on the seventeenth and replied the next day. She told Percy he needn't worry, what she meant by "we" was that she and Theo would split the cost of the work and Percy should start planning his season.[4] He breathed a sigh of relief and started packing his supplies for Egypt.

This wouldn't be the last time Emma would pay for an excavation for Percy. At the end of that season, she gave him another £100 ($12,775) of her own money so he could finish the work he was doing. With this money, she knew she was stepping into a usually male role in the field, paying for an excavation. She had opened the door to this exclusive patronage club, which meant that, later, other women could become direct, if unacknowledged, patrons of archaeological work.

The first laws regulating antiquities were enacted in 1835 by Muhammad Ali. Although they were vague, they did prohibit exporting antiquities without a permit. Most permits, before 1922,

allowed for a 50/50 split between the excavator and the Antiquities Department. It was a normal practice then, at the turn of
the twentieth century, for patrons to receive some of the artifacts
from the excavation. The original agreement between Percy and
Emma and Theo was no different. Theo frequently enjoyed cer-
emoniously rejecting all offers of artifacts from his excavations
while buying antiquities on the side or accepting only the finest
pieces from his sites. One of the prizes from Percy's first season
with them was a bronze bowl found in what turned out to be
a chapel to the spirit of Rekhmire (c. 1430 BCE), governor of
Thebes and vizier to Thutmose III. The bowl itself hadn't even
belonged to Rekhmire but had been left there by a tomb robber in
the time of Thutmose III. Despite its mixed-up origins, the bowl
was beautiful—and ancient.

In January 1901, Percy brought the bowl to Theo as he, Emma,
and their whole group were on their dahabeah.[5] Theo was excited
and grateful, and placed the bowl on the large piano in the center
of their boat's saloon as a showpiece. It is now on display in the
Metropolitan Museum of Art. Emma, who likely paid more than
Theo had for the excavation that year, was briefly thanked by Percy

Fig. 3.1: Votive Bowl, Metropolitan Museum of Art 30.8.67,
Theodore M. Davis Collection, Bequest of Theodore M. Davis,
1915.

in the publication of the site. This wouldn't be the first time Emma was left out of the story.

A Gilded Age Affair

Before she met fellow Ohio native Theodore Montgomery Davis in 1860, Emma Buttles Andrews was already a wealthy, married woman with a baby on the way. She had been born in June of 1837 to one of the wealthiest families in Columbus. Her father owned a number of businesses in that town and land in four different states. Two days after Christmas in 1859, Emma married Abner Lord Andrews, a lawyer whose family was even wealthier than Emma's (Lord was a family name and not a title). Emma met Theo, who was a self-made man and almost a year younger than she was, when he was on his honeymoon with his wife, Emma's cousin, Annie Buttles. Annie, twenty-four at the time of her marriage to Theo, was kind and gentle, and her personality seemed a good counter to Theo's brash and aggressive manners, but he must have had an instant connection with Emma.

Emma was educated, confident, and intelligent. She was short, topping out at five feet one inch tall, but she was feisty. They bonded more as friends than as lovers at first, but as Theo continued to visit Columbus every year after that for the next two decades, their relationship became a love affair. Theo made a lot of his money running shares scams in mining and logging properties in Michigan and Minnesota. He flourished as a lawyer, liquidating defunct banks in the financial crises of the 1880s. He was also a member of Boss Tweed's inner circle in the New York political scandal centered at Tammany Hall. In short, Theo's money was ill-gotten.

Emma, however, inherited money from her father, and upon the death of her even wealthier husband in 1897, she became even richer. Together the couple had had two children, a daughter who died in infancy, and a son, Charles, who died at the age of nine. This must have taken a toll on Emma's physical and mental health. Just a few years after they got married, Abner must have suffered a debilitating accident—possibly the same one that killed her son. According to an article in the August 29, 1897, edition of the

Cincinnati Enquirer, from the time Abner was twenty-seven, he was "confined to his bed and revolving chair, alternately, a hopeless paralytic."[6] Emma apparently "cared faithfully for her husband" in their home for twenty years. For some reason, possibly having become "tired of his utter helplessness" or having fallen in love with Theo, or both, "they mutually agreed to a separation." They made what the *Enquirer* called a "queer compact," and she was freed from the marriage before he died. He remained in the care of his sister until his death. Emma didn't go to his funeral.[7]

Throughout this time, Theo was visiting Emma regularly, and it quickly became clear that Annie had no interest in traveling anywhere. Emma, with energy and money to spare, wanted to travel the world with Theo. She moved into the Newport mansion in 1889 with Annie and Theo, making an awkward situation. At this point, Annie and Theo had stopped speaking to each other directly and would only communicate through a third party, even if they were in the same room together.[8] But they wouldn't get divorced. In the 1890 census, Theo is listed as the Head of House, with Emma listed as his cousin, which was technically true, by marriage. Annie was not recorded as being in the house. Emma and Theo started sailing in Egypt that same year.

After almost a decade of sailing up and down the Nile in their private dahabeah, the *Bedauin,* they decided to try what many wealthy travelers to Egypt did at some point, with varying levels of success: supporting excavations financially. This was where they found themselves when Percy's excavation was finished in the spring of 1901. Theo was supporting work in the Valley of the Kings, and Emma was involved in Theo's program. Emma chose to remain financially and philosophically committed to Percy's work, even visiting him on-site in January 1902. But by that fall, Theo himself had received permission from the Department of Antiquities to excavate the Valley of the Kings—the entire valley. This was *the* prized concession at the turn of the twentieth century.

The Wadi Biban el-Muluk, known also as the Valley of the Tombs of the Kings, is the resting place of most of the rulers of the New Kingdom (c. 1550–1070 BCE). Dug into the living rock on the West Bank of the Nile at Thebes are almost one hundred tombs, burial pits, and caches that occupy the eastern and western parts of the valley. The earliest burial in this place was possibly that of Amenhotep I (died c. 1504 BCE), but archaeologists aren't sure where exactly his original tomb is.[9] His successor, Thutmose I (died c. 1493 BCE), was initially buried in what is now called KV 20. The numbering system for the tombs was developed by John Gardner Wilkinson in the 1820s and is based on the order in which the tombs were found, uncovered, or cleared.[10] KV 20, then, is the twentieth tomb found in the modern era in the King's Valley. The valley is one of the richest sites in Egypt in terms of both information about the ancient past and the worth of its objects to modern sensibilities. When Theo got permission to excavate there, KV 42 had just been uncovered in 1900.

At this point in its history, the Department of Antiquities was led by French Egyptologists, dependent upon the British Egyptian colonial system to help support it. In 1904, the two countries signed the Entente Cordiale, which, among many other things, effectively enshrined political control of Egypt to the British while giving the French control over antiquities there. The department didn't have much of a budget, even for excavation, so when a wealthy patron wished to spend their money in Egypt on an archaeological expedition, they were rarely turned away. The patron was often assigned an archaeologist (not always well trained) to supervise the work, given a site or selection of sites, and released to find artifacts. This was much the same arrangement that Theo made with the director at the time, Gaston Maspero.

Over the next eleven years, Emma and Theo were responsible for funding and supervising the excavation of twenty-four tombs in the valley. Like Theo, Emma learned about archaeological methods by watching the local crew work; unlike Theo, she recorded important information about most of the tombs they dug, such as maps, lists of artifacts that were found, and a record of visitors to the sites. Her diaries are the most accurate record historians and archaeologists have for over a dozen tombs, and these include some information that Theo omitted in his few published sites.[11] Unlike Flinders Petrie, James Breasted, or Howard Carter, all of whom needed to publish to stay solvent, Theo didn't need to attract funding for the following year. He and Emma *were* the funding. We now know that real archaeologists—those excavating for the scientific knowledge of the material past and not usually for the fortune and glory—keep detailed and useful records for themselves and other archaeologists. Theo simply didn't need to publish reports for anything he found, so the fact that historians and archaeologists have those sources is remarkable. Keeping and publishing those records at the dawn of the twentieth century meant that Emma was, and Theo arguably was not, an archaeologist. Yet, it is Theo—a golden man in the "Golden Age"—we know the most about.

If Emma had been a man, we would know a lot more about her, and she would no doubt be in the Egyptological canon as an archaeologist. But she wasn't. In fact, there are no known existing photographs of her, she doesn't have an existing archive outside her diary, and Theo excluded her from his published reports.

Arguably, up to this point, women in Egyptology largely lacked formal training, but most of the men in this field lacked it as well. The first university department in the UK didn't exist until 1894,

Fig. 3.2: The *Bedauin*, c. 1900.

and the first in the United States opened in 1895; Germany and France had established university training earlier, but not for excavating. There was hardly time to have turned out fully formed, university-trained Egyptian archaeologists, so a lack of training wouldn't have been a barrier like it might have been in other sciences. It was in fact because of women like Amelia Edwards, the MBs, and Emma that more of the women who followed saw the possibilities of fieldwork.

Familiar Recollections of Egypt

When they arrived in Egypt in late 1889, Emma began her diaries there with the thought that it was "rather strange and interesting that we should have familiar recollections of Egypt."[12] She and Theo had visited Cairo before, possibly as part of a European Grand Tour the previous year, but had never been up the Nile. This year, they planned on doing just that. They had stayed at Shepheard's Hotel before, however, and Emma loved it as much as Amelia Edwards had. They were given sunny rooms that looked out onto the wide-open central courtyard with swaying date palm trees and birds flying and cawing.[13] She also enjoyed the famous dining room, which had undergone a major renovation since Amelia had been there. It was now a large room with high ceilings and whitewashed walls, against which potted trees and other tropical plants stood out in stark and colorful contrast. Emma marveled at the people from all over the world seated in the room—by now it could fit over three hundred—in evening dress or traveling clothes, some in military uniforms and others in turbans or fezzes, making it a bustling, diverse, and interesting place to sit and watch the people go by. But, like Amelia and others before them, she and Theo had an important question to answer: how would they get up the Nile?

First, the couple had decided to charter a small Thomas Cook's steamer, the *Sethi*. In the fifteen years since Amelia had derided Cook's tourists, travel had exploded on the scene in Egypt. By 1880, they had control over Nile steamers, and by the end of that decade, more than five thousand people per year were booking Nile tours from Cook.[14] They had a number of different-sized steamers, and while the *Sethi* was built for tourism and had room for twenty-six passengers, it could be booked for private trips up the Nile.[15] Emma and Theo had planned on traveling upriver with their guest that year, Mary Neil Buttles, Emma's niece, and a Miss Gibbs. Miss Gibbs backed down from the *Sethi*, possibly due to lack of funds, so Theo went to look at other boats. He soon became enamored of the idea of a private houseboat, and so he rented the *Nubia*, a fast iron dahabeah possibly belonging to a prince. It was an expensive boat, though, and Emma, ever the practical one, tried to keep Theo from paying too much to fix it up. They were excited to leave Cairo, as much as they loved Shepheard's, for parts farther south, and they did so on December 28.

As the group ate their breakfast at the hotel that winter morning, Emma was surprised when their dragoman, Mohammed Salah, appeared. He was in a hurry to let them know that there would be good wind to sail around 11:00 that morning. She looked out the window beside their breakfast table and saw only damp, cold fog. How could they have good sailing wind in just a few hours? They likely had hired Salah the year before as a guide and dragoman, so Emma trusted that he must be right. She recalled that he told them, "The sooner we settled ourselves on the Dahabeah the better it would be."[16] Not wanting to miss good sailing weather, Emma and Mary quickly finished their coffees and rushed to the shops to get a few last-minute items. When they returned to the hotel, their packages and suitcases were loaded in carriages, ready to depart for their boat at the Bulak. Along with Theo, they said a few hasty goodbyes and were on their way. They rode through markets and streets crowded with people, sheep, and camels all going about their daily business.

When they arrived at their boat, Emma was proud to see the American flag flying from the mast, which was a common practice for travelers up the Nile. They boarded the boat and inspected it. It was clean and comfortable, and many of their belongings had already been unpacked by the crew. At the time Mohammed had predicted, the wind picked up, and they began to sail. As they traveled on the Nile through Cairo, they heard the noon cannon from the Citadel on the hills above the city to the east. They glided past the Giza pyramids to the west and slipped past the city.

Emma and Theo quickly became a fixture on the Nile. By the end of their trip that year, in the spring of 1890, they knew they would be coming back every year. They started their time in Egypt as tourists, interested in seeing and buying antiquities. By 1891, they were holding court in the newly rebuilt Shepheard's Hotel with its purpose-built dining room and central gardens, wide corridors, and raised terrace. Then, in 1892 as they sailed along the river, Theo read Flinders Petrie's book *Ten Years Digging in Egypt* and became interested in the idea of digging and finding something—anything—important. Over the past few years, the couple and their friends had bought a number of antiquities from the Luxor dealer Muhammad Mohassib. Rumored to have started his career as Lucie Duff Gordon's donkey boy, he was a trusted merchant. He had also worked with Maggie Benson and Nettie Gourlay while they excavated the Temple of Mut, providing them with the best antiquities they could buy. Both Emma and Theo had their favorite kinds of pieces, and they counted on Mohassib to save them some of the choice items. In the end, however, Theo wanted to find the pieces on his own.

In 1896, they finally commissioned their own dahabeah, built in Cairo. They named it the *Bedauin*. It was eighty feet long and had rooms for Emma and Theo, as well as extra sleeping quarters for their guests. They furnished the large salon with a grand piano, the dining room with a crystal chandelier, and the library with hundreds of books. Now that they had their own boat, they joined an exclusive group of wealthy patrons in Egypt—but they needed Percy for the archaeology.

A few months after Percy presented the bronze bowl to Theo on the *Bedauin* in 1901, Howard Carter boarded the moored boat to talk to the intimidating man. An artist who had trained with both Petrie and Newberry, Howard had known Emma and Theo since 1899. As he sat on deck, he glanced over Theo's shoulder at the piano with the bowl proudly displayed on it. Howard smiled smugly to himself because it was he, in his role as Inspector, who gave Percy permission to let Theo have the bowl in the first place. So really, Theo should be thanking him.[17] The couple were delighted to see him on the *Bedauin*. Howard had been inviting them to lunches, teas, dinners, and, most importantly, newly opened tombs the entire season. They got private, expert tours, and sometimes they were the first ones in a tomb. Howard had a motive, though, as he gambled on their interest in Egyptian antiquities that season, and he was there to cash in his chips. He cleared his throat, ready to offer Theo something far more important than a measly bowl. Theo and Emma were ready for the offer.

Howard told them that the Egyptian government would allow him to excavate in the Valley of the Kings if he could secure funding. More importantly, he said, whoever he secured funding from would be the rightful owner of any duplicate antiquities of those excavations, if duplicates should arise. Howard was certain there would be duplicates and told Theo and Emma that they would be the owners of real artifacts, better artifacts than the bowl or anything they could purchase from Mohassib. They looked at each other, impressed with what Howard was proposing. He finished his oral application for securing their patronage by also assuring them that he was primed to discover at least one tomb the following season, if not more. And to top it all off, Theo's name would be on those discoveries. They happily accepted Howard's offer. How could they refuse? It was what Theo had been hoping for. From then on, their winters in Egypt would be dedicated to excavation—the funding, supervision, and recording of sites. Emma continued to support Percy's excavation for another year, too.

The *Bedauin* arrived in Luxor on January 7, 1902, just after noon. Emma would have gone to see Percy's progress on Malqata, the palace of Amenhotep III (c. 1400–1350 BCE), that very day, but she was tired from the trip and had a pile of mail to deal with. It had taken them almost four full weeks to get from Cairo to Luxor that year, and the last time they had gotten mail was in Sohag, a town about 130 miles north of Luxor, a week before. The next morning in Luxor, January 8, dawned bright and hot—just how Emma liked her Egyptian mornings—and after an early breakfast, they left the boat promptly at 10:00 A.M. They went with their servant Daniel

Jones straight across to the West Bank. They took a footpath that led through some fields near the riverbank to Medinet Habu, the mortuary temple of Ramesses III, and just slightly farther on to where Percy and Robb de Peyster Tytus, a wealthy American-trained archaeologist, were excavating.[18] In just a few days, Emma found that her investment was already paying dividends. Percy had uncovered a painted floor and decorated walls at the palace. Emma was shocked at the state of the colors after thousands of years of being covered by sand—they looked as though they had been painted the day before, when really Percy had just revealed them. She smiled as she talked to Percy about his finds and his plans for the rest of the winter. She looked around at the beautiful desert with mountains on one side and the river in the distance to the other. She could just make out where the *Bedauin* was moored on the eastern bank next to their friends on the dahabeahs *Scarab* and *Castle*. She wanted to live in these hills, but for now lunch and tea would have to do. They put up a tent near the site that week, and Emma could hardly be enticed to leave.

The end of that season was productive for Percy, Emma, and Theo. Emma had paid for Percy's work with Tytus at Malqata, and Theo had paid for Howard and Percy's excavations at some tombs in Abd el-Gurneh. He and Howard excavated the tomb of Thutmose IV, where they apparently found two mummified bodies. In 1906, he published a years-long study on scarabs, in which he thanked "My friend, Mrs. E. B. Andrews of 'The Beduin.'"[19] Percy soon moved on to a position with the Catalogue Général of the Department of Antiquities, and from 1906 was a professor and then honorary reader at the University of Liverpool, which allowed him to excavate in Egypt almost every winter season until 1949. He never dug for Emma and Theo again, but they maintained a warm friendship.

Emma and Theo continued to get to know the lay of the land and their diggers. By the time they left Thebes/Luxor for good that year in early March 1902, the barley fields they had walked through just two months earlier were in full head, ready for reaping. Emma's view of the rose-colored mountains had changed that season as well, from a beautiful backdrop into land ready to be harvested for antiquities.

Emma was also passionate about supporting women's rights and women's education. In Egypt, she had the perfect outlet for her patronage, the American Mission School for Girls. The school in Luxor was run by Miss Carrie Buchanan, who had been in Egypt for over ten years with the Mission, and Miss Jean Gibson. There were several American Mission schools all over Egypt, begun and supported by the United Presbyterian Church's Mission in the 1850s. Their main task was mission work, that is, converting Egyptian Muslims to Christianity. They also hoped to "civilize," which is to say Westernize, Egyptian men and women through various educational efforts. To achieve this goal, the Girls' Schools taught students, who ranged in age from five years old to adult women, to read and write as well as the domestic tasks of cooking, cleaning, and sewing.[20]

The school in Luxor had just been established in 1901 in a house in the village, and in that same year Theo had given land for a new school building. When Emma went to visit in February of 1902, bringing Theo with her, she noted that the original school was in "a very good native house—new and large. With a really pleasant sitting room belonging to Miss Buchanan and her friend." They had 130 students, including ten boarders from smaller villages outside Luxor, who were taught in five classrooms. In the mornings each girl had to pass a hygiene inspection, then they had reading and writing lessons, and in the afternoons they worked on domestic tasks. For their meals, which the students prepared, they were not allowed to eat "in Arab fashion" but were "obliged to eat in [a] civilized manner." That is to say, they had to sit upright at a clothed table, in chairs, and properly use forks, spoons, and knives. The students then had to clear the table and clean the dishes. Emma watched with excitement as the girls completed their tasks.

Emma had hope for the prospect of a civilizing education for Egyptian girls, and especially for her young servant Nubia. Nubia's parents had died, and she lived with her sister, so Emma and Theo had taken her on. Emma warned Carrie and Jean that Nubia was "a little savage," but Emma left her at the school after that visit with high hopes. In her diary she remarked, somewhat dubiously, "We will see."[21] Although it would never be explicitly admitted, the catch was that little Nubia and the other women at the school would never be truly or fully "civilized." They would always be Egyptian. Much like British civilizing efforts through mission work in India, the main goal here was conversion and coercion, never coopera- tion.[22] After just three weeks at the school, Nubia had shown "such aptitude and cleverness" that she became a boarder. What happened to Nubia after this is not clear—Emma didn't mention her again. What is clear is that, from that point on, Emma was a major patron of the Mission, and of the Luxor school in particular. Emma herself knew the value of a good girl's education.[23]

Emma wasn't the first millionaire to visit the valley, and she wasn't the first to excavate or fund an excavation, but she was the first woman who would do all of these things. Being first can his- torically be an important milestone or touchpoint for women, but when you really dig deep, it's the impact Emma had on the field with the work that she did that makes her significant. From 1900 to 1913, Emma was in the field, on-site, next to Theo, every step of the way. She may not have decided to dive headfirst into just-opened tombs, but that was often a wise decision on her part. While Theo frequently emerged from newly opened tombs covered in dust and hardly able to breathe, Emma sat under the shade of an umbrella, taking notes and drinking tea.

"There Is Everything There but a Grand Piano"

When the *Bedauin* arrived in Luxor in early 1905, her passengers went about their regular tasks—washing, collecting the mail, and visiting with old friends. Theo and Alice Wilson, the daughter of Theo's closest friend Nathaniel Wilson, went to visit Muhammad Mohassib, the antiquities dealer. Their old friend was still mourn- ing the loss of his son the year before. Emma had gone to see the progress on the new Mission school building in Luxor.

Through the chilly winds that still blew through the Nile Val- ley that January, Emma ventured over to the West Bank and the Valley of the Kings a few times to see what their excavator James (everyone called him Edward) Quibell had been doing. Howard Carter had left them in 1904 to move into the Inspectorate for

Lower Egypt, but Theo maintained the permission for the Kings' Valley. Emma was so upset to see that the beautiful fields of barley they had walked through just a few years earlier had been torn up in favor of irrigation canals for crops and railways to transport sugarcane through the area. She hated the loud, bouncing cars. The donkeys weren't used to the new noises and smells, and her donkey chair couldn't balance between the animals when the donkeys were distracted.

To add to all this disappointment, Edward Quibell hadn't found much in their old digging spot by the time they arrived to the valley on January 20. Theo decided he was tired of digging there and wanted to excavate in a new, undisturbed spot. It was a risk, though, since it was between the entrances to the tomb of an unidentified son of Ramesses III (KV 3, built c. 1150 BCE, open since antiquity) and Ramesses XI (KV 4, died c. 1077 BCE, open since antiquity), so surely someone would have found something if anything existed. Theo was well aware that if he had been an Egyptologist exploring with someone else's money, he would not have taken the chance on such a difficult but obvious spot.[24] But he knew "every yard of the lateral valley, except the space described, and I decided that good exploration justified its investigation, and that it would be a satisfaction to know the entire valley, even if it yielded nothing."[25] But that space was about to reveal the biggest, most complete, and most important discovery in the valley, until the discovery of King Tutankhamun's tomb in 1922.

February 6, 1905, was a windy day as Theo, Alice, and Jean Hardy, one of Emma's Columbus nieces, braved a trip over to the valley. Emma refused to go. The wind bothered her too much, and it had been unseasonably cold lately. She was also busy working her way through *Paul's Rose Catalog* to get ready for the summer garden season in Newport. She needed to pick just the right flowers for her garden. When Theo, Alice, and Jean arrived at the site, the diggers saw them coming and began cheering. The trio knew this meant something had been found while they were gone. They were right. For the last two weeks, diggers had been clearing debris and had just found a stone step in the dirt. It gave the hint of more steps below it (fifteen to be exact), and farther on, a passage and a tomb.

Theo told Emma about it that night, and they were very encouraged. Over the next few days, the diggers continued uncovering the steps. On the eleventh they found a portion of a door, and at the end of the day on the twelfth, they had revealed the door in its entirety. They thought it was the entrance to the tomb chamber itself, and luckily there was a small opening at the top of the door with just enough space for a small person to get through. Normally, Theo would try to go in himself, but they couldn't open the door any farther without fearing a full-on robbery in the night.

Theo could see into the corridor just past the door that the ancient tomb thieves had dropped a few tantalizing goods. The final diggers left on-site that evening—the reis and his son, the captain of the basket boys—were conscripted into service.[26] They tied the boy's turban under his arms and lowered him into the opening. The boy was terrified of evil spirits in the darkness of the tomb, and he kept begging to be let out, but Arthur Weigall, the incoming Department of Antiquities Inspector assigned to Upper Egypt, and Theo directed him to grab the objects for them. The boy managed to hand them a wooden staff, a heavily gilded chariot's neck yoke, a pair of sandals, and a large, gold-covered scarab.[27] Theo examined the pieces, and in the darkness of the evening was convinced the scarab was solid gold.[28] The boy, still crying, reported there were no reliefs to read, and he was finally pulled back through the opening and deposited safely into his father's arms. Theo paid no attention to the boy and his father but wrapped up the items and took them back to the *Bedauin*. Emma was still awake and delighted to see Theo pull out the "queer parcels." She was enthralled with the new pieces, and recorded:

> He first unwrapped a yoke of a chariot, finely decorated in gold and colour—in perfect condition, then a long baton, or wand of office—also finely decorated—then produced a large beautiful green, hard stone scarab, with gilded bands, beautifully inscribed even to the wings.[29]

They discussed the pieces with Maspero on the *Bedauin*, but even he didn't know whom they, and thus the tomb, could have belonged to. Maspero, his curiosity piqued, was as anxious to get inside the tomb as Theo was. Against what we now know as best practices, Maspero asked Theo to enter it the very next day.

Before Theo had left the site that night, they had all agreed that Arthur Weigall, photographer Joseph Lindon Smith, and Joe's wife, Corinna Smith, would spend the night at the tomb. No one really slept. It was cold. The site was spooky in the complete darkness, and Weigall kept everyone awake, talking excitedly about what he thought could be in the tomb.[30] Maspero had pointed out earlier that evening that if the tomb actually contained a chariot to go with the yoke, it would be only the second known example of an early Egyptian chariot; the first was in the museum at Turin.

The story of the opening of the tomb is confusing, however, because the firsthand accounts don't completely agree with one another. Emma had her own, as did Theo, and so did Joe Smith. The problem of few published sources means that there are conflicting timelines, events, and, of course, information about who was involved and when. Still, even with a few events that don't line up, it's possible to construct a fairly accurate chronicle of what happened.

Everyone—even Alice, who hadn't been well the past few days— joined the caravan to the tomb.[31] Theo arranged for a carriage to take Emma and Alice at least part of the way. When they arrived, a little past nine o'clock in the morning—quite late for most excavations as the sun had long been up—they found Weigall and the Smiths. Emma was slightly envious of their experience overnight, even though Corinna told her it had been cold and unnerving. The Egyptian Inspector was there as well, and they all waited for Maspero and his secretary to arrive. The day was already warming up, which was going to make going down into the rock-cut tomb difficult, to say the least. The inner door to the tomb was mostly bricked up and needed to be cleared, so Theo ordered the bricks to be taken down by workmen and inspected to see if there was any indication on them of the owner of the tomb. They bore no markings.

While the door was being cleared, which, in his publication, Theo claimed to be present for, he had in fact climbed to a spot in the valley that Maspero wanted to show him that could be a good digging spot later. They were gone for quite a while, leaving everyone else waiting on the rocks near the tomb's entrance. As the door was slowly opened, Alice and Emma were glad for their carriage's comfortable seats and the shade from the small roof. The horses that had pulled them had already been removed to get food and water. The Egyptian Inspector, who had been in charge of clearing the bricks, emerged from the passage and said, "The entrance is free." Weigall and Smith decided to go down into the tomb. Just a few minutes later, they came back out, out of breath and pale. They had quickly assessed the tomb and were pleasantly surprised at the state of it. Smith proclaimed, "There is everything there but a grand piano.,-the place is crowded with furniture and coffins."[32] The crowd outside the tomb was abuzz with excitement, but they still had to wait for Theo and Maspero to come back from their other explorations. Emma was ecstatic. Neither Maspero nor Edward Quibell had thought the site would yield anything. They were certain that no tomb could have survived the excavation of tombs KV 3 and KV 4 in antiquity. They were wrong, and Theo was right. His usual stubbornness in the face of expertise had worked this time as it had for the tomb of Hatshepsut (KV 20, died c. 1458 BCE) and Thutmose IV (KV 43, died c. 1390 BCE) the previous year. He was justified in his methods, for good or for ill.

Theo and Maspero arrived back from their long, hot exploratory hike to an anxious and jubilant group. The two men, along with Arthur Weigall, each got a candle and hurried down the passage, which was easy to access thanks to the diggers having cleared it out. There were about fifteen precipitous stairs to descend first, then a level path to a short, declining corridor going down farther into the earth, which led to another short set of stairs, then into the tomb. They were down there for a while; Emma wondered what they were doing. Theo would tell her later that, on the way down, they had found two red pottery bowls, one that had the fingerprint of the original potter preserved in the clay. These bowls were deposited near a wig and an armful of ancient flowers set in a niche carved in the wall. They passed all of this before reaching another sealed-off doorway with yet another slight hole at the top left. Theo and Maspero began removing bricks with their bare hands so they could peer inside the chamber. They agreed that they didn't want to disturb anything, but they simply had to be the first ones to look inside. Theo and Arthur helped Maspero through the opening, then got through themselves. It was "as dark as dark could be and extremely hot."[33] But Maspero was able to make out one name: Yuya. Once they came back up, Emma went down to see for herself—and she did so with relish.

Corinna, and not Emma, had been the first woman in the tomb that day and, as Maspero pointed out, the first woman alive *ever* to be in the tomb.[34] Emma, hoping to see what Theo saw, also took her candle carefully down the passage. One of the staircases was situated so vertically into the deep tomb that it was almost like a ladder. As she arrived at the hole in the door, she used her flickering candle to try to get a glimpse of some of the furniture. She saw what every Egyptologist hopes in the depths of their hearts to see as they peer into millennia-old darkness: gold. Everywhere she moved her candle, she saw the glistening gold of the tomb's remains. There was tomb furniture, like the chariot Maspero hoped would be there, a gilded chair, and more, along with a confusion of coffins, some of which were already revealing their human contents. Before the group took a break for lunch, they arranged for electric light to be installed as they ate.

The whole group climbed the long incline from the floor of the valley up to the Thutmose IV tomb (KV 43), near where their butler had prepared lunch for them. They ate, talked, and rested in the shade. Their view from the plateau at KV 43 was clear and bright all the way down to the excavation site, so Theo could keep an eye on progress but still relax in the cool shade. It really was amazing to Emma that the carving-out of KV 3 and KV 4 did not accidentally destroy this tomb. She was lost in reverie about the tomb's placement, and Theo never took long enough for lunch. As she roused herself from her thoughts, she suggested that Theo should eat more slowly and enjoy his tea and after-lunch cigar. He refused. He was too excited about the tomb. Could what Maspero said be true? Could this be the first, and likely last, virtually undisturbed tomb in the valley? If so, he would get credit for this find and be even more famous than he was already. Maspero had offered him a share of the artifacts, even though, technically, the permission didn't really allow for anything but duplicates. No, Theo had said, this should all go to the Cairo Museum together. Maybe *now* he would be more respected in the Egyptological community for his unusual digging techniques and generally sloppy methods. He could only hope. He ate quickly, which made everyone else eat quickly.

After lunch, they all went back to the site so Theo could go back in, although Emma said it was too hot. She wanted him to stay and sit in the shade with everyone. She told him to wait for England's Prince Arthur, the Duke of Connaught, third son of Victoria and brother of King Edward VII, to arrive, which should be around 4:00 P.M. Instead, Theo and Maspero went in with the other Egyptian crew. After about twenty minutes, one of the diggers ran back out of the passage, frantic to get water and brandy back to Theo in the tomb. Emma sighed and shook her head. She knew that Theo had fainted. Again. He'd done it a few years ago, too—pushing himself too hard in the morning and heading straight into a newly opened tomb in the heat of the day made the prime conditions for him to lose consciousness. She went into the tomb a few steps and could see him from there. He lay at the bottom, barely conscious but held up by two men while being doused with cool water and sipping the reviving spirits. He called up to her that he was "quite all right," but she wondered to herself why Theo limited her time in a new tomb, while he regularly emerged short of breath or even fainted. He came out of the tomb on his own and sat in the shade of the carriage. Alice, still ill from the week before, had to make room for him to rest and recuperate. By 4:00 P.M., when the duke and his entourage arrived, very excited to see the tomb, Theo was ready.

Before the Duke of Connaught arrived, however, Joe Smith recalled that another Duke, Spencer Compton Cavendish, and the Duchess of Devonshire had shown up, quite conspicuously, at noon, before lunch. Cavendish was distinguished as the former leader of the House of Lords and held many other political offices throughout his life. While Maspero was down in the tomb with Corinna, the duke rode up on a donkey. He was tall, so he dismounted by simply straightening his long legs and letting the donkey walk out from underneath him. It wasn't the most dignified of dismounts, but neither was it dignified to ride a donkey. The duchess attempted to be more imposing than her husband, so she was carried in on a chair by eight Egyptian men. She was unprepared to dismount this contraption, so she shouted to the men in the front, "Down!" They dropped down as quickly as they could, but the men in the back didn't follow suit, so the duchess was dumped out of the chair, rolling on the ground to the duke's feet.[35] He was not impressed with his wife. The crew finally retrieved Maspero to meet the duke, who had become extremely impatient at the lack of grace he was being shown by the Egyptologists—some of whom had the gall to be Americans! The Duke of Devonshire, however, was denied entry into the tomb until the Duke of Connaught had shown up, because, as the brother of the king, he had to officially open the tomb.

When Connaught arrived promptly at 4:00 P.M., possibly with Devonshire (according to Emma's diary on the day, but not according to Joe Smith's memory years later), Connaught and Maspero went into the tomb. When they emerged, Connaught congratulated Theo as if he had done the work all on his own. Edward Quibell then arrived on the scene, having missed all the excitement. He was extremely upset that people had been allowed in the tomb before he had even seen it. It was irresponsible of Maspero above all to do this, knowing how they were supposed to handle new tombs. Theo didn't care. He had found a remarkable tomb and wanted everyone to know.

Maspero announced that day that the tomb was that of Yuya and Thuya (c. 1375 BCE), the parents of Queen Tiye (died c. 1338 BCE). Tiye was the wife of Amenhotep III, the mother of Akhenaten (died c. 1335 BCE), and grandmother of Tutankhamun (died c. 1323 BCE). It was, in fact, as Theo had hoped, a virtually undisturbed tomb, and Maspero further announced that this was one of the most complete finds in the valley, ever. Emma recorded that day that "all the objects so far as they have been seen, are in perfect order and good and very beautiful."[36]

Over the next few days, a parade of dignitaries came to see the Egyptians whose remains were still in their ancient tomb. Some of them were working on the tomb—Maspero, Archibald Sayce, Weigall, Smith, and Egyptologist Edward Ayrton. Many of them were famous visitors to Luxor at the time, and their prestige added to the excitement of Theo and Emma's work. The nonroyal tomb brought all sorts of royalty to see it, and Theo and Emma were not about to turn them away. The Duke and Duchess of Connaught returned to see it with their daughter, Princess Margaret. Emma was impressed by their interest in the objects, and she was flattered that they thought her room on the *Bedauin* was "lovely." The Empress Eugénie also came to visit, as she had been in love with Egypt since her first visit in 1869 for the opening of the Suez Canal. Prince Gustaf Adolf of Sweden, its future king, also visited, and he and Theo became friends. It was also on this same trip that Gustaf Adolf and England's Princess Margaret met and fell in love at first sight. They would be married just four months later in St. George's Chapel at Windsor Castle. Margaret died fifteen years later of sepsis, but she gave birth to five children, one of whom would become Queen of Denmark, and another who would father King Carl XVI Gustaf of Sweden. Devonshire and his wife returned to see the tomb, as well. A few years later, Devonshire died after sailing up the Nile to help relieve symptoms of tuberculosis.[37]

Despite all the excitement, oddly, just a week after the tomb had been opened, Emma and Theo left for Aswan. Emma didn't want to go. Why leave Luxor when they'd just found an amazing tomb? She thought Theo might just need the rest. He had been at the tomb all day, every day since the steps were discovered. But Arthur Weigall had been sleeping there every night as well as working all day. He surely needed a break. And shouldn't they stay with their find? Still, Emma couldn't complain much. She liked the relaxing time on the boat, being free of all the people who competed for their attention. It took them a few days to sail to Aswan, but they moored in familiar places and visited people at the Cataract and Savoy Hotels. They recharged and were back in Luxor two weeks after they left.

They consulted with Arthur, Edward Quibell, Maspero's student Pierre Lacau, and others about the tomb, revisiting it once more. As Emma prepared the *Bedauin* for the journey back downstream to Cairo, she watched as all the boxes were brought from the tomb of Yuya and Thuya to a waiting boat, bound for the train station on the other side of the Nile. She wondered how the diggers could carry all those precious boxes while walking on burning sands. After a total of five weeks and three days in Luxor, on March 6 they finally left for the long journey home. Nine days later they arrived at Bedresheyn, where Emma dreaded seeing automobiles, brand-new to Egypt. This was evidence of civilization she deemed "horrid" after weeks of blissful time in the desert.

They arrived in Cairo a few days later, and one of the first things they did was take the antiquities they had carried from Luxor on the *Bedauin* to the Cairo Museum. They had brought the most delicate pieces, even though the rest had come by train from Luxor. Emma was glad to get rid of them. Having such valuable pieces in her care was more than she could handle. But when she got to see them unpacked and displayed, in their own room at the museum, she was so happy that others could enjoy them. Maspero renamed that particular room Salle Theodore Davis to honor Theo and hopefully continue to cultivate his patronage. The room, the first and only one in the museum to be named after a patron, excavator, or Egyptologist, was dedicated first to the artifacts from KV 46, including the mummified remains of Yuya and Thuya, who had special cases R and S in the middle of the room.[38] Theo wished to have the whole assemblage together in one place, seeing how it was an important and unique tomb, and he "contented himself with four funerary statuettes, which the Egyptian government presented to him as a souvenir."[39] The whole group left Cairo on April 3, making the best crossing from Alexandria to Brindisi that Emma could remember. About a week later, Percy Newberry came to stay with them in Venice so Theo and Percy could work together on the publication of the tomb.

They used Emma's records of these excavations almost exclusively. She was the only one who had taken detailed notes. Not only did she show the human side of excavations—both in those who visited the sites and those who dug them—but she also showed that more than just the white men were doing work. While Quibell published his own account of the excavation and the tomb, today Emma's journals are important for inclusion and understanding participation on-site. When Percy and Theo were working with the notes, they left out the personal details, only focusing on the heroic work they had done.

"By Jove, Queen Tyi, and No Mistake!"

The 1905–6 season went relatively smoothly and uneventfully for Emma and Theo. They finally hired their draftsperson, E. Harold Jones, to do full-time drawing after several months of part-time work. He had come to Egypt in the winter of 1904, also looking for the change-of-air cure, and ended up being a central figure in their excavations in the valley from 1907 to his death in 1911, even becoming their excavator in 1908. During the 1905–6 season, Emma, who was sixty-eight at the time, fell ill with a cold. It got worse, and she battled a bad bronchitis that kept her in bed for four weeks. She was more ill than she had ever been in her life. She recalled it as "a weary time."[40]

Theo, on the other hand, was "very busy with his work." It was mainly Theo's diggers and Edward Ayrton who found and cleared tombs KV 47 to KV 53. The most important tomb that year was KV 47, the tomb of Siptah (died c. 1191 BCE), "an unimportant king of the XIX dynasty."[41] Harold Jones worked in this tomb full-time, painting copies of several of the walls. In 1909, J. P. Morgan commissioned Jones to copy some of the doorjambs in the tomb, and those paintings were gifted to the Metropolitan Museum of Art upon Morgan's death in 1912.[42] Because Emma was so ill, she didn't record very much activity that season, but she complained that, because of the tomb uncovering, they had a lot of visitors to the *Bedauin.* The stream of visitors would often arrive at breakfast and last through tea and dinner. Emma would sit with them to be polite, but that winter she spent most of her time waiting for people to leave her in peace so she could convalesce in bed.

The following two seasons, however, that of 1906–7 and 1907–8, a total of five more tombs were uncovered, and four in very quick succession. Emma was in full health during these two seasons, feeling energized by the work and being in Egypt. Everyone was excited with the flurry of activity, but also by this time she and Theo were both seventy years old and tired (Theo would never admit it). She was sad they'd had to leave Newport in the winters before she could finish planting her garden, so she decided to manage by "long distance planning," which likely meant writing to their gardener to direct him about what to plant. She also missed her dog Toby, who was getting too old to travel with them.

They arrived in Egypt toward the end of November 1906, in a torrential downpour at Alexandria. They just caught the train to Cairo and made it to Shepheard's by the afternoon of Monday the twenty-sixth. The hotel had been fully torn down and rebuilt in 1891, but 1906 was the year the hotel added another floor, and another seventy-five rooms, complete with bathrooms. Emma fell right into making sure everything was ready for travel, or, as she noted, their maid Amelie did that work. They were fully ensconced in the Egyptological circles to which they had become accustomed, the ones in which they were often the center. Friends came to see them at Shepheard's, and they met with their archaeologists and did a little shopping. That year, they traveled as far upriver as Abu Simbel before coming back down to rest in Luxor by December 28.

On January 7, 1907, after they'd been settled in for about a week, Theo went over to the valley in the late morning to see what Ayrton had found, if anything. He had been digging, with Emma and Theo's financial support, for several weeks before they arrived. In fact, a few days before, Ayrton had excitedly written to Theo declaring he'd found a tomb, but that turned out not to be the case. He was embarrassed by his rush to judgment and the fact that he had had to write a second note saying he was wrong. He didn't want to bother Theo again with something he wasn't sure of. So, on this hot Monday, when Theo went over to the valley, he found Ayrton in the midst of a new tomb. Theo understood why he hadn't been notified. He was a little disappointed he was so late to the site, but he would never let Ayrton know that. Theo stayed all day and came home late in the evening, tired from the sun and work. Emma had been on the boat most of the day but had gone with Nettie to the Luxor Hotel around 3:00 P.M. to meet friends for tea. There the women had run into their old friend Howard Carter and brought him back to the boat with them.

The following day, Tuesday, January 8, everyone went with Theo to the valley. Emma, Jean, Nettie, their maid Amelie, and their butler Daniel Jones were all happy to be in the valley again. It was just as hot as the day before, but the diggers were hard at work, and they thought they had cleared the entrance to the entire tomb. Emma and Theo were happy that it turned out to be just an entrance to a tomb corridor. The possibilities the tomb contained were limitless, given what they found in the space leading up to the door: a broken vase and bits of gold foil. It is hard to overestimate the excitement that Theo and Emma must have felt. Even being old hands by this point, they surely dreamed of more gold and another fuss being made over something they were able to reveal. The work slowed considerably because of the difficulty in clearing the corridor and entrances of millennia of debris. Once the gold was found, work halted for the day because it was too late to open the tomb. The slightest hint of gold would draw out people from all over, so they called security, and Weigall slept by the tomb as he had done two seasons earlier to protect Yuya and Thuya.

The next day, which was a warm Wednesday, they were able to open the tomb. Emma rode there early in the morning of January 9 on her donkey chair, as usual, with Theo, Amelie, and Jones, as well as Hassein, a figure who shows up only a few times in Emma's diary but was one of their Egyptian workers each year. Emma preferred the warmer days, and she had the shade from her donkey chair to help. The chair can best be described as a litter, but instead of people carrying Emma, one to two donkeys were placed at each of the four corners, strapped to wooden poles. They would slowly walk, carrying the rider in a chair. It was more dignified than simply riding astride a donkey, and it gave Emma a high status among visitors. As a woman who had just entered her seventies, Emma needed the relief that the change of air and sun brought to her joints and her breathing, and the relaxing ride of the donkey chair.

It seemed the crew had been at work during the evening and dawn hours clearing the steps down to the door as well as the doorway. The crew were proudly waiting for Theo to arrive to the site so he could make his customary grand entrance. Emma silently prayed he wouldn't faint this time. Ayrton and Weigall had waited for them, and, with Theo, they began the scramble through the corridor to the tomb. Emma waited on the rocks outside and above the tomb, likely in the shade, with David Erskine, a Liberal member of Parliament who was in Egypt at the time. Emma described him as a "nice, big, handsome Englishman."[43] Also there waiting were Arthur's wife, Constance Weigall, and the Lindon Smiths, anxiously anticipating any news from inside the tomb.

The entrance, Emma recorded that day, would prove to be "very difficult." The corridor, which sloped steeply downward, was filled with stones and other rubble almost to the ceiling. "On this pile of stones," Theo later recalled, "were lying two wooden doors, on each of which copper hinges were fixed. The upper faces of the doors were covered with gold foil marked with the *name and titles of Queen Tiyi* [*sic*]."[44] One door was large—about fourteen feet long and six feet wide—from a large wooden shrine, and the other door was much smaller, about two by four feet. They couldn't get any farther in the corridor without damaging the doors, but they couldn't move the doors until Maspero had seen the state of the uncovered tomb. Theo really wanted to go into the tomb, so "with the skill of the native captain, we got a beam about ten inches wide between one wall and the golden door. On this beam," Theo wrote, "I managed to crawl over, striking my head and most of my body but without damaging the doors."[45] Ayrton, Weigall, and Lindon Smith went in with him. By the time they had crawled almost seventy feet along the top of the stones filling the corridor, they found that the tomb chamber itself was largely untouched by that kind of debris.

All four men were shocked by what they found. Emma recalled that the group waiting outside the tomb strained their ears "to catch the broken exclamations that reached us from below."[46] The men inside yelled out "Aton!," "The rays of the Sun!," and even "Tut-ankh-amen!" until finally Emma could hear Theo shout, clearly above all the others: "By Jove, Queen Tyi and no mistake!"[47] The smaller door they had found on top of the corridor debris was the key to these men identifying the tomb so quickly. That door contained cartouches that were of Tiye and her husband, Pharaoh Amenhotep III. These were the parents of Akhenaten, the grandparents of Tutankhamun. Yuya and Thuya, whose tomb they had found around the corner in 1905, were the parents of Queen Tiye. In the end, the initial identification of the occupant of this tomb, the fifty-fifth tomb uncovered in the Kings' Valley, would turn out to be an egregious mistake, leading to decades of debate.

The tomb itself was relatively small, completely undecorated, and in considerable disarray. The shrine, or what was left of it, was broken apart, with pieces lying on the ground or propped up on the wall. The sarcophagus and the body in it were strewn about the floor, as well. It looked like the tomb had been abandoned quickly or robbed in antiquity, or both. Although Emma didn't go down into the tomb that first day, Nettie, Constance, and Jean Hardy made the arduous climb and went in. Theo made sure that Nettie was the first woman in the tomb.

Tired from the exertion of getting into the tomb and the excitement of what they thought they had found, everyone soon stopped and ate lunch. The Department of Antiquities had set up a dining room in a tomb nearby with tables and chairs for excavators. They ate in the sloping entrance hall of KV 10, the tomb of Amenmesse (died c. 1198 BCE), the father of Siptah, possibly a grandson of Ramesses II, but he was later seen as a usurper of Seti II (died c. 1197 BCE). Just a short walk from the new tomb they were working on, across the wide, uncovered space in the middle of the wadi, number 10 had been open since antiquity but not yet fully

Fig. 3.3: Valley of the Tombs of the Kings, Thebes, c. 1882.

cleared.[48] Where three thousand years ago mourners finally sealed the tomb door (which didn't remain sealed for long), Emma, Theo, and their entourage excitedly talked about what prospects the newly found tomb on the other side of the pathway held for understanding ancient Egypt, and for bringing fame and recognition to the Americans.

Throughout the next week, Theo and Emma's entourage went about their normal business of shopping and dining in Luxor, meeting with friends, and eagerly awaiting the arrival of their old friend Gaston Maspero. They couldn't wait to show him all the treasure they had found. He arrived in Luxor on the fourteenth, sailing on his own dahabeah, the *Miriam,* about a week after Edward and Theo had breached the tomb.[49] That day dawned, showing off the rose pink mountains of the West Bank at sunrise. The main peak, called El Qurn (the Horn) by modern Egyptians, had been known as Meretseger by ancient Egyptians. The ancient name meant "She Who Loves Silence." Hymns were written to her, and shrines were dedicated to her as the resting place of the ancient kings of Egypt. Emma looked out at the peak, pyramidal in shape itself, and enjoyed the silence as they rested on the *Bedauin* that Monday. Emma wrote letters home and updated her diary as Theo went to Maspero's boat to break the news of the tomb. Maspero was delighted by and surprised about the new find. Other, more immediate work took his time those first few days, so he didn't visit the tomb until the sixteenth. Despite the rain that day, Maspero's wife joined them and borrowed Emma's donkey chair for the trip.

The next day, Thursday the seventeenth, Theo and Jean Hardy went to supervise the clearing of the tomb. Particularly difficult for them was bracing the wooden shrine for transport out of the tomb and to the museum in Cairo. Emma didn't go to the tomb that day but instead went with her niece Nettie across the river to Luxor. They took a carriage to tour the Temples of Luxor and Karnak. She also went to Muhammad Mohassib's shop for "a little visit," but she probably did some shopping there as well. After they rode out to visit Carrie Buchanan at the Girls' Mission School, they hosted Howard Carter for tea in the afternoon.

Emma's busy social calendar kept her from being in the photo-

Fig. 3.4: The Weigalls, Theo (holding hat), and Edward Ayrton, outside KV 2, January 17, 1907.

graph of Theo taken that day. While it is the most reproduced photo of Theo, we don't have any extant photos of her. The Weigalls and Ayrton are also in the photo. The caption, on the bottom left of the photo, reads, "This is Tomb no. 2 and used by Mr. Davis and Mr. Ayrton as a [unreadable]."

The crew needed for an excavation was massive. Ayrton was in charge of the work, and Theo was paying for it. For better or worse (usually worse), Theo was also an active member of the crew—as active as he wanted to be, anyway. If Emma contributed financially to the excavation, she never said so. Even though she missed several days on-site, she meticulously recorded the events at the tomb and the attention that came after it was opened. There is little to no mention of the Egyptian workers who did the backbreaking work of digging, lifting, dumping, and crawling.

Joseph Lindon Smith was also there much of the time. Theo was lucky to have him. By the time Maspero arrived, they hadn't cleared much room in the corridor to crawl—only about eighteen inches

between the rubbish and the ceiling—and Joe's smaller physique
lent itself to cramped spaces more so than his colleagues', and especially more than Maspero's, so he was tasked with entering the
tomb to draw anything he could. He wiggled across the makeshift
bridge as carefully as possible and supported himself on his elbows.
He drew quick sketches of a few cartouches with names in them,
so Maspero could know who they were dealing with. Maspero was
so pleased with the cartouches—they were indeed of Queen Tiye—
that he asked Joe to return and report on the state of the rest of
the tomb. Maspero was concerned that Theo had pronounced the
owner of the tomb too quickly, and he wanted to make sure all the
evidence was accounted for. Joe was told to examine the tomb and
its contents—which included the golden doors, now propped in
the tomb itself, alabaster jars, a coffin with the lid partly off, and
exposed mummified human remains—for water damage. To everyone's surprise, there was a lot of water present.

The third time Joe went down, workmen at the surface held
mirrors to reflect sunlight into the tomb. This was how ancient
Egyptians lit the tombs as they worked. Like the Palaeolithic artists in caves at Lascaux and Altamira, ancient Egyptian craftsmen
would never have seen their work illuminated by a bright electric
light. They had intended the art to be viewed only by the tomb
owner in the context in which they had created it. Joe was surprised
that this ancient lighting system "gave a steady and brilliant illumi-
nation that brought out details not visible by flashlight."[50] With it,
he sketched the coffin lid and returned to the surface.

On the nineteenth, Emma went down into the tomb that was
now called KV 55, but Maspero and Theo were still debating the
tomb's inhabitant. Emma could easily get down there because the
corridor had finally been mostly cleared. She saw the tomb and was
surprised at its disarray. As she carefully walked in, Emma "saw the
poor Queen as she lies now just a bit outside her magnificent coffin, with the vulture crown on her head—all the woodwork of the
shrine, doors, etc. are heavily overlaid with gold foil . . ."[51] Despite
the state of the tomb, Emma thought the queen looked stunning.
But in the last twelve days, the outer air had infiltrated the tomb,
interfering with the preservation process of the last three thousand

years. The gold foil was coming off the shrine, and Emma, despite taking care in her step, was walking all over small pieces of gold. One of the crew had pieces in his hair. Other visitors to the tomb felt as though they were breathing in the gold—one reported that when he sneezed after being in the tomb, he found seven or eight small pieces of gold in his handkerchief![52] Theo was infamous for his terrible conservation efforts, when he even attempted them, so the tomb and its contents—that is, all the evidence about the occupant of the tomb and their life and death—were quickly deteriorating.

Emma, on the other hand, was able to quickly record the only surviving map of the tomb and its original layout. The map below was adapted from her map of KV 55, drawn on January 19, 1907. Emma noted rubbish strewn about the floor, and her labels include: (1) "mummy of Queen," partly underneath the coffin; (2) and (3) large doors or panels with gold overlay, "the one with the x has a beautiful portrait of Queen." The Xs near the back wall are large panels, each with inscriptions and overlaid with gold. The niche to the right contained the four alabaster jars with painted lids. Archaeologists still use this map as a starting point because the excavation and subsequent conservation of the objects were so badly done—and not just by today's standards.

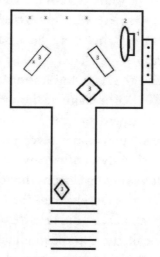

Fig. 3.5: KV 55 reproduction (author's own). Redrawn from Emma Andrews Diaries, American Philosophical Society.

While Emma was down there, she saw that they were working to preserve the shrine doors, with whatever gold was left on them, by spreading paraffin wax all over them. Harold Jones, their artist, was hastily copying a number of the objects from the tomb. He did this so well that his are the most detailed records of the shrine doors. Joe Lindon Smith was taking photographs and painting copies, and a photographer had come down from Cairo to take photos, too. But the clearing of the tomb was still chaotic, all because of Theo's stubbornness.

The clearing and packing happened very quickly, which is to say it didn't happen with the greatest of care. Theo brought home objects for safekeeping on the *Bedauin,* a practice Emma wrung her hands over. Theo brought what he called the "vulture crown," actually a pectoral (chest piece), back to the *Bedauin* for Emma to store in a box at the head of her bed. She admired it for hours, writing in her diary, "It is of solid gold, and represents the royal vulture, with out-spread wings and meeting behind the head, beautifully done in a fine répoussé style—every feather perfect."[53]

The debate over whose tomb it was continued. Theodore Davis, American millionaire, was sure the mummy was an old woman, the Queen Tiye: wife of Amenhotep III, mother of Amenhotep IV/Akhenaten (the heretic king), and grandmother of Tutankhamun. Maspero and others kept warning him not to jump to conclusions so quickly, but he just *knew* he was right. To ease Theo's worry, and to stop the daily arguments they were having about the identity of the tomb's owner, Arthur Weigall did the only thing he could think of: he arranged to send the body to Grafton Elliot Smith, a physician and anatomist living in Cairo at the time. Elliot Smith had worked closely with Maspero and the Department of Antiquities for years and had already unwrapped several mummies for them.

Elliot Smith was slightly confused when he finally received the body, months after its removal from the tomb, and unwrapped it. He examined the bones closely, then focused on the head. He stepped back from the remains—did he have the correct bones? He turned to Arthur Weigall, there in the room with him, and asked if these really were the remains that were found in the tomb. Weigall assured him these bones came out of the coffin in KV 55. Elliot Smith nodded, then told him the shocking news. These weren't the bones of an old woman, he said, so they couldn't be those of Tiye. What lay before him were the bones of a younger man.[54] Elliot Smith showed Weigall how the skull had evidence of hydrocephaly, a condition that causes a build-up of cerebrospinal fluid and may have resulted in the mummy's head becoming misshapen and the bones aging slowly. Elliot Smith concluded that the body could be of a young man around the age of twenty-six, but could also be much older.[55]

When Theo learned of this news in July 1907 back in Newport, he was shocked that an anatomist could get it so wrong. He told Elliot Smith not to present any of the details of his examination for the site report. Theo wasn't wrong, he told Elliot Smith. He knew what he had seen. He blocked Edward Ayrton from contributing any evidence to the contrary of his own initial assumption in the site report, or at all.[56] In the end, Elliot Smith's conclusions were included in the report as purely speculative. Theo would continue to maintain that the person interred in the tomb, the coffin covered in gold, inlaid with lapis and other precious stones, with a golden vulture on her head, was indeed Queen Tiye, and *no mistake.*

This tomb, KV 55, has had more written about it than almost any other tomb in the valley, mainly because of how mysterious Queen Tiye, the daughter of Yuya and Thuya, was at the time. Also, because of how badly the excavation went, how poorly the materials were handled, and how mistaken Theo was from the very beginning about whom the tomb belonged to. There are plenty of written accounts of this excavation, but it's not clear which is the most accurate.[57] Emma's diary, however, was the only one that included daily notes of the activities, but at the same time it was not written for public consumption. Theo clearly used her records for his published reports, lending more credence to hers being the most accurate. In the end, Emma's work has become invaluable for Egyptologists, historians, archaeologists, and biographers who want to trace the activities of this group for the twenty-five years they excavated in Egypt.

"The Valley of the Tombs Is Now Exhausted"

As often happens when diarists travel multiple times to places and become familiar with their surroundings, Emma's diary entries in Egypt became less and less descriptive as time went on. The pair's final major tomb find had been the Gold Tomb, KV 56, in January of 1908, as Ayrton was finalizing the clearing of KV 55. It was called the Gold Tomb because it contained some of the most remarkable gold and silver jewelry ever found in Egypt, including some alabaster jars inscribed with the names Seti II (r. 1203–1197 BCE) and Ramesses II (r. 1279–1213 BCE). But it was and still is unclear whose tomb it actually was.

Even though the Gold Tomb was their last big tomb, they continued to excavate in the valley for the next five years. They had built a dig house in the valley in 1905–6 for their archaeologists to stay in, and they continued to use it as long as they were in Egypt. Ayrton lived in it first. Theo enjoyed staying in the dig house, and Emma liked to host people for tea or lunch. Their subsequent archaeologists lived in it over the next seven years as they continued to clear other tombs. Harold Jones died in the house in 1911 from tuberculosis, surrounded by his brother Cyril and his friend Howard Carter. In December of 1911, at the start of their season, Theo stayed in the house for several weeks, working in the valley. Emma wrote that "Harry Burton and Lancelot Crane are there and hard at work, and Theo says the little house is in fine order, cleaned, disinfected, colour washed etc. and that it is comfortable and pleasant."[58] It was a relatively uneventful season. They visited with friends, including financier and Metropolitan Museum of Art board president J. P. Morgan, who was on a Nile cruise, and watched a graduation ceremony for the students at the Girls' School. The pair left Egypt on April 3, tired and ready to be home. They made their way through Italy, France, and into London, leaving London on May 29. Emma noted that their trip across the Atlantic would take longer than normal that spring, "as all the boats take a long southern course, to avoid possible ice" after the sinking of the *Titanic* on April 15, 1912.[59]

Theo's final publication appeared in 1912, detailing the tomb of

Horemheb (died c. 1292 BCE, KV 57, found in 1908), which he declared to be shared with the tomb of Tutankhamun. In the site report, he announced, in his usual confident finality so that no one could argue: "I fear the Valley of the Tombs is now exhausted."[60] Maybe he was just referring to himself. Maybe he was stating definitively what he believed. Today, we know Theo was wrong. The last tomb Theo and Emma had fully uncovered—excavated by Harold Jones in January of 1910—was numbered 61 in the valley; archaeologist Howard Carter, their old friend, would take another a decade to find the next tomb in the series: KV 62, the Tomb of Tutankhamun. But in 1912, Theo didn't know what waited in the Valley of the Kings.

Both Emma and Theo loved the thrill of discovery, so they returned for two more lackluster seasons in the valley. Both of them were seventy-four years old when they arrived for the 1912–13 season. Theo's health was deteriorating more and more, so Emma's diaries don't really record much excavation work for that year, and she didn't record the 1913–14 season at all. In 1912, with Harold Jones gone, Harry Burton was working for them. He cleared KV 3, KV 6, KV 7, KV 8, and KV 47. He didn't find much more than what had already been known, and in his excavation journal he closed out the 1913–14 season with the statement: "Nothing of importance." Thus ended Theo and Emma's time in the valley.[61] When they returned to Cairo in March of 1914, Theo told Maspero he was done in the valley and relinquished what had been the most coveted and productive excavation permission in the history of Egyptian archaeology.

Lord Carnarvon, another millionaire patron, was granted permission to work in the valley just a few months later, in June of 1914, with Howard Carter working as his archaeologist. Carnarvon was granted a share of all finds in order to repay his efforts for digging, except in the almost impossible event of finding an intact tomb. When this event actually happened in 1922, with Carter presiding and Harry Burton on loan from the Metropolitan Museum of Art to photograph the excavation of KV 62, what turned out to be King Tutankhamun's tomb, Harry used KV 55 as a darkroom for developing his photographs.

As they made their way out of Egypt for the last time in 1914,

Theo and Emma tried to sell off everything they knew they had to leave behind. Since 1896, they had traveled tens of thousands of miles on their custom-built dahabeah, the *Bedauin*, and Emma wanted to make sure they sold it to someone who would love it as much as they did. That person was none other than Percy Newberry, their first archaeologist. On March 28, 1914, before Emma and Theo left Cairo for their Newport mansion, they signed the contracts handing over ownership to Percy. He had a permanent position at Liverpool but needed a place to live and use as transportation when he came to Egypt in the winter. Newberry paid £1,100 for the boat and all its contents, the equivalent of around £104,000 or $130,000 today.[62] By 1929 he would return to take up a full-time teaching position at Cairo University.

Percy boarded the *Bedauin* as it was moored on the Gezireh bank of the Nile, across from the new Semiramis Hotel. The bowl he had gifted Theo and Emma was long gone, but it didn't escape him that he had just purchased the place he first met with them. They were the patrons whose generous support had funded some of his early excavations that helped keep him in the field for a few seasons as he was in between institutional positions. The contract was signed by both men, Percy's young hand contrasting with Theo's shaky signature. As good as the records are at the Griffith Institute, which holds all of Newberry's surviving correspondence—thousands of documents, letters, and photographs—there is no record of what happened to the *Bedauin* after Percy purchased it.

Emma's Legacy

Emma was back in New York in the autumn of 1916. The leaves were changing in Central Park, and she had just met with Head Curator Albert Lythgoe and Caroline Ransom at the park's museum. She had visited to see that the collection she and Theo compiled was on display. Caroline was delighted to show her around. Emma loved seeing the displayed pieces because they brought back the warm, sunny, and sometimes windy memories of where each object was found, who handed each piece up out of each tomb, and how each was stored on their dahabeah. Emma thought she could almost smell the air around her in the Valley of the Kings, tinged with sweat, flowers, and her four donkeys as she sat in her chair in the shade. She could see, as if it were yesterday, Theo, dusty and happy, clapping his hands on his pants and laughing in excitement about his latest discovery.

Theo had died more than a year earlier, on February 23, 1915, and Emma still missed her partner daily. He had left his entire collection of Egyptian antiquities as well as his classical antiquities, European paintings, furniture, and more to the Metropolitan Museum of Art. His nephew, Theodore Davis "Terry" Boal, with Annie Buttles Davis's approval, immediately began contesting his uncle's will. Emma couldn't help but be reminded of this when she read the small labels, stating that the objects were "on loan" from Theo's collection until probate could be sorted out. She didn't know that would take another fifteen years.

While Emma was at the museum, Albert asked her if his secretary could type up her diaries from their time on the *Bedauin*. She was thrilled at this idea and agreed right away. Even if Annie and Terry somehow won their legal battles and got to keep the artifacts they didn't even help collect, at least her legacy and that of her dear Theo would be intact in her journals.

It took two years to complete the transcription and typing of the journals, and Albert hand-delivered the originals back to Emma at Newport in the cold winter of 1918. When he arrived, she had honored Albert's work and friendship by gifting him one of the last bookplates she had saved from their library on the *Bedauin*, thinking it would be fitting for it to go at the front of her journals. Albert agreed. They ate, drank tea—as was their custom—and laughed and reminisced about their lovely days on the Nile. As he left, he assured her that her diaries would be kept safe and that her record of their archaeological work would be a testament to her life and to Theo's. Upon Emma's death in 1922, the museum received $25,000 from her estate, the equivalent of over $400,000 today.

Emma's life and work are bound up within these journals. They aren't just charming recollections, and they don't just contain Theo's work. They contain hers, too. There are few surviving letters from her to anyone, and there are no existing photographs of her that we

Fig. 3.6: *Bedauin* library bookplate.

know of. She was an expert gardener, and maybe if she had stayed in Newport, that would be her legacy. But instead she followed in the footsteps of Amelia Edwards by going to Egypt. She followed women like Maggie Benson, not necessarily excavating on her own but paying for a number of sites to be uncovered and published.

Emma also had a major impact on the community in Luxor. She was a longtime financial supporter and advocate for the Girls' Mission School in Luxor, allowing the students to grow in so many ways. By 1904, they reported having 278 girls at the school, up from 130 just a few years before; 52 were boarders in 1904, which allowed girls from distant villages to "reach higher standards than ever before possible."[63] In 1905, the new school building that Emma and Theo had poured so much money into opened just outside the village of Luxor, along the road to Karnak. The Luxor school was so successful in educating Egyptian girls and women that former president Theodore Roosevelt came to visit in 1910 and gave a speech at the school. He told Carrie Buchanan that he was pleased with her work in making girls into women who could be "the intellectual equal of husband or brother, so that she can take her part in the family life, so that she can be a wise adviser, a wise friend, a member of the family who must be consulted in all manners that concern the family."[64] Carrie Buchanan remained at the school until 1912, when she was transferred away to another town in Egypt. She died in 1927, but even before her death, the Luxor school had been renamed the Carrie M. Buchanan School for Girls. It isn't clear when the school shut down, but it is possible that it continued for several more decades. Emma's recollections are some of the only evidence we have that she was a patron.

It is also because of these journals that we know the names of so many people who were ignored by others—Hussein, their dragoman and *Bedauin* captain Mohammed Salah—and we know more about their old friend, antiquities dealer Muhammad Mohassib. Emma included details that never occurred to Theo to record, much less make public. There are plenty of names that appear within the pages of her journal but don't appear anywhere else, and, because of Emma's detailed note-taking, their impact on Egyptology can be seen. Despite the impact she had on the discipline, it is largely because of these journals that we know about Emma at all.

4

Margaret Alice Murray

By November 19, 1902, we were off, and in Cairo on the 26th.... Hugh Stannus came out to plan the temple work, Miss Murray, my colleague, came out to help with the Osireion.

—Flinders Petrie, *Seventy Years in Archaeology*

Margaret Murray woke with a start. She could have sworn she heard a dog barking outside her window. But where was she? The sun wasn't up yet, so she had to wait for her eyes to adjust to the darkness of the room. The curtain on her long, narrow window was blowing in the light breeze, and she was warm. This wasn't London. She saw her clothes hanging on nails driven into the mud-brick wall, and her bedside table was made out of packing boxes. Margaret sat up in her bed, which was hardly a bed—just a thin mattress on top of a simple wood frame—and she could clearly see the outline of her steamer trunk in the corner of the room. In the fog of waking, she remembered: Abydos. She was finally in Egypt! After eight years of studying and teaching at University College London, she could hardly believe it when Professor Petrie invited her to come to the field and excavate with him and his crew for the 1902–3 season.

They had left London later than they'd hoped due to a cholera outbreak near their site, but once it had subsided, the professor started making plans. Hilda was there, too. Despite the fact that Flinders Petrie's wife of five years was sometimes difficult to get along with, Margaret and Hilda worked well together, and Margaret looked forward to learning from her. Today would be Margaret's first day working on-site and, as the professor had told her, also her first day with the workmen. Petrie's trained workmen from the village of Quft, or the Quftis, as they had become known over the past eight years, were the best-trained excavators in Egypt. Petrie had begun training them almost ten years earlier on his excavation in Naqada, and they were so good at the work that he used them for decades thereafter. Petrie had promised Margaret that she would get to lead the crew today—but how? She didn't know the first thing about leading an expert crew of male diggers in the desert.[1]

She took a deep breath and climbed out of bed, mentally breaking the day down into easy tasks. Step one—get dressed. She had gotten dressing tips from Hilda. That first day, and every day after,

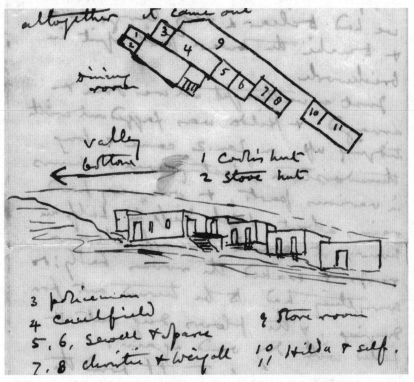

Fig. 4.1: Petrie's journal drawing of the huts they lived in at Abydos from 1902 to 1908. Rooms 1–3 were for the Egyptian cook and policeman. Rooms 4–8 were for excavation staff; 9 was a storeroom, and 10 and 11 were Flinders and Hilda's rooms.

she put on a simple cotton dress and added cotton trousers underneath. Hilda rarely wore trousers under her own galabeya, but
if Margaret were leading an excavation crew today, she knew she
would have to wear trousers. Cotton, a natural fiber, would keep
her cool in the hot sun, unlike the woolens she would have been
wearing if she had been in cold November London. She stepped
out of her tiny room, one of many in a long row, which was next to
a storeroom soon to be stacked with pots, skeletons, and cases. Her
room had a reed mat over the doorway to keep out nightcrawlers,
but no real door to speak of. The Petries' rooms had doors, and the
storeroom had two doors. No one had a toilet. That, she knew, was
the wide desert.

Step two—breakfast. Margaret had heard the horror stories
from her students and friends about food on Petrie's sites, so she
was a little nervous as to what awaited her. She knew that, just a few
years earlier, Edward and Annie Quibell had met and fallen in love
during terrible cases of food poisoning from the rotten food on-site
at Hierakonpolis. They got married, sure, but they had barely survived. Petrie had been digging at Abydos for three years, since 1899,
so he had implemented his now infamous practice of saving food
(and money). At the end of each season, he would bury leftover
tins of food in the desert. The following year, the crew would dig
up the food and test its fitness by throwing the tins against rocks.
The ones that exploded were obviously spoiled, full of gasses from
the rotting food, and couldn't be used. The ones that didn't explode
were considered good enough, even if they were bloated. The crew
had already tested the tins of food when they arrived on-site. Several tins of beans survived the test, so those would be added to the
boxes of food sent in from Cairo. Otherwise, they would have to
wait until market day when they could purchase meat, milk, cheese,
and produce if it was available and not too expensive. The cook
sometimes had fresh eggs.

When Margaret arrived at breakfast, Flinders and Hilda were
already there. She looked at the table with the food. Her choices
were: strong tea, biscuits, meat or fish, and beans. Looking Flinders
right in the eye, as she had become accustomed to doing in the
department at UCL since they met, she said, "Good morning, Pro-

fessor Petrie, Mrs. Petrie." They replied with a curt "Miss Murray," and continued eating. They were already making the day's plan of work and were in the thick of discussion. Margaret was famished, so she grabbed her plate, chose her food from the trestle table on one side of the room, sat down at the rough-wood bench that served as the dining table, and tucked in. Others trickled in to breakfast, including the male students Petrie had invited to Egypt that year and two other women, the medieval historian and suffragist Lina Eckenstein and artist Freda Hansard. They were friends of Hilda's who came to help with the work but soon became friends and confidants of Margaret's as well.

After their perfunctory breakfast, everyone was ready to work. So, Margaret was on to step three, the one she was most excited about—training. She knew the academic side of Egypt better than probably anyone on-site, including the professor, but she did not know how to dig. Professor Petrie pulled Margaret aside that morning and gave her some minimal training. He told her (rather than showed her) how to clear a site, how to choose a good spot for the rubble heap (you don't want to cover up another possible site), and how to fill out one of his new tomb cards. A few hours of training later, with a slight smirk on his face, he told her that she was ready to lead a crew. She asked, surprised, "What about Mrs. Petrie?" He told her Mrs. Petrie had other tasks that day and could not be spared to help her. She walked away, shaking her head in disbelief. She knew she had learned more in that morning than she had from all the books on excavation she had read over the previous few years. She was surprised, though, that everything went so quickly. How could she have gotten enough training that morning when Petrie would spend at least the next several weeks training the men he had brought from London for the same job? She brushed it off, but the all-male Egyptian crew could tell she was worried.

As she moved on to step four—the work—she led them to their digging spot. But the men refused to work with her or do anything she asked of them. These men, Petrie's famous Qufti crew, were superbly trained field experts, and they assumed she hadn't earned this job. Margaret had to think quickly. If she yelled or threatened or forced them to do anything, she knew they'd always give her trouble.

So instead, she marched them straight back to Petrie. He saw her coming and chuckled to himself, setting down his pencil, waiting for her to complain. Instead, she walked right up to Petrie, pulling herself up to her full height of four feet eleven inches, and said, "I'll have nothing to do with them for the rest of the day, they might come tomorrow." The men—all of them, including Petrie—were dumbfounded. The crew knew they would lose their entire day's pay, so they started shouting, clamoring, explaining, and imploring. While Margaret walked away, Petrie calmed them down. He was also worried about losing a whole day of work, but he saw that Margaret could handle herself. This wasn't the first—or the last— test Petrie would put Margaret through, and she knew how to get results.

During the rest of that 1902–3 season, Margaret had no more problems with the crew. In fact, she passed what was probably the happiest winter of her life. She was in Egypt; she was excavating; she got to sleep in the desert and do the work she had been training for the last eight years. Her responsibility was a temple known as the Osireion, a site that was important but not well understood at the time. In this season, Margaret was able to work with Hilda, Freda, and Lina, digging and mapping the site, making copies of inscriptions and art, and collecting and cataloguing artifacts. The women did more work that season than the men Petrie had brought. The men supervised diggers and thought and talked about the items coming out of the ground, but they did very little of the administrative work. From that season, Margaret published a groundbreaking site report called *The Osireion at Abydos*. She argued that "this was the building for the special worship of Osiris and the celebration of the Mysteries. . . ."[2] Her claims and her investigation of the site were so influential to Egyptology that *Osireion* became the main source for the site for at least the next thirty years.

She did such a good job, in fact, that the Petries invited her to the field the next season, 1903–4, to copy tombs at the funerary site of Saqqara. She worked with Freda Hansard again, along with another copyist, Jesse Mothersole. Margaret had the time of her life seeing Athens and Crete on their way to Cairo, then got herself settled on-site at Saqqara, twelve miles south of Cairo and firmly within the long stretch of the pyramid field on the West Bank of the Nile. This site was usually the first stop for Nile travelers, like Emma Andrews and Theodore Davis as they sailed on dahabeahs or steamers, and she probably met a lot of travelers that season.

Her rooms at Saqqara weren't as plush as her rooms in Abydos. In fact, she described her bedroom as being "cold draughts with a few stones between." Their job that year was to clear several of the early tombs at the site, known as mastabas, and copy and possibly correct older copies of the inscriptions. Working with one servant, a twelve-year-old boy, a reis named Rubi whom Auguste Mariette had used fifty years earlier, and Rubi's son Khalifa, the three women were shown the best tombs to open and copy. Often, they copied walls that were bulging inward from the weight of the stones and sand on top of them, and to get to the sites they slid down hills of flowing sand. In the end, they produced a report entitled *Saqqara Mastabas,* which contained copies of ten complete tombs, three of which hadn't been recorded by Mariette, and several that contained corrections. That was to be Margaret's last work season in Egypt. She loved the field, but the professor needed her in London.

Egyptologists know about Margaret Murray mainly because she worked with Flinders and Hilda Petrie. Only recently have they begun to pay attention to the work she did at UCL curating and administrating from 1898 to 1935. Her biggest impacts on the field were simply not the exciting, dirty work that histories count on for an action-packed story. But her work at UCL made digging in the field possible for Flinders and Hilda for over thirty years. Margaret founded, developed, and taught most of the courses for the first two-year training program for students wishing to excavate. It was because of teachers like her that British Egyptologists were educated in theory and method, so they would know that the pieces they pulled from the ground were important, and why. By the early twentieth century, university training in the field, as well as experience in-country, were prerequisites in the rapidly professionalizing field of Egyptology. Margaret and women like her were the teachers who made this happen. Her work in London with her students is where she left her main legacy.

London Calling

Margaret returned from her time in the field to the small Egyptology department at UCL in the late spring of 1904. Her mother's health was failing, and her older sister, Mary Slater, was in India with her husband and children, so she was left to care for her mother in London for the foreseeable future. She didn't really mind. London was home now and had been for the last ten years.

Margaret was born in Calcutta in 1863 at the height of the British Raj. Her mother, Margaret, had been a missionary in India, her father, James, a well-respected businessman, and she and her older sister lived within the trappings of middle-class British colonial life. Like most India-born British subjects, Margaret didn't go "home" to London until she was seven, when she went to live with her uncle and go to school. Even then, she moved back and forth between Calcutta and London until she was in her late twenties. By the time Margaret's father died in 1891, neither Murray girl had had any formal education. It didn't matter so much for Mary, who was married by then and living back in Madras with her colonial bureaucrat husband and their children. Margaret, on the other hand, didn't really want to get married, or at least she didn't have any good prospects. Any suitor would truly have had to be a strong candidate for her to give up her desire to do *something* useful. At the end of the nineteenth century, when women got married, they usually had to give up their own work for their husbands and children. The best-case scenario for someone like Margaret would have been to marry someone whose work she could have participated in, like Hilda Urlin Petrie and Kate Bradbury Griffith would ultimately do.

Margaret had always wanted to be useful. Her father, a "true Victorian gentleman," didn't want his daughters to work for pay. When Margaret turned twenty, they compromised, and James allowed her to volunteer as a nurse in Calcutta for three months during a cholera outbreak. Although she and her sister had been well provided for during their youth in India and England, their father's money wouldn't last forever after his death. Margaret was looking for something to do both to cure her boredom and to support herself in the long term. Her sister and mother had suggested she go to UCL: it was one of the few universities in the UK accepting women as full members of the university. Right after Flinders Petrie had been named the Edwards Chair of Egyptian Archaeology, Mary had read in the *Times* of London that he was not merely accepting women students in his department but welcoming them.[3] Mary told her younger sister that she *must* attend those classes. Margaret's future was clearly decided for her.

When she first arrived at UCL in early 1894, she braced herself as she walked up the spiral staircase to the new Egyptology department. She was thirty, slight, and soft-spoken, but driven to succeed. On that first cold January day, the dingy rooms of the department didn't offer a reprieve from the gray outside. She first met an older gentleman, Dr. James Walker, who was the librarian. They hit it off immediately. Then Margaret met a young, poor, balding linguist named Francis Griffith. She and Frank were about the same age. He had been educated at Oxford but had taught himself Egyptian, as there was no program for the script until he developed it at UCL. He had worked with Petrie for the last ten years. The two men welcomed her into the department, where, as one of several women, she started taking hieroglyphics classes from Frank immediately. Kate Bradbury was in and out of the department on a regular basis, as she continued to work as the executor of Amelia Edwards's will. She was responsible for getting the books bound and ready for the library, as well as making sure her dear Amelia's money was spent according to her stated wishes. Nettie Gourlay was there, too. She had been one of the first students in the department under Petrie and hadn't yet gone to Egypt to meet Maggie. Margaret found it easy to make herself comfortable there. Margaret excelled in her classes and got along well with her cohort, even though she was thirty and, except for Nettie, they were all younger than she was.

All was going well, until one day in late spring of that year, Margaret arrived to the department to see a tall, bearded man storming around as if he owned the place. She strode over to Dr. Walker, who seemed to be almost cowering at a table in the corner, and demanded to know who this man was. "That," he replied, "is Professor Petrie." Later in life, she chuckled as she relayed the story during a BBC interview, but on that day she was furious. Petrie sort of did own the place—he was the Edwards Chair of the department, his appointment made possible with Amelia's money. He was already the Father of Scientific Archaeology in Egypt, the problem child of the Egypt Exploration Fund, and the wunderkind of Amelia Edwards, and he played the part. When the two met, Margaret was just a regular student among perhaps a dozen that year. But Flinders noticed something in her that made her different from the others.

He tested Margaret's abilities and tenacity right away. In what would today be a sure case of sexual harassment and discrimination, Petrie tasked his newest student with placing labels on tablets and other items inscribed with the god Min, whose overlarge erect penis made him somewhat of a prized figure in many Victorian Egyptian collections. Margaret was a little surprised at this, but she worked quietly without complaint; that is, she passed the test with flying colors. In order to try to cover up the many penises, she placed each inscribed paper label strategically. Petrie smirked to himself as he checked her work, but he was impressed. Her fate was sealed from that point on. She had begun to earn the respect of Flinders, but it's unclear if she ever fully had it. Within a few years, he had her working on his annual exhibits, and she started getting paid for

Fig. 4.2: Margaret Alice Murray,
c. 1928 (age sixty-five).

teaching hieroglyphs to incoming students. Even though she could have earned her degree at UCL, there is no record that Margaret ever officially completed the work for it. No matter; she worked as an instructor in UCL's Egyptology department for over forty years.

Her students loved her, recalling that "Miss Murray" always began her seminars by passing around boxes of chocolates and talking about witches, one of her favorite topics of study. Over the years, her classroom saw the likes of future archaeology giants Reginald Engelbach, Gertrude Caton-Thompson, Myrtle Broome, and Guy and Winifred Brunton walk through the doors. Many of them returned to UCL to become faculty themselves, and some made major names for themselves in archaeology and Egyptology. They could follow that path because they first had a solid academic foundation. With the help of other women colleagues and students, Margaret trained dozens of Egyptologists whose collective impact on the discipline is immeasurable.

Teaching the Gang

All of the students sat in their seats. They couldn't speak from all the confusion that muddled their thoughts. They looked askance at one another—did anyone actually understand this? It was silent in the room, except for Frank Griffith scratching his chalk on the blackboard at the front. Frank was undoubtedly a gifted linguist, but his teaching style was, well, difficult to follow. He tended to write a hieroglyphic inscription on the blackboard quickly, with very little context, then translate it for the class. He would scribble notes on the board, mutter things to himself such as "That's not quite right," erase his work, and begin again. All the while, Margaret and her fellow students tried their best to keep up with the chicken scratch and mumbled instruction. By the end of each lecture, the students had to meet separately to compare notes so they might get a semblance of a solution. Not one to suffer these situations for long, Margaret chose to work through Adolf Erman's *Egyptian Grammar* on her own, just to get ready for class.[4] Erman's book is a classic text, but it's difficult to use without direct instruction. Margaret, however, was a quick study with a sharp mind. Within a few months, much to her fellow students' relief, she had taken over the class from Frank, substituting when he was away in the field. By 1896, with Flinders's blessing and a little cajoling, Kate Bradbury had agreed to marry Frank, and the two moved to Lancashire, leaving Margaret to teach full-time. By 1898 she was appointed Junior Lecturer.

Just four short years after arriving at UCL, Margaret was doing much more teaching, staffing the museum, and dealing with correspondence while Flinders and Hilda were away excavating in the winters. She had some misgivings about this new post. She worried about her credibility, knowing she had never even sat an exam much less had any kind of college degree, but she was more prepared than she gave herself credit for. The struggles Margaret had dealt with and overcome in Frank Griffith's early classes equipped her to guide students through similar difficulties and make them successful. As a Junior Lecturer, she was paid £40 per year (the equivalent of close to £6,000 today) out of Flinders's annual salary to do the lion's share of the work in London. The college terms ran from October through May or June, the same months that the professor was in Egypt, so Margaret not only organized and scheduled the courses, she also taught most of them.

Flinders Petrie, on the other hand, was a digger. He had started his career in Egypt as a digger and would always be a digger. He was chosen to be the first Edwards Chair at UCL because of his success in excavating in Egypt, and because Amelia Edwards liked him. However, Margaret knew that an academic department needed an organized course of study. Early in his career, Petrie was known to believe that a big mistake in field archaeology was thinking an "excavator must needs be a scholar," but even Flinders counted on Margaret's sharp mind and teaching prowess to "separate the sheep from the goats."[5] In the end, though, he found he wanted field excavators who had enough training in the history, language, theory, and method of Egypt and archaeology so that when they came to the excavation site, he could give them the appropriate archaeological experience. This became Margaret's main responsibility.

Except for 1902–4 when she was in the field, and until 1911, Margaret created curriculum that would prepare students to go into the field with the professor. Based on requirements from Flinders, and pulling from her experience on excavation, she built a two-year training program that gave students a grounding in a number of disciplines. It was the first program of its kind in the UK and was an example to other programs across Europe that were language or script based. Classes ranged from anthropology, anatomy, geology, mineralogy, languages, and pottery to the history and religion of pharaonic Egypt. After completing the coursework—a combination of in-class lectures, hands-on work with the department collections, and trips to the British Museum just down the street—students took a series of eleven exams. If they passed successfully, they were awarded the College Certificate in Egyptology. Throughout the course of the two-year program, Margaret flipped the focus of Egyptological training from the field itself to the university classroom. She knew from her own experience that students had to have a foundation of knowledge before they went to the field or else they wouldn't know about anything that came out of the ground. Once they finished in London, students went to the field to train with Flinders. After their field training was complete, they would be known as Petrie's Pups.

Margaret, tasked with the intense classroom training to prepare future Pups for the field, wasn't bothered by the work, but she was a little annoyed with how much she was teaching. She was able to publish her two site reports, *Osireion* and *Saqqara Mastabas,* requirements of excavating with the Petries' Egyptology Research Account (the EEF's main competitor), but she did little other writing, or little else at all. At one point she was teaching six courses per term, which, not counting lecture preparation and grading exams and papers, took between twenty and thirty hours per week. This left precious little time for research or writing, not to mention excavating—the kind of work that would get her name recognition in the male-dominated field. Instead, her students would get the name recognition as Pups, and she couldn't have been prouder of them.

The first class of students to come to UCL to take advantage of this new training program arrived in 1911. Margaret called them the Gang, and they included Myrtle Broome, Guy and Winifred Brunton, Reginald (Rex) Engelbach, and Georgina Aitken. Rex is likely the most well-known of this group because from 1919, after his service in World War I in the Artists Rifles in France and Gallipoli, he remained in Egypt. He worked with Petrie from 1919 to 1920, then as the Chief Inspector of Upper Egypt until he became Assistant Keeper at the museum in Cairo in 1924. In 1931 he became Head Keeper, a position he held until his death in 1946. As Keeper during a contentious time in Egypt—laws around antiquities were changing rapidly, thanks to nominal independence from Britain in 1919 and a nationalist movement to keep the entirety of the contents of the Tomb of Tutankhamun found in 1922—he maintained good relations with European Egyptologists and was especially supportive of his Egyptian colleagues. Most of his career, then, was centered not on excavation work but on museum administration and organization along with script decipherment. He learned all of this from Margaret at UCL.

When Guy and Winifred Brunton arrived at UCL, they had already been married for five years. They trained with Margaret, then went to the field with Rex and Flinders, digging at Lahun in 1914. There they found the tomb of an unnamed twelfth-dynasty princess buried during the reign of Senwosret II (c. 1897–1878 BCE). It had been plundered in antiquity but still had enough jewelry, including beads, bracelets, amulets, and a gold diadem with precious stones inlaid, for Guy to call it a treasure.[6] Guy had to carefully extract these pieces, including about ninety-five hundred loose beads, from the mud. To do this, he had to lie flat on his stomach in the low-roofed tomb and rest on his elbows while he pulled out each piece, one by one. After the war, Guy worked on several early sites, and by 1931 he was working with his old classmate Rex as Assistant Keeper of the Egyptian Museum. Together, they substantially rearranged the collections and published a complete catalogue of the museum. While Maspero and Mariette had published short lists, none were as complete as the one that Rex and Guy published. It was the first of its kind for the collection in Cairo.

Winifred was an artist in her own right and was Guy's chief illustrator on excavation; she also took over organizing artifacts and administrating their careers. She painted landscapes of excavation sites and portraits of workers, like Ali es Suefi, Petrie's Qufti reis, but as an archaeological illustrator, she was trained by Margaret at UCL. Together, the Bruntons were a productive scientific couple. Winifred also published some of her own paintings, the most influential of which was her *Kings and Queens of Ancient Egypt* in 1926.[7] Margaret provided two chapters for that book as well.[8] The Bruntons maintained a close relationship with Margaret for the rest of their lives. Winifred even painted a portrait of Margaret that now belongs to the Petrie Museum at UCL.

Myrtle Broome was another integral part of the Gang who also became an artist in the field. Like Winifred, Myrtle was likely one of Margaret's favorite students, and they continued a close relationship for decades. The two women were kindred spirits—artists working successfully in the field without a husband at their side. As it happened, Myrtle followed right in Margaret Murray's footsteps. She became well-known for her work in Abydos about twenty years after Margaret worked at the site. Working with Amice Calverley from 1929 to 1937, Myrtle formed an ideal partnership with her that lasted almost a decade. Their story continues later, but they copied scenes in the Temple of Seti I, giving some context to the Osireion. They wanted to fully publish the temple, but the work ended in 1937 with only four volumes produced. Their efforts set "a standard of excellence which, in the absence of special funding and of the artistic skills of the two ladies involved, may be difficult, if not impossible, to match" today.[9] Margaret's students, especially the women, truly took over Egyptology in the early years of the twentieth century.

Georgina Aitken was another member of the Gang whose career probably most clearly shows what Margaret was working so hard for at UCL. The truth is, we don't know that much about her. She began taking evening courses with Margaret but quickly joined the Gang in 1911, probably due to encouragement from her longtime family friends Guy and Winifred Brunton. She was the one who introduced her friend Rex Engelbach to the training program at UCL. Aitken's social connections made up half the Gang. Her lecture notebooks, now in the archives at the Petrie Museum at UCL, show that she was attentive and talented in terms of hieroglyphs—she took copious notes in Margaret's many classes. It is hard to trace her trajectory, though, despite the fact that she was well-connected to Margaret and the Gang. This is mainly because, like a lot of women at the time, she didn't have a permanent position anywhere. By 1919, Georgina was an Honorary Assistant and recognized as an official member of the faculty in the department at UCL. To take some of the pressure off Margaret, Georgina taught the evening elementary hieroglyphs class. By 1924, she was excavating with Petrie at Qau, an early site, but after that she disappeared from the work for the next five years. By 1929, she had returned to the department to fill in for her old instructor again when Margaret was in Finland giving a series of lectures. Georgina is virtually unknown to historians of the discipline, but she was an indispensable asset to the department as they worked to train productive Egyptologists.

The various disciplinary links to Margaret's work are solid, even if they're hard to find. Not everyone acknowledged her impact on their careers. Sidney Smith was a student in 1913–14 and went on to be the Keeper of Egyptian and Assyrian Antiquities at the British Museum from 1931 to 1948. Raymond Faulkner was one of her most gifted students after World War I. Later on, he dedicated his *A Concise Dictionary of Middle Egyptian* "To Dr. Margaret Murray, who first taught me Ancient Egyptian, in gratitude and affection."[10] Faulkner's dictionary became well-known for providing a vocabulary reference as well as the important addition of textual and bibliographic references for complex Middle Egyptian terms and signs. Margaret Drower, Flinders Petrie's biographer and one of Margaret's last living students, arrived in the department in 1931. She remembered Margaret's love of chocolates and talking about witches.

Margaret continued to mentor students both inside and outside the classroom throughout her time at UCL. With the success of her Gang, Margaret was given quite a bit of latitude by Flinders in her curriculum. By 1916, she added new components to the certificate, such as organic chemistry; her two-year program continued until at least 1935. The curriculum was progressive in its outlook, allowing students to have some experience among the growing museum collections, handling and learning how to organize artifacts, while learning theory and methods in Egyptian archaeology before heading out into the field. Margaret was extremely successful in training countless archaeologists, curators, writers, linguists, and more. UCL today has many similar components in its Egyptian archaeology program, like hands-on work with collections and acknowledging the importance of knowing the foundational information before going into the field.

Margaret's legacy was in those students she taught. One of her closest friends and mentees was a woman in Manchester named Winifred Crompton. The two women had known each other for years but became close friends in 1906 when Margaret went to the Manchester Museum to help accession and organize the Egyptian collections there, and Winifred was then an assistant. There was so much material from Flinders Petrie's most recent excavation that they needed extra hands to help, so Flinders sent his one, consistent, trusted colleague. Margaret loved museum work, but not as much as she loved teaching. She went where she was needed, though, and used every opportunity for education.

The Tomb of the Two Brothers

Margaret was dressed in a white apron that covered her dark, long-sleeved dress. The cuffs were fastened at her wrists. Her hair was pinned back, and she was not wearing gloves. She watched as more than five hundred people gradually filed into the chemistry lecture theater at Manchester University on that cool spring day, May 7, 1908, for the monthly meeting of the Manchester Egyptian Association. The end of April had been surprisingly snowy in London, with some of the heaviest spring snowfalls ever recorded. Manchester, in the northwest of England, had been colder than London but strangely had thunderstorms, not snow.[11] As she glanced around at several familiar faces in the crowd, she wondered if it was the warming weather that had gotten people out and about. Then again, she thought, it was probably the mummified human remains that lay on the table before her.

Margaret had to smile to herself, though, as she recalled that the

Professor had never brought so many people into this room for one of his talks. No one had. She turned and studied her team. Mr. Standen and Mr. Wilfred-Jackson were fussing over Khnum-Nakht, the mummy they were about to unwrap, while Miss Wilkinson and Miss Hart-Davis were busily collating Margaret's notes, wiping down the lab table, and making last-minute adjustments to the supplies at the front of the room. Her dear friend Winifred Crompton was not part of the team performing the unwrapping that day; she was serving as the secretary of the Manchester Egyptian Association and was in the audience. She found Winifred in the crowd and they gave each other quick nods hello.

It was standing room only as Margaret took her place behind the table. All these people were here to watch her and her team take all the linen wrappings off the body of Khnum-Nakht, the half brother of Nakht-Ankh.[12] She had to stand on a box so she was tall enough to reach the parts of the person she needed to unwrap. Petrie had found the funerary equipment, including the coffins and remains of the two brothers, in a rare, undisturbed Middle Kingdom (c. 2030–1650 BCE) tomb at Deir Rifeh in the 1906–7 excavation season. Always looking for ways to fund his excavations, Petrie beseeched his longtime supporter, and friend of Amelia Edwards, Jesse Haworth. Haworth, a cotton yarn magnate from Lancashire and partner in a Manchester cotton firm, had already contributed thousands of pounds to Petrie's efforts in Egypt and to the Manchester Museum. Decades earlier, he had been inspired by the thousand miles Amelia had sailed up the Nile and immediately began his own vast personal collection of antiquities.

When he found the tomb group, Petrie wrote directly to the museum committee at Manchester. He wrote that he would give the whole assemblage (all the artifacts) of the tomb to the museum if they would give him five hundred pounds toward the following year of work. The committee quickly raised the money, which fully supported the excavations. The Two Brothers arrived in Manchester in late 1907.

The Manchester Museum, which at this point was underfunded and understaffed, relying mostly on volunteers and underpaid women to do the work, needed more help in processing the artifacts. Petrie loaned Margaret to Manchester for months at a time to do this. She enjoyed the work and did it very well. She loved working with Winifred. The two women accessioned the tomb and all its contents, catalogued them, and set them up to be displayed in the already cramped galleries on Oxford Road. The location itself didn't do any of the artifacts justice. The museum was full to the rafters. They needed more space.

It was decided that the museum needed a spectacle—something big to bring in a lot of people to see the new artifacts so the museum committee could justify a bigger building. Since the laying of its first stone in 1882, there were plans to expand the building itself, and in the age of wealthy cotton industrialists wanting to make a name for themselves as civic-minded citizens, textile magnate Jesse Haworth was heavily involved in the museum's expansion. The growing collections included geology, mineralogy, and natural history specimens such as a horse that lived to the age of sixty-two and a sperm whale skeleton hanging from the ceiling.[13] There was so much there that they needed more exhibit space. But they had to demonstrate that Mancunians would use the space to view the objects the museum held.

In England and the United States, public unwrappings of human remains had been extremely popular crowd draws, especially around the turn of the nineteenth century. Usually, unwrappings were private, invitation-only affairs for the upper-middle and upper industrial classes. They would be performed by medical doctors or antiquarians, often in someone's home as part of a party. Very little was published about them, though, in the end. Thomas Pettigrew was infamous for his unwrappings in the early part of the nineteenth century, but at least he published a memoir about them, *A History of Egyptian Mummies, and an Account of the Worship and Embalming of the Sacred Animals by the Egyptians*, in 1834. He wished to turn his private spectacle into a scientific study, and, while he wasn't quite successful in that endeavor, the Manchester Museum took a cue from him and others to attract attention.

Other human remains had been unwrapped in Egypt by Maspero, Victor Loret, Elliot Smith, and others in an attempt to figure out the identity and biological sex of the human remains. In early

1906, Emma Andrews and Theodore Davis had asked for the person in KV 55 to be unwrapped to try to validate the identity as Queen Tiye. It wasn't the queen, and Maspero and Elliot Smith had confirmed it was the body of a man. In November of 1925, Howard Carter, Douglas Derry, and Salah Bey Hamdi would unwrap the mummified remains of King Tutankhamun over the course of several days inside a nearby tomb in order to perform a scientific examination. These were both private affairs, with a small, select audience of scholars and scientists. In Manchester, however, this would be the first public unwrapping in Britain in several decades, and it would also be the last. The unwrapping and the subsequent publication, *The Tomb of the Two Brothers*, had exactly the desired impact on the museum, as well as on Egyptology itself.

Before the display, Margaret knew she had some public relations issues to tackle first. For the last several weeks, members of the public had written letters to the *Manchester Guardian* decrying the public unwrapping, saying that Khnum-Nakht should be left alone. Margaret was not particularly sentimental, however, arguing that the best way to preserve the remains was to study them, carefully, and to record any and all information about them "without sentimentality and without fear of the outcry of the ignorant."[14] She wanted to educate people with this display and entered the room with that expressed goal.

As she stepped up on the small box behind the table on which the remains of Khnum-Nakht lay, she waited for the crowd to quiet. Figure 4.3 shows this scene and contains a depiction of human remains. Some students in the back row cracked jokes, and some nervous laughter peppered the crowd as they waited for the presentation to begin. Margaret cleared her throat and began to speak in her small voice. She found she had to yell, and people had to be silent, almost straining from the back rows, to hear her. Despite the public outcry against the event, people in the room were listening with rapt attention.

She began with a brief presentation about how important it was to expose the ancient remains. The purpose, she argued, was threefold, but she only shared two of these reasons with the audience. First, it would help researchers learn more about a then relatively unknown period in pharaonic history, namely, the Middle King-dom period. Knowing more about how mummification processes had developed over time from the earliest days of ancient Egypt would help scholars to understand what Egyptians believed about life after death and their mortality. The second reason was tied into a major tenet of the Manchester Egyptian Association's mission: to educate the public about ancient Egypt. The size of the crowd spoke to their success. Margaret's report on the unwrapping would allow the public and scholars who weren't there in person to experience it, too. Third, the more people who learned about ancient Egypt in these demonstrations, the more public financial support the disci-pline would likely receive. Margaret was focused on public support for the Manchester Museum, the university, and the Manchester Egyptian Association. Much like she had been doing in her class-room in London, she pushed for expanding the education of anyone who was interested, which would grow these institutions as a result.

Only a few photos survive from that day, as Margaret and her team painstakingly removed twenty-six long pieces of linen from

Fig. 4.3: Chemistry Theatre, unwrapping Khnum-Nakht. Image depicts human remains.

the body of Khnum-Nakht, a Middle Kingdom great wab priest of Khnum. His title meant that he performed various rituals and maintained the cult temple of the god Khnum at Shashotep, a district capital and administrative center just a few miles south of Asyut.[15] He was the half brother of his tombmate Nakht-Ankh, through their mother, Khnum-Aa, who came from a family of high status and had also married into wealth. Some historians have argued that they weren't brothers but rather lovers. Recent DNA testing has shown that they were, in fact, brothers who had different fathers. Nakht-Ankh, twenty years older than his half brother, was the son of a governor; Khnum-Nakht was the grandson of a governor. But together they grew up and lived in relative comfort in the town of Shashotep.

Khnum-Nakht was the brother chosen to be unwrapped, Margaret later wrote, because his mummified body "was absolutely dry, and the tissues had resolved into a fine powder which rose in clouds when the mummy was handled."[16] Nakht-Ankh's remains, on the other hand, were wetter and stickier than those of his younger brother. Margaret and Winifred thought that the resin used in his embalming process would make removing the bandages much more difficult, not to mention the aroma they knew might accompany wet human remains. Later, behind closed doors when Nakht-Ankh's wrappings were removed, their theory was proven correct.

Removing Khnum-Nakht's bandages went quickly and smoothly, but some in the audience felt like his spirit was there— just as curious about his audience as they were about him. One reporter wrote, "As the last wrap left his forehead his head turned slowly over, and his sightless eyeholes looked full on the silenced onlookers before him. Then he lay still again. The clang of a passing tram startled all but him."[17] Being in the room watching mummified human remains be uncovered for the first time in over two thousand years would have been a wondrous event.

Margaret closed the presentation with a few remarks: the remains of Khnum-Nakht turned out to be simply well-preserved and dried out, so they had not gone through the entire mummification process. Obviously there was still much to be learned about the drying process in this period, and about the brothers' lives in general. That work would happen later. The audience, not knowing about the in-depth study that still needed to be done on the remains, filed out of the room. They were given the opportunity to record their name and address on a list so they could receive a souvenir from the day—a piece of linen that had been pulled from the body.

Public concern for the mummified brothers was even more pro-nounced after the unwrapping than before. The *Manchester Evening Chronicle* printed this poem the day after the event, written by a reader:

> You went to sleep, poor lump of clay,
> Beneath old Egypt's silent skies;
> And now we wake you up to-day
> To gaze on you with morbid eyes;
> When science says "Just take a peep,"
> I s'pose one cannot well object,
> And yet—they might have let you sleep,
> Khnumu Nekht![18]

In her report about the event and the tomb itself, Margaret got the final word on the public's concerns:

> To most people there are few ideas more repugnant than that
> of disturbing the dead. To open graves, to remove all the ob-
> jects placed there by loving hands, and to unroll and inves-
> tigate the bodies, seems to many minds not merely repulsive
> but bordering on sacrilege. . . . To those, however, whose ob-
> jections are not of the purely sentimental kind (dictated by
> a momentary feeling passing through an otherwise vacant
> mind) I wish to offer a short explanation of the reasons for
> the action of archaeologists throughout the world.[19]

She continued, writing that archaeology is a science, and science is the pursuit of gaining knowledge. In unwrapping these mum-mified remains, Egyptologists could gain knowledge about ancient Egypt, thereby better understanding its history, culture, and practices moving forward. While the unwrapping was a fantastical display of a human body treated as an object to garner public interest, Margaret's report was scientific. Others, such as Rosalie David and Campbell Price of the Manchester Museum, have built on Margaret's work considerably.[20]

Egyptologists have done significant study on the remains of both Khnum-Nakht and Nakht-Ankh. They have found that Khnum-Nakht was probably ill and in pain for most of his life, which ended when he was in his forties. He had issues with the bony structure of his body, and at the time of his death, he probably had to walk almost completely doubled over. He may have used a cane or been carried by servants. Nakht-Ankh, who was in his sixties, had died about a year after Khnum-Nakht. He had been much more active in life than his younger brother, but being in your sixties in the ancient world brought aches, pains, and, finally for Nakht-Ankh, probably a heart attack. He was buried with his brother.

The scientific spectacle indeed had the desired effect on the museum. In the end, Haworth gave more than £5,000 (the equivalent of almost one hundred times that today) to the museum to house the newly popular and rapidly expanding Egyptian collections. Others donated smaller amounts, and it added up to a new section of the building. The day the new expansion opened, October 30, 1912, there was a large ceremony with a packed audience. The brothers were displayed prominently, then as they were for the next century, in the center of the room in a large glass case so they could be seen by patrons from all sides. Notably, the people sitting on the dais that day were all men. Flinders Petrie and Jesse Haworth were in the middle of this prestigious group, along with Grafton Elliot Smith, who, among other things, had studied the remains of KV 55. Absent were the women like Margaret and Winifred who actually did the daily work. They were used to not being invited into certain spaces, but they didn't have to like it.

Margaret Murray, Suffragette

About a year before the unwrapping in Manchester, on the wet and cold afternoon of February 9, 1907, a group of women were preparing to trudge through the streets of London from Hyde Park, via

Piccadilly, to the Strand, near the Houses of Parliament. Thousands of women were gathered, lined up along the route, with their torch-bearers out front, leading the charge—Millicent Garrett Fawcett, Lady Frances Balfour, and Lady Jane Strachey. A band began to play, the women held banners aloft in the pouring rain, and they marched. Margaret Murray may have been surprised to find herself in this crowd, but there she stood, shivering against the rain that was making the ground beneath her feet muddy and slippery. As they passed by hundreds of spectators, most of them out to see if the women would really march, Margaret saw a large, drunk man fight his way to the corner pavement closest to her. She and the women around her worried that he might start shouting, or worse. Violence against women asking for the right to vote had become standard, after all. This time, though, the man was simply there to support his wife as she passed by in the march.

So they made their way through the muddy London streets to the Strand. Later in the day, as they continued to get soaked, there were talks in Trafalgar Square nearby, within view of both the Houses of Parliament and Buckingham Palace. While papers like the *Daily Mail,* the *Daily Mirror,* and the *Times* of London reported on what became known as the Mud March and gained the suffrage movement a lot of publicity, the march itself failed to move the legislative needle on the topic.

For Margaret, her activism had slowly been building since her father had kept her from training as a nurse in Calcutta twenty-five years earlier. She had volunteered, but only for three months—she knew she wanted more. Then, her mother and sister sent her to UCL ten years later where, much to her surprise, one of her first assignments was labeling penises. Then on her first day in the field a few years after that, she rebelled against the poor leadership of her mentor. She was close to a breaking point but wasn't sure how to go about contesting that kind of treatment.

Luckily, that year at Abydos, Hilda had brought a few of her radical friends with her. Medieval historian Lina Eckenstein and political activist Sarah Amos were both suffragists (people who supported including women in the right to vote), and they were active in other social movements as well. Both women were leaders in Millicent Garrett Fawcett's National Union of Women's Suffrage Societies (NUWSS) at the time. The people in that group included several prominent men, as well as women. They pushed for the vote in a law-abiding, peaceful manner, which included holding rallies, writing letters, and giving speeches. Around the campfire at night, Lina and Sarah had talked to her about the vote, suffrage, and what the Bill, as it was called, would mean for women in the UK. Without the right to vote, women were second-class citizens, living in bondage with no path to social, political, or material equality. Margaret knew distinctly what that felt like, so it didn't take much convincing for her to want to work for the vote.

She returned to London in 1904, and though teaching and caring for her mother took over for a while, she quickly joined a small suffrage society at the encouragement of Lina and Sarah. Suffrage societies proliferated in Britain during this period, especially in London. By 1897, most of the smaller, local societies had joined the larger NUWSS coalition. Soon, however, Emmeline Pankhurst had grown weary of all the talking with no action being done. With her daughters Christabel and Sylvia, she founded the Women's Social and Political Union in Manchester in 1903. The WSPU's motto "Deeds Not Words" meant that acts of violent civil disobedience were sometimes needed to push back against a violent parliamentary resistance to the women's franchise. Margaret's Manchester counterpart, Winifred Crompton, became an early member of the WSPU and brought Margaret into this group at some point, possibly as early as 1904. By 1910 Winifred had invited Margaret to speak at a WSPU event in Manchester. It's not clear if she spoke about Egyptology or about suffrage, but her name appears on the record for the meeting. By the time Margaret marched in the Women's Coronation March in 1911, the largest joint suffrage march ever to take place in the UK with more than forty thousand women in attendance, she had a lot to say about women's rights. Like a lot of women in a similar position, she couldn't be too vocal, but she could be quietly subversive.

Margaret wasn't the first woman in Egyptology to fight for the inclusion of women in mostly male institutions. Amelia Edwards had done so, and she had given money for women's inclusion in her bequest to UCL in 1892. It is possible that wealthy archaeologists like Maggie Benson, Nettie Gourlay, and Emma Andrews had donated money for suffrage causes. Winifred Crompton was obviously active as a suffragette. Margaret was one of the first prominent woman Egyptologists to join public, disruptive, feminist work for the specific cause of women's rights.

Especially at UCL, Margaret also seamlessly integrated the fight for women's rights, especially the right to vote, into her daily work. World War I started in 1914, changing the landscape for women's suffrage (finally granted to all women over the age of twenty-one in 1928). The war also scattered faculty, staff, and students, including Margaret, but she used this to her advantage. She began investigating several different lines of research, much of it having to do with anthropology and folklore, specifically witchcraft. She chose witchcraft because of the ways she found that women could take control—over their choices, over their lives, and over nature.

She thought about her newest project—studying a prominent witch cult in Western Europe—as she sipped her tea in the Ladies' Common Room one afternoon, not long after the end of World War I.[21] Once faculty and students had returned to the college after the war, Margaret took delight in the fact that the daily tea break was still a tradition she could enjoy, even if some of her friends, colleagues, and students never returned from the front. When she had arrived to the room that day, one of the two chairs in the back had been open, so she sat down quickly as she watched other women come in for their tea. There was hardly room for anyone to stand, much less sit, in the long narrow room, which seemed more like a hallway. It had a slate slab that ran down one half of the room, which took up most of the space but allowed for a heating apparatus for water and a small area to make tea and coffee. At most, about six people could be in the room at a time. It wasn't comfortable, and it was difficult for anyone to talk to anyone else. It was akin to sitting at a bar.

The Men's Common Room, on the other hand, was practically palatial. Most of the women had heard about the comfortable chairs with tables. There was rumored to be a selection of newspapers, tea, coffee, and cakes available to their male colleagues while they sat and chatted after lunch. All the while, the university women were struggling to find the elbow room to pass a coffee cup. The women had been applying to the administration for a larger room for weeks, but they kept getting rejected. They simply wanted to have a comfortable space for breaks, and they were tired of being second-class citizens at the college.

But there was some hope. World War I was over. Women over the age of thirty had just won the vote in the UK. It was the early 1920s, and, buoyed by some newfound momentum, Margaret had been working on a plan with her good friend and kindred spirit, Winifred Smith, the tutor to women students at UCL and a fellow member of the radical suffragette WSPU before it had been disbanded in 1917. Margaret and Winifred invited the provost, Sir Thomas Gregory Foster, to join them in the common room for the after-lunch coffee tradition. He was delighted to accept. Margaret, Winifred, and the other women made sure he would be welcomed with open arms—even if there were no open seats.

As he arrived that day, he was shuffled through the room and seated in the place of honor, one of the only two chairs at the back of the room by the fire grate, with Winifred seated next to him. The women passed around coffee cups, and the room soon filled up, with a long line outside waiting to get in. As people finished their coffee, the whole room would be emptied to allow more people in. The provost sipped his coffee and made polite conversation, but he watched with interest and amusement the situation that was obviously set up for his benefit. Women chatted and shuffled, a few coffees were spilled, and the hospitality limitations of the room became clear.

The plan worked. A few weeks later, the university women again applied for a larger room, and the Ladies' Common Room was allotted a much larger area for their purposes. Margaret had taken control over the situation and gotten results. The women used the larger room until 1969, when the common rooms were finally desegregated. The room was then renamed the Margaret Murray Room, and it remained so until 1989 when administrative offices took the space and the nameplate was taken down. Her visible name was gone, but her legacy lived on.

Margaret continued to work at UCL and connect with all her students. She built relationships with so many of them outside the classroom because of the way she integrated her university instruction and public education. Margaret was only one woman, with a quiet voice, but her real presence was much larger than her person. She cared about her students and wanted to see them succeed.

Margaret finally left UCL in 1935, after Flinders Petrie had retired and she disagreed with their choice of his replacement. Her career had been rich, but she cried as she ran down the stairs of the Edwards Library for the last time after over forty years. Surprisingly, she realized, "My tears were flowing not for grief at leaving the place where I had spent so many happy years but because I was glad to escape from what was now a prison-house, full of bitterness and frustration."[22]

Margaret's life, and her career, connected so many women in Egyptology. She worked closely with Kate Bradbury and Emily Paterson of the Egypt Exploration Fund. She had been a colleague of Nettie Gourlay. She must have met Emma Andrews as she made her way up the Nile around the turn of the century. She taught Myrtle Broome how to draw and must have met Amice Calverley. She probably knew Caroline Ransom Williams, given that Caroline had traveled to London several times to work in collections there. Margaret's work spans seventy years and several disciplines, and she impacted lives with her activism. Margaret died in 1963, just a few months after her one hundredth birthday. She was still working.

5

Kate Griffith and Emily Paterson

My Katie, Nov.ʳ 1891. A.B.E
—Inscription in Kate Bradbury's personal copy of
Pharaohs, Fellahs and Explorers

Kate Bradbury stood next to the obelisk that soared into the sky over Amelia Edwards's grave. Situated so close to the church of St. Mary the Virgin in Henbury, Bristol, the large stone obelisk almost touched the outer stone wall. It towered above where Kate's friend and confidant lay, next to her own partner Ellen Braysher. The ankh lying on top of the grave was a brand-new addition—her dear Amy wanted the ancient Egyptian symbol of life there—but the obelisk was original to their joint resting spot. For now, the ankh was made of beautiful flowers, but soon it would be made of stone. Kate slowly read the words on the obelisk that she was made to have inscribed: "HERE LIES THE BODY OF AMELIA ANN BLANFORD EDWARDS NOV-ELIST AND ARCHAEOLOGIST . . ." She stopped reading. She couldn't believe it. Kate and Amelia only had five years together. They had known each other since 1887, lived together since 1888, and traveled most of the United States and parts of Europe together in that short time. They worked together side-by-side almost every day for the Egypt Exploration Fund during those five years. Somehow, without Amelia, Kate would have to carry on Amelia's legacy.

As she said goodbye to the other mourners, which included the ever-present Percy Newberry, Kate made her way home from the churchyard to the Larches, about five miles away, with Emily

Paterson. Emily was another of Amelia's protégés who joined the Fund team in 1888, about the same time as Kate. Brought together by Amelia and their enthusiasm for her legacy, Kate and Emily would work closely together for the next decade. Emily had been trained as Amelia's private secretary to handle the correspondence with field Egyptologists, so the two women already knew each other well. They mourned, of course, wondering what would happen to the Fund now. Emily was the new General Secretary of the Fund, taking over for Amelia, and Kate was the executor of Amelia's estate. There were letters to write, money to disburse, excavation permissions to support, and general business to do to keep the Fund, and Egyptology in Britain at the time, operating. It would be up to Kate and Emily. It is not that Kate Bradbury's and Emily Paterson's lives started right when Amelia died. In fact, they each had full lives before meeting Amelia. But it took Amelia's death for their true impact on the field to become visible.

As the two women rode in the horse-drawn cab toward the Larches, they talked, remembering their friend. Kate also considered her next steps. She told Emily she would have to pack up Amelia's things, however long that would take, and move to London full-time in order to complete work on Amelia's estate. Amelia was a forward-thinking woman who left most everything to various institutions. Importantly, much of her Egyptian collection, hundreds of books, and money to fund the first department of Egyptology in

Fig. 5.1: Grave of Amelia B. Edwards, Ellen Braysher, and Sarah Braysher.

the UK went to UCL. Kate would have to work much more closely with Amelia's protégé Flinders Petrie and his student Frank Griffith. She got along with both of them pretty well, and she hoped she would simply be able to move into Amelia's place in their work lives. In turn, Emily recounted to Kate a list of all the letters she needed to write and respond to and the meetings she needed to set up to make sure Egyptology would continue running smoothly through the Fund. In their grief, they just took care of business.

The Egypt Exploration Fund may have been presided over by men from its founding in 1882, but on the ground it was run by women. Both Kate and Emily were the hubs of this massive network of Egyptologists, far-flung in the ancient Near East. These women would have been known by all Egyptologists working with and through the Fund. They were the administrators, facilitators, diplomats, organizers, check writers, and curators of the collections and people that moved through the Fund's hands and lists. Yet, historians hardly talk about them. While Kate's and Emily's lives are embedded in earlier parts of the story already chronicled here, their cooperation after Amelia's death shows the power of women working together in the professionalization of the discipline of Egyptology. Especially in the early days of the field, women were effective and absolutely necessary. Their collaboration, care, and "behind-the-scenes" work meant that the men were free to excavate and find the objects that shaped Egyptology, academically. They were not women behind the men; they were, however, overshadowed. These women were the physical, financial, and institutional backbone of Egyptology.

Building a Dream Team

Kate was born August 26, 1854, to a wealthy cotton merchant, Charles Bradbury, and his wife, Elizabeth Ann Tomlins, in Ashton-under-Lyne, just outside Manchester. Like Marianne Brocklehurst's, Kate's family being in the Manchester textile world meant wealth and a good education for her and her younger siblings, Harold and Emma. When they were younger, Kate and Emma attended a local school, Miss Ashton's, and Kate went to a finishing school in Switzerland; Emma went on to earn certificates in art and several sciences at South Kensington.[1] It was probably in Switzerland where Kate became fluent in German, a skill she later used to translate German Egyptology scholarship into English. The Bradburys were likely acquaintances, if not friends, of the Jesse Haworths, the MBs, and other textile magnates in the northeast. They certainly socialized in the same circles and held many of the same interests, including education for women and Egyptology.

Kate's mother died when she was young. Emma died in 1879, and Harold died almost exactly two years later, but the cause of neither sibling's death is clear. Kate and her father were very close, but she didn't say much about her stepmother, Mary. By 1882 the family was living in Riversvale Hall, a large home on a parklike estate near Manchester.[2] Kate herself, by now almost thirty years old, had traveled extensively and had an interest in Egyptology before she met Amelia. It is likely that Kate met Amelia during Amelia's northern lecture tour in the winter of 1887–88. Egyptology and mutual admiration united the two women. Kate had just suffered a broken heart, and her friendship had impacted Amelia's life quickly enough that Amelia was writing to Stuart Poole about the affair. She instructed him, however, to burn most of the pages she had sent about Kate. By May of 1888, Kate was staying with Amelia and Ellen at the Larches, helping to address subscriber envelopes for the Fund and perform other administrative tasks. Kate became so close to Amelia that her work, and her companionship, were soon indispensable.

Amelia was overwhelmed with the Fund in the spring of 1888. Even with the assistance of her salaried personal secretary, Hellier Gosselin, along with Kate, the load was too much. On July 11, 1888, in some frustration, Amelia wrote a private statement to the Committee of the Fund. She shared her opinions on the work that Hellier Gosselin was doing to the tune of fifty pounds per year. He simply wasn't pulling his weight. There was only so much she and Kate could pick up for him. They needed someone else. "And as I personally like Mr. Gosselin," Amelia wrote,

I am bound to say that I think he does not give us the full value of that money and that the affairs of the Society would undoubtedly

be better attended to had we a more businesslike Secretary installed in an office of our own.[3]

The Fund didn't have offices of its own, yet, but its staff often worked out of Poole's office at the British Museum. Amelia continued her letter by saying that she had already been "carefully training Miss Paterson in the work of the Fund."[4] It was, in fact, Poole who had recommended Emily Paterson in the first place.

Emily was twenty-seven years old when she was hired as Amelia's private secretary. She was a rapid and accurate dictation taker because she was proficient at shorthand. She was professional and intelligent. She had a great memory for particular subscribers and their "various peculiarities." Amelia emphasized that Emily's understanding of the annual work of the Fund was as thorough as Amelia's herself—high praise from the founder. Most importantly, Amelia wrote,

> *she gets through a large amount of correspondence daily and is at the present time employed in extending the connection of the Fund by writing numerous letters to persons likely to become subscribers. This was what I promised should be done by any Secretary placed under my direction. . . . It was in this way that I first succeeded in getting at a large number of the present subscribers and in this manner I now hope very materially to enlarge our subscription list.*

Emily worked well with Kate and fit in as part of their team. After Amelia died, Kate and Emily, together, grew the Fund over the next several decades into the main professional society of Egyptology in Britain. But even before that unexpected loss, they were a well-oiled international machine.

Coming to America

As Kate packed her and Amelia's trunks, she glanced over her long list of supplies. She was tasked by Amelia with making sure her lantern slides were arranged so they wouldn't break. She also had to make sure to include plenty of warm clothing for both of them. It was mid-October 1889 in England, so the cool autumn temperatures had only recently set in. They would soon be traveling through the northeastern United States from November through March. They were warned of frigid air and almost constant snow on the ground, but Kate was used to some cold. She'd lived in Switzerland, been to both the French and Italian Alps, and had traveled all over the UK with her father. Even though her uncles William and Frederick had lived in the United States since before she was born, Kate had never been across the ocean. She also checked over the list of all of Amelia's salves and pills. Her dear Amy had just recovered from typhoid, and she wasn't getting any younger. At fifty-eight years, Amelia wasn't old, necessarily, but she was not in the best of health.

Kate also needed to remember to take plenty of paper for writing. She could buy some, she presumed, at a stationer in New York City, but she had promised her family she would write every day, and she planned to start on the boat. She would also need to write to Miss Paterson, who was staying behind to manage the Fund's daily business until Kate and Amelia returned in March. As she stowed more and more in their steamer trunks, she wondered if everything would fit. Would the trunks be too heavy to drag from one hotel or house to the next? She was sure they could buy things as they needed in America, but Amelia had said they wanted to conserve as much money as possible. As Kate kept packing, she flinched every time she added more.

The whole endeavor began as an idea proposed by the Rev. William Copley Winslow of Boston to garner interest about ancient Egypt in the United States. He also wanted to raise funds for the American branch of the Egypt Exploration Fund, of which he was treasurer and secretary. Lecture tours like this were common before the American Civil War and were even more so now. With the secession of the Confederate States in 1860 and the war from 1861 to 1865, travel to the United States from the UK and Europe essentially stopped. In the years after the Civil War, more and more wealthy Americans worked to bring British and European scholars to the United States. The purpose was threefold: to repair diplomatic relations with the UK, which had fallen apart because Britain had sided with the Confederacy; to rebuild educational institutions; and to create a truly American tradition of intelligentsia.[6] Eminent scientists like Thomas Huxley, John Tyndall, and others toured the United States in these later years of the nineteenth century. By 1889, Amelia was one in a long line of scholars brought to the United States through the cooperation of institutions and wealthy private citizens.

Sometime in the mid-1880s, Copley Winslow had extended the tour invitation to Amelia. She had been wanting to go to America for years. She saw the potential in meeting with already established branches of the Fund to cultivate new and existing subscribers. But, she feared her health wouldn't be good enough for her to go on her own, and she was worried about Ellen's health. By early 1889, with things running smoothly at the Fund, she accepted Copley's invitation.[7] Amelia actually looked forward to the trip. Kate was happy to travel with Amelia, care for her, and serve as her assistant along the way. Kate ensured that Amelia would always be organized, supported, and never lonely. In turn, Amelia depended on Kate for almost everything on the trip, from laundry, correspondence, and meals, to hair and makeup.

Amelia was drawn not only to the prospect of spreading interest about ancient Egypt in the United States and getting subscribers for the American branch of the Fund but also to the income she could generate for herself. Copley Winslow practically assured her of a small fortune, writing, "You will have larger fees than any of your predecessors . . . ever had . . . except Dickens."[8] In turn, Amelia wrote to Flinders Petrie in April 1888: "The truth is that I want the money very much. This house wants repairing, much renewal of furniture, &c."[9] The promise of the honors and accolades US institutions would bestow upon her didn't hurt either.

Once universities, arts institutions, museums, and other wealthy individuals found out she was coming, Amelia received over three hundred requests for lectures. They all took advantage of the fact that she would finally be on their side of the Atlantic. All speaking requests were handled by the Redpath Lyceum Bureau, which managed her schedule, travel arrangements, and guides and chaperones, and paid Amelia five hundred dollars per week plus expenses. She also received equipment to show her lantern slides and a projectionist who traveled with the equipment to make sure it operated as it should.[10]

Amelia's engaging lectures drew record crowds and record fundraising, but the trip itself happened because of Kate Bradbury.[11] It was Kate's presence and her work on the US trip that made Amelia's tour possible. In fact, Amelia did not keep much of a record of her whirlwind journey through America, but later, with Kate's help, she did publish some of her lectures in *Pharaohs, Fellahs and Explorers*, in 1891. Notably, she did not thank Kate in the author's brief preface, contributing to her erasure from the story. Instead, we find Kate in her own words: starting on October 26, 1889, at 7:00 P.M., just after dinner had been cleared on the RMS *Etruria*, to March 24, 1890, when they only had four days left in America, Kate weaved a story of friendship and adventure in letters back to her family.

After about a week of being tossed upon the Atlantic, the women arrived at the coast of New York on November 3, 1889. In the cold rain in New York Harbor, they first spotted the Statue of Liberty. Just three years old, Lady Liberty was still copper in color, not yet turned green with oxidation. Like so many others who would come to the United States, Kate was excited about finally seeing the statue. She "called out to Miss E who said: 'Well, she's a brute.'"[12] Kate agreed that "she is a very <u>bourgeois</u> goddess, it is true, with little dignity. Her crown of light by night is a crown of thorns by day, out of which it would not be hard to make a parable or poem."[13] Once off the boat and having gotten their luggage, trunks, and most importantly lantern slides through customs, they were hounded by the press at the docks. Printing what they wanted about Amelia, they were worse than paparazzi and bothered them the whole trip.

With their first handler, a Mr. Bowker, they drove over the almost brand-new Brooklyn Bridge in a horse-drawn carriage. Later that afternoon, they arrived at the Hotel St. George in Brooklyn, one of the nicest hotels in the city at the time. Kate remarked that the rooms were always too warm and the heated air too dry, but neither of them missed England's radiant heat because they both loved not being cold all the time.

Even if the rooms were not up to their expectations—rarely anything in the US met with Kate's approval—they loved the views from the Hotel St. George. From her window to the southwest, Kate wrote that she could

> see the bay, and Liberty's torch as the dark comes on. Had we been one storey higher, the view would have been fine. To-night, Sunday, there was a grand sunset over the river, and below the clear and brilliant scarlet orange and eau-de-Nil blue, deep chocolate-crimson clouds passed. As the sunset faded and the moon rose, these turned copper-colour, absolutely metallic in lustre, and covered all the sky that I could see.[14]

She was astounded by the clean air in New York compared to the coal smoke of Manchester and London. "The nights are so clear," she marveled to her father, "the moonlight is like stage moonlight especially as the buildings upon which it falls are of most varied architecture . . ."[15]

Despite being enthralled with the colors of sunrise and sunset, Kate didn't like New York City at all. She thought "it was strange to walk along a street with a railway overhead in the middle, and trams running under it. Telegraph, telephone, and electric light wires run overhead too." She noted, too, that "the telephone wires are not insulated, so occasionally, they rust and drop."[16] To get around in Brooklyn, they had to walk "along the narrow, unfrequented, horribly paved streets, with trees either side, old-world looking streets, with a Dutch suggestion about them."[17] Her first opinions of New York may have been impacted by her travel exhaustion—except that they remain the same throughout the whole five-month tour. The rough crossing didn't allow much sleep that week, and both Kate and Amelia needed some time to rest and recover from colds they had caught on the ship. So for the first few days in the United States, they were both laid up breathing the doctor's vapors and eating the "most peculiar" Concord grapes. By the time of Amelia's first lecture, though, the women were both ready to take America by storm.

Amelia's first talk was at the Brooklyn Academy of Music on Montague Street in Brooklyn Heights. It took place on November 7, just four days after they arrived in the United States. The doctor's vapors had indeed worked wonders. Amelia's voice had returned just in time, and she went on to become one of the greatest science orators in US history. There were around twenty-four hundred seats to be had for her first talk, "The Buried Cities of Ancient Egypt," and it was probably sold out.[18] The *Brooklyn Daily Eagle* reported the following day that "Amelia B. Edwards delighted and instructed an Academy full of people last night with her first lecture in this country."[19]

For several weeks after they arrived, Kate and Amelia used New York as a base for travel around the area. They went to Yale, in New Haven, Connecticut, where Kate raved about the grand elm trees. They went to Boston, a six-hour train ride away, where Kate wrote that Amelia "carried them all captive" as she was growing "increasingly, phenomenally popular."[20] The morning following her Boston talk, the New England Woman's Press Association gave a reception for Amelia, with over four hundred women in attendance. In Boston, they also toured the Museum of Fine Arts and met with dignitaries such as Oliver Wendell Holmes. They traveled to several women's colleges in the area—Vassar, Smith, Bryn Mawr, Mount Holyoke, Wellesley—and were received by their administrators and presidents. In each town, they either stayed at a hotel or in someone's home. Kate always liked the homes best.

During their time in New England, a typical day would involve a small breakfast in their rooms, sometimes with wine, as Kate wrote letters home and to Emily Paterson. Kate mentioned "Miss P" in several of her letters back home, which meant that Emily was still working diligently while Amelia and Kate were on the lecture tour. Often, Kate would let Amelia sleep in and rest; other times, Amelia needed to review or copy out her lectures. They would usually have guests or be guests for a larger lunch with several of the community leaders who had brought them to town. These were often long and relatively fancy affairs, with oysters, soups, bread and butter, cold meats and cheeses, coffee, tea, milk, and often wine. If there wasn't wine, Kate could quietly arrange for both of them to have teacups with a little claret in them. Kate was often impressed by the amount of ice cream available at the meals. But it was winter, so frozen delicacies were easier to make and preserve even without artificial refrigeration. Kate would do their laundry or send it out if they had time and were in town for more than a day or two.

Most lectures began around 7:00 P.M. and would last for an hour or so, so they had to be at the lecture hall by 6:30 at the latest. Kate had to begin doing Amelia's hair around 5:30 P.M., often while Amelia was still copying out lectures or making notes and practicing her delivery. The women would get dressed, rush into a carriage, and usually get to the lecture hall on time. Kate made sure everything was prepared at each venue—that the projectionist had the slides ready, Amelia's notes were available, and everything started without a hitch. Kate did not stay for every lecture, choosing instead at times to take a walk through town or go back to their hotel to rest, write, or prepare for the reception and dinner that inevitably came after. A few times, when Amelia was too ill to speak, Kate gave the lecture for her. Other evenings, she had to sit near the front and wave a white handkerchief ten minutes before they had to leave to catch their train to the next stop. Afterward, if they had time, they would attend the reception, where they both were overwhelmed with flowers, cards, well wishes, and questions.

In Boston, Philadelphia, and New York, as well as other towns, they were given tours in already-established museums. In early December, they were given a tour of the University Museum at the University of Pennsylvania. Kate remarked that it was an interesting tour, and she highlighted that they had a "magnificent clay cylinder bearing a list of the buildings of Nebuchadnezzar, which the British Museum had accounted themselves too poor to buy."[21] The women had gotten a lot of unexpected attention from the provost of the university during the tour, but he really wanted to talk to Amelia about getting Egyptian pieces for their museum and ask her about becoming a separate branch of the American Fund. The Philadelphia branch didn't want to have to answer to Copley Winslow, who had become overbearing in his leadership.

Barely a week into the new year, on January 7, Kate and Amelia were back in New York, where they went to the Central Park Museum, also known as the Metropolitan Museum of Art. In 1890 it stood in its current place, on Fifth Avenue and 82nd Street. They drove through Central Park in a carriage, marveling at the quiet. There were no bigger transverse roads from the west side to the east side of the park yet, so they had to ride along the smaller pedestrian paths. Kate thought the park was "very beautiful, and all made ground of carted soil, except that some of the great bare rocks are left standing."[22] They went to the museum, which had started as a Gothic Revival–style building, and already by 1890 the building was being expanded. It was four stories high, built of red and gray stone, and had an imposing front entrance off Fifth Avenue.

As for the collection itself, Kate had little to say about it the day they saw it. The Egyptian collection at the Metropolitan was in the entrance corridor in 1890, and not very extensive. However, on the next day, January 8, they saw the Abbott Collection at the New-York Historical Society. Much to Kate's delight, the Abbott Collection held over one thousand pieces of Egyptian material. Collected by British physician Henry Abbott during his twenty years living in Egypt, the materials had been displayed from 1853 to 1860 in the Stuyvesant Institute on Broadway in Lower Manhattan. After Abbott died in 1859, the collection was sold to the New-York Historical Society—the only serious museum in the city at the time—in 1860.

Abbott himself had written the first catalogue in 1854, but it was sloppy and needed to be redone. Most of the items were not out for view, but Kate noted several of her favorites, which included jewelry, wooden pieces, and gold. She lamented that the "whole collection is huddled away, much of it is quite out of reach of daylight, and very ill catalogued. . . . The Historical Society must build a Museum."[23] More than two decades after Kate rightly criticized the catalogue, Caroline Ransom completed a partial one in 1924. They never did build a museum, but in 1937 the New-York Historical Society permanently loaned the collection to the Brooklyn Museum, where it is now.

Historians have argued that American interest in Egyptology

exploded in the prairie town of Chicago with the display of Cairo on the Midway Plaisance at the World Columbian Exhibition in 1892. Some have claimed that American Egyptology officially arrived when the University of Chicago was founded. However, it wasn't wealthy men who started building Egyptology in Chicago; it was in reality the work of Amelia Edwards and Kate Bradbury five years earlier, in 1890. In fact, the Chicago they arrived in by train in February of 1890 was still recovering from the Great Fire of 1871.

They arrived to a flurry of new buildings, wealthy donors, innovative educational efforts, and brand-new municipal works. The rail lines that had originally connected Chicago to Galena, Illinois, had been destroyed during the fire. They were rebuilt because of new commercial efforts in meatpacking, mostly pork, with the stockyards and slaughterhouses quickly making Chicago an American metropolis in the middle of the country.

In this new, bustling city, the women stayed with the wealthy and influential family of Wirt Dexter, a prominent Chicago attorney who had helped in recovery efforts after the fire, and whose family had a history of being benefactors of educational institutions like Harvard. Now in the Prairie District of the city of Chicago, in 1890 the Dexters' New England–style farmhouse at 1721 South Prairie Avenue would have been almost outside city limits. Set back around two hundred yards from the lakeshore, they would have had sweeping views of the sunrise over Lake Michigan every day. Kate thought that the house was "very comfortable" and the interior "very picturesque."[24]

Amelia and Kate were celebrated at several receptions both at the Dexter house and at the Art Institute of Chicago about a mile and a half away, which already had a few Egyptian pieces. In Chicago, the Art Institute raised more money to grow its collections. Community leaders began to push for a university to be established to bring more people and prestige to the city. (This would become the University of Chicago, in 1894, funded by John D. Rockefeller. A Semitic-language scholar from Yale became its first president, who then hired James Breasted as its first Egyptologist.) They were also lunched by other prominent ladies in Chicago such as Mrs. Marshall Field (Nannie Douglas Scott), whose husband's store

Fig. 5.2: Kate Bradbury
(Griffith), March 1890.

had been rebuilt at State Street a decade earlier. They met so many
wonderful women, Kate could hardly list them all and her favorite
things about them. In the end, she thought Chicago was a "great
city . . . and so well paved."[25]

As the tour wound down, the pair became tired of hotels and
rooms, packing and unpacking, and riding in carriages and trains.
They had seen and done so much, both enjoyable and excruciating.
Kate closed out her last letter to her family by saying, "Now we have
but four whole days in America—it seems so strange."[26] Interest-
ingly, when they were in Chicago, they were only an overnight train
ride away from Kate's cousin Jane, who lived in Topeka, Kansas,
near Kansas City, Missouri. They were lifelong correspondents, but
there was no mention of her trying to see Jane at all.

At the start of the tour, Amelia was criticized for being a bit
wooden and stiff, but by the end, she had gotten very comfortable
with the large audiences. The last lecture of Amelia's tour also took
place at the Brooklyn Academy, on March 10, 1890. It was attended
by some of the wealthiest people in Brooklyn and Manhattan. For
others who could get tickets, the academy was standing room only.

To celebrate the end of the tour, New York's Sorosis Club, the first professional women's club in the United States, honored Amelia with a lavish luncheon.

These two talks at the Brooklyn Academy, and the groups Kate and Amelia were celebrated by, were perfect bookends to their US tour. The main point of having this final talk in Brooklyn was to raise money to purchase art and artifacts for what would become the Brooklyn Museum. Just twelve miles away from the Metropolitan Museum of Art in Central Park, Brooklyn wanted to be just as big and just as important as the Central Park Museum. In the end, they didn't quite get as big as the Metropolitan Museum, but their fundraising for a new building was successful. The Brooklyn Museum was built in 1895 in part due to the money that poured in after Amelia's visit. By 1916, they accepted a major donation of Egyptian artifacts from the family of Charles Wilbour, and in 1937 they received the Abbott Collection, solidifying their place in world-renowned Egyptology collections.

In the Gilded Age tradition of British scientists on the American lecture circuit, no one had done it the way Amelia and Kate had done it.[27] Before them, the lecturers had been men like Charles Dickens, John Tyndall, Thomas Huxley, Alfred Russel Wallace, whose goal it was to educate the public in their fields of literature, physics, and biology. For Amelia and Kate, the main purpose of their tour of the US was to fan sparks of interest in ancient Egypt into flames. They did so well that their audiences were bigger than those of any previous visitor—except Dickens, of course—and they left a trail of financial and civic support for Egyptology everywhere they visited. Amelia and Kate were welcomed by the public with open arms from New York to Chicago, from St. Paul to Cleveland. Their impact in some places was felt immediately through ticket sales and building fundraisers. In other places, the financial support for the Fund in the United States and for its several branches was growing. They were poised to have a long-lasting partnership with the UK.

Some establishment figures in the discipline of Egyptology criticized the tour as not being a serious endeavor because it was done by a woman, and an untrained one at that.[28] Even though Amelia hadn't had university or field training in Egyptology, very few of her critics had, either. Today we might call Amelia a "crossover" phenomenon. Like Margaret Murray did twenty years later by unwrapping a mummy, Amelia excited interest from both scholars and the public. She was responsible for raising money across the northern United States in support of academic and public interactions with Egyptology on a scale not seen before her. Copley Winslow had been right about her. He had known that Amelia "could strike the right balance between 'sparkle' and scholarship."[29]

The Fund After Amelia

After what was arguably one of the most influential Egyptology lecture tours ever undertaken in the United States (possibly second only to Howard Carter's 1924 lecture tour after the uncovering of King Tutankhamun's tomb), the women arrived home in early April 1890. Amelia was in rough shape. She had begun the US tour with a cold and had lost her voice, due to the mix of warm dry air inside and the cold weather outside. Toward the end of the tour, in March, she had fallen down a short flight of stairs in Columbus, Ohio, and had broken her left arm. It was set immediately, and, astonishingly, she was able to lecture that same night. Everything seemed okay, but then on the boat ride back to England, they were blown by a gale for days, and Amelia was thrown about in her stateroom, further injuring her arm. Three days after they were back in England, she fell again, possibly because of exhaustion and weakness. A few weeks later, she had a surgery, probably to remove a benign tumor in her breast, and she was finally able to rest.[30] Kate and Emily took over most of the Fund work.

In that resting time, Amelia worked on the final step of all American lecture tours: writing up her lectures for publication. Kate helped her edit, research, and rewrite the lectures for the reading public. They worked day in and day out. By November of 1890, Amelia and Kate went north for another lecture tour, although they were both greatly in need of a break. Not much is known about this tour, and by Christmas Amelia was back at the Larches. Kate remained up north to visit her father and stepmother at Riversvale, but she rejoined Amelia by January of 1891. The two were planning a trip abroad to help ease Amelia's many ailments. This doctor-ordered change-of-air trip to warmer climes would take them to the South of France, Sicily, and back through Italy and Switzerland. These were well-traveled roads for both Kate and Amelia, but this was the first time they were in these places together. Oddly enough, Amelia felt her best in Switzerland, where it was the coldest.

The rest of 1891 for Amelia, Kate, and Emily was full of work. *Pharaohs, Fellahs and Explorers* was published at the end of that year, which was cause to celebrate. It did very well with both public audiences and the scholars who sought to communicate their ideas more widely. On the other hand, Emily and Kate were also trying to keep Amelia comfortable, all while trying to care for Ellen Bray-sher. Ellen, herself eighty-six that year, was a difficult patient. She was nigh unmanageable for Amelia. She suffered from what Kate called "brain failure," which was probably dementia, and only had brief moments of lucidity. Christmas of 1891 was very stressful for Amelia, and for Kate, who worried about her friend. Ellen's death on January 9, 1892, was a slight relief to all of them. Amelia seemed to be happier, even though she missed Ellen dearly. Unfortunately, she continued to suffer from various chest infections, and her health failed rapidly after Ellen died.

During these final weeks of Amelia's life, Emily tried to keep people at the Fund updated on her health. On New Year's Day, 1892, she wrote to Reginald Stuart Poole, "Miss Edwards who is still very ill in bed requests me to thank you for your letter, and to send her best wishes for the New Year to you all."[31] Things only got worse. In February, she wrote to him, "I do not see Miss Edwards at all now for fear she should think of work. . . . Quieter & nourishment better retained."[32] At the same time, Kate fretted. She reflected on her love for her friend, and wrote to Flinders: "Her love for me, & her seizure of me—unwilling—almost at first sight, has always been to me one of the strangest things I have known—so strange that I dared not refuse it either, or its consequences. . . . Of course I have grown to love her with a love as great as hers has always been for me, I think."[33] As tended to be the case with Amelia's loves, Kate didn't quite return the same kind of love Amelia had wanted from her.

Amelia died not long after Ellen did, most likely from lung issues, like bronchitis, that weakened her, and ultimately from the flu, on April 15, 1892. Several friends, family, and neighbors came to pay their respects. Kate was there, of course, and she laid an ankh made of pansies on her dear Amy's coffin. Emily Paterson was also in attendance, along with Percy Newberry and the Jesse Haworths. Lucy Renshaw sent a wreath from her nursing home.[34]

A few months after Amelia died, in October of 1892, Kate wrote again to Flinders, reflecting on her relationship with Amelia: "Ah! how loveable she was after all is said and done, all that I now know. She was always worrying me with—'if there *is* a next world, will you stand by me in it?' and trying to secure this from me. I will, and said so."[35] Kate mourned her dear Amy, and continued to mourn her as she worked to follow the instructions given in her will. This was when Kate's most impactful work for Egyptology, especially with Emily, really began—and that is saying something.

Amelia's will established a chair of Egyptology, named for her, at UCL. This was meant to be occupied by Flinders Petrie. Amelia's small but important collection of antiquities, amassed over her twenty years of work in the discipline, was also bequeathed to the college, along with several books. Some books went to Somerville College at Oxford, along with some of Amelia's personal effects and documents related to her fiction writing. Kate received a lump sum payment from Amelia of five hundred pounds, not that she needed money, and some of her Etruscan antiquities. Emily received twenty pounds.[36] Even though Amelia had a lawyer, Kate was the one who executed the plans in Amelia's will and did most of the work to get the items where they needed to go.

She worked closely with Emily as well as with Percy Newberry, who was digging for the Fund at the time. Kate and Amelia had agreed, before Amelia died, that Percy would be a great addition to the Fund's Committee, and Kate told him as much in a letter in May 1892. In that same letter, Kate then asked him to help catalogue the books and antiquities in Amelia's house. She reminded him, "I ask, because you told me that you would help me." She continued trying to entice him to the Larches to stay and help for several days: "I have no cook there now, but I would find you something to eat at proper times."[37] He must have agreed to it and done quite a lot of work because in July, she thanked him for all the help he gave her in fulfilling Amelia's wishes. She thanked him especially "for the crowning mercy of this catalogue."[38] With all the other paperwork and packing and unpacking Kate had had to do, along

Fig. 5.3: Amelia Edwards's study at the Larches, c. 1891. This shows only a portion of the books and antiquities Kate, Emily, and Percy had to catalogue and pack.

with running the Fund with Emily, Percy's book catalogue was a huge help to her.

After the materials were delivered to UCL in 1893, Kate continued to work with that group. She personally paid for several display cases at the new department at UCL to make sure Amelia's collection was properly housed. She also paid to bind several of Amelia's books for the new library at UCL, as well as at Somerville College in Oxford.

This entire time, Emily Paterson worked right alongside Kate. The women were close friends after having been with Amelia and the Fund since the late 1880s. Emily's administration of the Fund after Amelia's death ran so smoothly that she made herself nearly invisible. Yet her mark is literally everywhere in the archives: her name appears on almost every piece of correspondence that left or arrived at the Fund for over twenty years. From the late 1880s, she had taken over daily correspondence with the Fund's excavators and subscribers from Amelia, who had grown tired of all the work. Emily quelled worries, encouraged excavators, and, importantly, made sure that everyone got paid so that British Egyptology could continue on without any hitches.

In the 1890s, after the US tour, Emily worked closely with Marie Buckman, Secretary of the American branch of the Fund, based in Boston. The American branch was always struggling with subscriber numbers and finances, as well as infighting among the group. In February of 1897, the Rev. James Carter wrote to Emily and asked her to "exert your influence powerfully" over a governance matter in the US branch.[39] The matter was an old one that Emily and Kate were used to: some of the subscribers wished to have William Copley Winslow as the head of the committee, and others did not. Emily attempted to fix what she could from London and wrote to Marie about it. Marie responded to Emily in March that "your letter leads me to hopefully anticipate a wise adjustment of all difficulties by the Committee (London)."[40] What she could do immediately wasn't clear to Emily, but she tried. In the end, however, Copley Winslow left under a cloud, but published all the gossipy details about the US branch of the Fund in 1903, dedicating his book to the memory of Amelia Edwards.[41]

Women's Work

Once everything in the new department at UCL was stable enough
and students were regularly joining classes, Kate let herself fall in
love. After forty-two years of living mostly with her parents and
then with Amelia, Kate was as surprised by this as anyone. It was
never a situation she had planned for, and, from a young age, it was
one she was completely against. When she was twenty-four, she
wrote about her "ideal" life to her American cousin Jane:

> You live quietly you say—it is my opinion the most desirable
> life—a life of habit-propped undisturbed monotony amid beau-
> tiful & appreciated surroundings is growing my inglorious ideal
> of "happiness." (For all that my _theoretical_ contempt for this same
> "_happiness_" is as good as Carlyle's.) It would suit me very well to
> live quite alone.[42]

She wasn't really against marriage; it just had to be the right kind
of marriage. She continued explaining to Jane:

> I agree with you, women, as a rule have narrower interests when
> married. Is it of necessity I wonder? I am afraid so because of the
> children. Childless married life a woman might make another
> thing. She _might_, but often she doesn't.[43]

A few months later, she and Jane were still on the subject of
marriage, possibly because of Jane's impending engagement, when
she responded to another question of Jane's:

> For living alone, then—my ideal of it does not exclude ~~company~~
> servants nor visits paid & rec'ed of hours, days, or weeks—nor
> travelling—it is the noise & friction of many people _tied together_
> & therefore careless of being en deshabille[44] with each other that
> I hate so.[45]

Obviously, as a young woman, she wanted to maintain her privacy, her habits, and her own study. All of that had, decidedly, been

blown after meeting Amelia. Not that Kate minded being tied to Amelia or the Fund, but she liked to go home every so often even when she was in the throes of caring for Amelia full-time.

Then she met Frank Griffith. They met when Kate started working closely with Amelia in 1888. Apparently Frank was immediately smitten, but Kate had been clueless. In fact, she was so certain of her singleness that Frank needed some help from Flinders in convincing Kate to marry him. Six months after the couple got married in April of 1896, she wrote to her aunt Mary, "... he has wanted what he won at last long before I had a suspicion of his mind in the matter."[46]

Frank wasn't the only one who got what he wanted in this match; Kate got what she wanted, too. She didn't want to give up all her efforts just to have her name and labors be subsumed under a man's work. Kate helped Frank with his writing while getting on with her own. She told her aunt that they were "very happy working hand in hand" and that now that they were married she was "free to do nothing but work with him, which will be joyful."[47] To keep free from distractions, and be close to her father and stepmother, the couple decided to move back to Riversvale full-time. They were

Fig. 5.4: Kate and Frank Griffith, c. 1899, in Riversvale Hall.

able to depend on Kate's father's wealth so both could devote all their time to study. They had a loving and mutually respectful relationship, and Kate was equally as smitten as Frank. She shared with her aunt that her new husband was "good to look upon (this is not my verdict only)."[48]

Using the German she learned while in school in Switzerland, Kate translated Alfred Wiedemann's *Egyptian Doctrine of Immortality* (1895) and *Religion of the Ancient Egyptians* (1897) into English.[49] She also collaborated with her new husband in his translations of Egyptian texts. These were published as "Egyptian Literature," in *A Library of the World's Great Literature* (1896), and Kate was second author to Frank. We know from Margaret Murray's estimation of Frank that he might have been a brilliant linguist, but he wasn't a good teacher. Knowing what we know about women's work in archaeology, we can wonder how much work Frank actually did on this book.

They were very happy, and both professionally productive, but not for very long. In late 1901, Kate suffered an unknown medical episode, and Frank took her to a nearby hospital for an emergency operation. She never fully recovered, and she died in March 1902. Frank, devastated by Kate's death, continued living at Riversvale, caring for her father, Charles, and working as much as he could. At this point in his career, he was an honorary lecturer in Egyptology at Manchester University, not far from Riversvale, and Reader in Egyptology at Oxford. Kate left over £30,000 to Frank upon her death, and Charles left over £40,000 more to him when he died in 1907. This left Frank with the equivalent of around £5.5 million today. He had gone from a relatively poor scholar to a very wealthy man in a short period of time, thanks to Kate and her family.

Frank married another wealthy woman, Nora Cobban, after the death of Charles Bradbury. Upon Nora's death, long after Frank had died, a large bequest, combining her money and Kate's, was made to the University of Oxford that established what is now the Griffith Institute there. Frank's judicious choice in spouses had allowed him to work in the field, which wouldn't pay him much salary. Like UCL, the Griffith Institute is a salient example of the fact that it was women in Egyptology whose money and intellectual and physical labor made it possible for many of the famous men to accomplish anything. Indeed it was Kate's work to keep the Fund running that was crucial to its survival after the death of its founder. Her translation work, her assistance to Frank both intellectually and financially, and her care for Amelia and her wishes meant that both the Fund and the new department at UCL, headed by Flinders Petrie, would remain afloat for the next 130 years and counting.

Emily and the Fund

Kate died in early 1902, and there was a short obituary about her in the Fund's report from the 1901–2 season. Working as she did, essentially, behind the scenes, Kate would have been a relative unknown to many in the British and European Egyptological communities. To a person, however, they all depended on UCL and the Fund, but Kate's work ended up hidden behind her husband's name and Amelia's endowment. Kate's good friend Emily was saddened by her death. As she had had to do when Amelia died, Emily mourned but continued working. She was with the Fund until 1919.

There are no extant photographs of Emily Paterson that we know of. In fact, there is very little information about her life outside of the Fund's offices. Most of what we know about her comes directly from the fact that she left so much professional correspondence behind and that the Fund saved most of it in its archives.

Emily attended many lectures at UCL with Flinders Petrie, Frank Griffith, and Margaret Murray as her teachers. She started attending as early as 1902, but possibly earlier, and continued until at least 1908. Her lecture notes, in a notebook about 1.5 inches thick with each page completely full, are mostly in her neat shorthand.[50] They show her attention to detail, and she likely used them, and what she learned in those classes, in her scholarship. She published articles, including a poem, "On a Mummy Bead."[51] She gave several lectures, especially during World War I, including one in March of 1916 for the Fund, at the Royal Society's rooms, entitled "Animal Worship in Ancient Egypt."[52]

In the midst of her studies, she corresponded with Egyptologists, managed meetings, and gave and published reports. The conflicts of negotiating within local committees, distributing field finances, and dispersing of objects never ended. To parse through her correspondence alone would result in a detailed history of the Fund during the thirty years she was the General Secretary, and that history still needs to be written. Topics within the letters addressed to Paterson included such mundane issues as publication proofs, travel arrangements, meeting attendance, and generalized complaints and gossip. Letters from the field tended to focus on administering money, working with subscribers and patrons, and partnering with curators, Egyptologists, and donors. The biggest problems from the field that she dealt with were permissions (or lack thereof) from the French-run Department of Antiquities.

Emily's greatest achievement and contribution to the Fund was her institutional memory, combined with her decades of experience in the discipline. As General Secretary, she was in contact with everyone who dug for the Fund, as well as scholars from all over England and the rest of the world. Every Egyptologist would have known who she was. Often they came to her with questions. Other times she had to push them in the right direction. In January of 1915, she wrote to Alan Gardiner, an Oxford-trained linguist who was much younger than Emily and much less experienced. She had heard that Gardiner had "suggested at the Publication Sub-Committee [meeting] that I should be 'directed to send Negatives to Collotype makers always in the future.'"[53] She continued, "May I tell you how it is the practice was given up?"[54] Emily then explained how irreplacable negatives were often lost or broken in the process of making the collotype prints. This process for photograph printing, developed in the middle of the nineteenth century, allowed for high-quality reproductions to be printed for mass consumption. These prints were most often found in postcards and books. Emily argued that if she simply sent the positives the quality of the photos would remain high, and the Fund could keep its negatives intact. She closed the letter, "Of course, I am only too anxious to act as the C[ommit]^tee wishes; but I thought you might care to know what over 20 years experience has taught me as to the possible gain & certain risk [to the negatives]."[55] Gardiner wisely acquiesced, and Emily's procedure was the chosen one moving forward.

Emily also oversaw several physical moves for the Fund to different offices around London. The first move was from Reginald Stuart Poole's office at the British Museum, which had been their home from their inception in March of 1882 to sometime in 1883, to the Larches until 1892. Emily wasn't there for that move, but in 1892, the Fund finally moved to a central office. The first was at 37 Great Russell Street, near the British Museum, giving easy access to Egyptian collections and curators. In 1919, the Fund moved to 13 Tavistock Square and changed its name to the Egypt Exploration Society (EES). That was also the year that Emily retired and Mary C. Jonas took over.

By 1919, the Egypt Exploration Society had survived its first star excavator leaving, its founder dying, and a world war changing not only the geopolitical and physical landscape of Europe but also that of the British Empire. Britain had given nominal independence to Egypt, and they responded by shifting and tightening antiquities laws for everyone. All of this happened while the steadfast work of Emily Paterson continued, day in and day out, in the institutional center of British Egyptology. By the time she retired, she was almost sixty. She was ready for a break, but it wasn't easy. She had been with the Society for thirty years and knew everything about everything there. The Society recognized her service and honored her with a pension of £175 per year.

After Emily's retirement, Mary C. Jonas sat at her predecessor's old desk and loaded up the typewriter with another blank sheet of paper. She had already written so many letters that day. Still, she needed to write to Percy Newberry to tell him about her meeting with Lord Carnarvon. The man who had sponsored Howard Carter the last six years in the Valley of the Kings had just returned to England and wanted to deliver the news about the uncovering of the tomb of Tutankhamun.

Just four days into 1923, Mary found herself completely snowed under. Emily warned her about the busy times, so she should have expected this. But, to be fair, no one could have anticipated this. The tomb had just been uncovered a few months before, and the excitement had yet to reach its zenith. And now Carnarvon had told her that he wanted to address the next meeting of the Society, where

Percy was slated to speak on the tomb. There was so much to do—write the announcement for the *Times*, make sure the venue was large enough, and of course let Percy know about the new plans.[56] She wished Emily could be there to help her.

.She dashed off a letter, detailing the news of Carnarvon's participation and alerting Percy to the fact that he had said they might have royalty in the audience.[57] They moved the lecture from their normal borrowed room at the Royal Society to the larger Central Hall in Westminster.

The next day, she wrote to Percy again. This time she only had time for a postcard:

> *Tickets have gone today like hotcakes. I have had a thoroughly* <u>*hectic*</u> *time. All are sold, but I can still manage one or two for special guests or lecturers friends. /Mary C. Jonas.*
> *& I expect an enormous post tomorrow*[58]

The event went off without a hitch, showing that Emily trained Mary very well, and that she was up to the task. Mary continued to write to Emily for years. She would answer questions as she could and would sign all her letters, "Love from yours very sincerely . . ." Mary appreciated Emily's friendship and support; her institutional knowledge was invaluable. Emily frequently came to see the Society's exhibits and she continued to offer help, such as when she offered to catalogue the library as a volunteer—some of the books were probably from her own extensive library. She even attended the fiftieth anniversary celebration of the founding of the Society in 1932.[59] But she really wanted to live a quiet life. She gradually moved from Highbury in London to Cornwall to be with her longtime companion, Miss Margaret Taylor.

The private lives of women in the early twentieth century are difficult to piece together, but we know that Emily and Margaret lived together or near each other in London. By 1935, Emily was living in the Manor House, Redruth, England, with four other women: wealthy "spinster sisters" Emily and Edith Swindells, pianist Manya Seguel, and her own partner, Margaret Taylor.[60] Here they lived the rest of their lives together.

When Emily was alive, the Society seemed to remember her in many ways. Along with her pension, in 1928 they offered her an oil painting of Amelia Edwards that had hung in the office (it is the same one that still hangs there).[61] In September 1931, excavator and benefactor Robert Mond invited Emily to an exhibition of some of his Theban finds. She took the opportunity to write back to him, gently admonishing him for not mentioning Amelia in a summary he wrote of the work of the then-Fund. She wrote, "Of course this does not matter to her now she is no more with us, but many of her old friends and original subscribers do not like it)."[62] She continued the letter by giving him a short summary of how the Society originated. He responded by writing, "You may rest assured that Miss Edwards' work will not be forgotten, nor will your own as Secretary of the Society for such a long time."[63]

When she died in September 1947, the Society was sure to send a wreath to her funeral in Cornwall. A few days later, Mary Jonas received a touching letter from Margaret Taylor:

Dear Madam
As the oldest (of 57 years standing) and only friend of the late
Miss Emily Paterson I wish to thank the Officers of the Egypt
Exploration Society for the beautiful wreath which they kindly
sent for her funeral which took place last Saturday.[64]

It was almost as if that was all she had the words to say about the loss of her dear partner. Emily left much of her Egyptian collection, what there was of it, to Margaret. Those pieces ended up in the Camborne Museum, which dissolved in 2005, and subsequently moved to the Museum of Cornish Life.[65]

It wasn't long, though, until the institutional memory that Mond had assured Emily of died. Later in 1947, the news of Emily's death got only a passing mention in the *Journal of Egyptian Archaeology*, the scholarly journal published by the Society. Volume 33 from that year has a brief note at the end of the editorial foreword, on page 2: "... while the older members will regret the passing Miss Emily Paterson, for many years Secretary of the Society under its old title of the Egypt Exploration Fund." She didn't even get a whole sentence to let members know of her death. The EES *Annual Report* from 1947 does her a little better service. She received a whole paragraph's worth of room:

> With the death of Miss Emily Paterson at the age of eighty-seven the oldest link with the early days of the Society disappears. Miss Paterson had worked in close association with Miss Amelia Edwards. From 1888 to the death of Miss Edwards she was her private secretary, appointed specifically to assist Miss Edwards with the work of the Egypt Exploration Fund. Miss Edwards had a very high opinion of her work and intended her to become the General Secretary of the Fund. Miss Paterson's work was not confined to ordinary secretarial work. She lectured and wrote articles on the work of the Fund. In 1892 on the death of Miss Edwards she became General Secretary to the Egypt Exploration Fund and she served first the Egypt Exploration Fund and then the Egypt Exploration Society until her resignation in 1919. In recognition of her thirty years' devoted service she was made a Life Member and was awarded a pension.[66]

The fact that they didn't really discuss her passing, or her career, is a feature of women in Egyptology in the mid-twentieth century. Emily was not one of the field archaeologists and was therefore seen at the time as a supporting character. But just because someone doesn't get lengthy elegies in multiple sources does not mean she (usually the person is a woman) is not important in her discipline. In doing her work at the Fund, Emily was one of the main administrators of a central scholarly group in London, then the center of the British Empire. Everyone who wrote to the Fund wrote directly to her, meaning she was obviously a main character in the development of the Fund and Egyptology as a discipline, not just in the UK but also in the rest of the world. She was a mainstay in the offices for three decades and someone who could be depended upon to perform tasks quickly and well. The implications of her work would connect and influence a number of people outside of her time as the General Secretary, as well.

Emily and Kate were truly the last of the early women of Egyptology. They knew Amelia Edwards, Marianne Brocklehurst, and Gaston Maspero. They worked with Maggie Benson, Nettie Gourlay, and Emma Andrews. They saw the start of professional Egyptology in Britain and formed the center of the network that made this possible.

6

Myrtle Broome and Amice Calverley

We were now fortunate enough to secure the additional services of Miss Broome, whose artistic skill is not inferior even to that of Miss Calverley, and henceforth these two ladies have borne practically the whole brunt of the work . . .
— *The Temple of King Sethos I at Abydos, Volume I*

Myrtle Broome sat down to write to her mother for the first time in a few days. She made writing home a habit on her first trip to Egypt with Olga Tufnell in 1927, and she wanted to keep the habit this season. She was close to her mother and father. They were her confidants. They loved getting letters from their traveling daughter, telling them all about her adventures. Her first season of what would be almost a decade at Abydos was so different from when she was with Olga at Qau el-Kebir. Mother wouldn't believe what she had done that day. Myrtle could hardly believe it herself. "I have had the thrill of thrills to-day," she wrote. "I rode on a real desert camel."[1] She paused and put her pen down, needing to stretch her tired fingers. She had been bent over paper all day long, copying and correcting copies of drawings of temple walls, so she was already tired. But she wanted to tell the story just right.

The camels they rode that day had been used to deliver a few supplies, but the camel man had remembered Myrtle taking photographs of his camels a few days earlier, when he had brought other stores. He asked her when he saw her again if she wanted to ride the camel. "You may be sure I did not say no," she wrote to her parents.

Myrtle and Amice Calverley, her supervisor, copying partner, and friend, wasted no time in mounting the camels.

It's never a dignified business for visitors to mount a camel. In order to ride a camel, then, as today, everything had to go just right. Their respective camels first knelt on the floor of the desert waiting for Myrtle and Amice to climb on. Then the camels heaved their back legs up first, nearly launching the women forward. They had to be very careful to lean back, far, so as not to go head-over-heels over the camel's neck or hurt the animal while remaining in their seat. Then the camels had to get up on their front legs. Myrtle knew that riders would slide off the back if they weren't careful, so she had to lean far forward and hold on to the camel's neck. Once the camels' backs were even, with all four long legs steadied underneath them, the women could relax a little bit. They'd have to repeat the process—in reverse—when they got down, but for now Myrtle and Amice both settled into their saddles, sat up straight, held the reins, and felt the "long swinging stride . . . [which] was perfectly wonderful[.] the easy swinging motion going up & down the sand hills without a sound, it was fine being able to view the desert from such a height."[2] Myrtle loved the fifteen-minute ride so much that, later that season, she and Amice embarked on an arduous twenty-two-mile, six-and-a-half-hour ride that no one thought they would finish. That was the first of many camel excursions Myrtle and Amice would make—both together and separately—throughout their time in Abydos.

Another crew member that first year, a Mr. C. Beazley, had been extremely bored in the desert. He refused to join Amice and Myrtle, preferring crossword puzzles to camel rides. Myrtle and Amice were far from bored. They were energized by their work and their useful, productive lives in the desert. Myrtle loved taking advantage of every delight the desert offered her. Starting with her first field season in Egypt with Olga Tufnell from November 1927 to January 1928, Myrtle regularly wrote to her mother and father, and sometimes friends back home, about life in Egypt. Until she left Egypt for good in 1937, she had written over four hundred letters to her parents back in England.[3] They are, like Amelia's travelogue, Emma's diaries, and Kate's journals, a mostly one-sided version of what happened at a particular place and time. Amice wrote some personal letters back to "Ma and Pa Broomie," but she wrote mostly to Egyptologists James Breasted and Alan Gardiner about the daily work and other administrative issues on-site. Myrtle's letters were more about the happenings of life at their site house and interactions with the nearby village than they were about the work they did in the temple.

There is often a stark difference between the field records men and women left behind. While men left journals about what work they performed, whom they paid, how much they paid, and what their thoughts about the site were on any given day, women, as we have seen, tended to write about daily activities on- and off-site. We can conclude that this is because men served as field directors and women were either not officially part of the work or they were considered to be less valuable. Women were certainly archaeologists and Egyptologists, but their record-keeping habits, in this period at least, differed from men's. We need both sides of the story to construct a complete picture of life on-site.

For the Temple of Seti (Sethos) I at Abydos project, the field director was a woman, Amice Calverley, and the correspondence that she left is largely that of a field director. She had written personal letters to Mary Jonas of the Egypt Exploration Society, for example, but most of Amice's existing letters are to her bosses. Myrtle simply told stories about her day to her parents. It seemed she was trying to help them not to worry about her and to entertain them at the same time. She detailed their caring for villagers in "hospital parades," the tourist and Egyptologist visits, and the sparrows and owls in the temple. She wrote a bit about their work, but most of Myrtle's letters gave the flavor of life on-site during those eight years.

The result of their isolated project was four volumes of beautifully rendered copies of the walls in the Temple of Seti I at Abydos. At the start of the project, they had enough material for at least eight volumes, but, so the story goes, World War II and a lack of funds put an end to any possibility of producing more publications. But that's only part of the story. It turns out, Amice was banned from Egypt in the 1950s, thus putting an end to any more copying. There was a fifth volume that made it as far as the proof stage, but it seems like the lack of time and interest, as well as a lack of money, kept it from production. The impact that these volumes have had on the preservation of the art at the Temple of Seti I cannot be overstated. Researchers have a glimpse into what the temple looked like one hundred years ago, and even two thousand years ago, with the bright colors and clear lines lending an air of newness to the artwork. Myrtle and Amice, with their training, craft, and tenacity, produced and published some of the best-known work on this temple at Abydos, allowing so many others to continue to work to understand its mysteries.

A Match Made in Egypt

Myrtle was born in London in February of 1888, and later her family moved to Bushey, just outside London, to build a house. She grew up comfortably middle class (they had two domestic servants), and, as the only child, she was very close to her parents. Her father, Washington Herbert Broome, was a book publisher and craftsman who used his talents to decorate the inside of their new home. Myrtle first studied art in Bushey but then honed her artistic talents with her father as they worked together on decorating the new house on Avalon Grange Road. She created the mantelpiece in their home, a stunning display of woodworking that is still there, and designed the textiles used in the decorations. Myrtle's mother, Eleanor, or Ellen, didn't have her own career, like many middle-class women at the time, but was always supportive and proud of Myrtle's talent and hard work.

When Myrtle was twenty-three, she became one of the original members of the Gang at UCL, the group that Margaret Murray taught in the first official year of the Egyptology certificate. She had two years of training in the collections at both UCL and the British Museum, with Margaret's guiding eye on her art. In 1913, she finished her certificate, along with the rest of the Gang, who all went their separate ways—Rex, Guy, and Winifred went straight to Egypt, but Myrtle stayed in England. She had grown close to Miss Murray, as she called her for the rest of her life, and remained so when she stayed near London. She continued working with her father, and the two started a business called Designers and Workers in Metal and Enamel.[4] They kept up with the housework and decoration, and Myrtle later designed textiles for the fashion house Liberty of London. As most women had to do in this period, Myrtle was simply trying to stay connected to the field, so she did odd jobs for other Egyptologists who needed copy work done. Margaret Murray, knowing what Myrtle was going through, wanted to support the work of a talented artist when she saw one, so she had Myrtle complete some drawing projects for the department. In her late thirties by now, she assumed this would be her life—working alongside her father and doing Egyptology as the opportunities presented themselves. But everything was about to change for her.

In 1927, because of her talent and her continued connection to UCL, Petrie asked Myrtle to come out to the Qau el-Kebir site to copy rock-cut tombs with Olga Tufnell, Hilda Petrie's former secretary and another Margaret Murray student.[5] The ancient site was Tjebu, today known better as El Etmannyieh, and it contained Middle Kingdom tombs that Petrie and his team had excavated a few years earlier. By 1927, because they were open to the elements, the tombs were in danger of deteriorating beyond repair. He knew they needed to be copied before they were destroyed—there was only so much rescue work they could do—and he needed the best copyists he knew. Knowing Margaret Murray, who, at the age of sixty-four, was still running the department in London, was unavailable, Petrie asked Myrtle and Olga. Soon, they were on their way to Egypt, together. Later on, Olga Tufnell would become well-known in Palestinian archaeology, but this was both her and Myrtle's first trip to Egypt.[6] Petrie fully depended on them to do this detailed work—they were essential to the team—but he didn't mention them in his report of the site from that year.[7]

In 1905, James Breasted had begun what would become, officially in 1924, the Epigraphic Survey based at the University of Chicago's then Oriental Institute (now the Institute for the Study of Ancient Cultures, henceforth the Institute) in Luxor.[8] He knew that when an ancient tomb is opened to the outside air after two or three millennia of being sealed off, the delicate painting and other artwork often deteriorate very quickly. For temples, the decay was ancient and ongoing. The main goal for the Survey was to "record the inscribed content of these monuments, along with their architectural context, at an optimum level of accuracy, creating a definitive and permanent record that will serve as a primary resource for academic research and will stand in the place of the original monuments themselves, as their physical deterioration takes its inevitable course."[9] Whether protocols for preservation of the original artistry were ignored (as in Theo Davis's case) or observed, rarely could ancient art be protected without modern techniques. In the 1920s and 1930s, some excavators were still using paraffin wax, plaster molds, and plaster squeezes. All of these methods were at least partially destructive, meaning the art would not survive unscathed, but they still allowed archaeologists to take pieces home with them. The only method that could conserve the artwork without destroying it at the same time was photographing or copying by hand. As Harry Burton's photographs from the 1922 uncovering of the tomb of King Tutankhamun show, field photographs were still only done in black and white. While the quality was getting better, the process of capture alone was labor intensive, yet not as detailed or reliable as a human copyist.[10] Enter the women.

The season with Petrie went well enough, with Myrtle and Olga completing the copying and having a few adventures of their own. Myrtle went to Luxor to tour several temples and to the Valley of the Kings to see the tombs. She celebrated Christmas at the lavish Winter Palace Hotel, where Howard Carter took a break from Tutankhamun's tomb to judge the fancy dress competition. On the way back to Cairo, Myrtle decided to stop back by Qau el-Kebir to visit a police chief by the name of El Gerzawy. The two had met while Myrtle was on-site with Olga, and he had been asking her to come back and visit. He hosted her at his police outpost—something that was frequently done for European visitors who were in transit. The places were safe and clean, even (somewhat) for women.

Over the course of two days, Gerzawy wooed and courted Myrtle. He gave large, impressive dinners in her honor, introduced her to all the local community leaders, and showed her how he could beat up a person who had just been arrested. Then, he asked her to marry him. She wasn't particularly surprised by the proposal, but she wasn't sure what to do. She told her parents it was "frightfully difficult to refuse [because] he really is one of the finest characters I have ever met. I like him immensely. the [*sic*] only thing against him is his Nationality. . . . I am afraid he thinks I may reconsider it if he lives in England & if he only were English I believe I would."[11] She refused to be married to an Egyptian man in the end and went home.

At the end of January 1929, though, she was on her way back to Egypt with her uncle Jim. They boarded the SS *Largs Bay*, bound for Port Said, Egypt, and ultimately the small village of Vicha el-Kubra, now called El-Mahalla el-Kubra, about eighty miles north of Cairo. It is situated well in the fertile Nile Delta region. It is no longer a small village, and its cotton textile industry remains the leading industry in the area. Myrtle and her uncle were able to stay in a house in the village for a short time, hosted again by El Gerzawy. Their trip was soon cut disappointingly short by Myrtle's would-be betrothed. After almost two weeks of adventures in the village, seeing the new textile mills and getting to know the people who lived there, Gerzawy told Myrtle and Uncle Jim that they would have to leave town, immediately, saying that Ramadan, the Islamic holy month of fasting and prayer, was about to begin. He may have been devout, wanting to follow Islamic practice closely with as few distractions as possible. It is also possible that Gerzawy thought that Myrtle would marry him upon her return, and when she refused again, he simply asked her to leave. From Myrtle's side, she and her uncle were confused and "bitterly disappointed" when they returned to Cairo to make arrangements to come home. They spent several days sightseeing in Cairo, but by February 18, they were on a boat home. It was too short a stay, and Myrtle was determined to get back to Egypt.

Myrtle had the education and she knew she had the talent to work in Egypt long term. Plenty of men with less talent than she had done it. She had the necessary connections, too. Her old friend from the Gang, Rex Engelbach, was now in Cairo, working as the Assistant Keeper at the Egyptian Museum. Guy and Winifred Brunton were in Cairo, too, excavating, and by 1931 Guy became the Assistant Keeper when Rex was promoted to Keeper. Including

Myrtle, more than half of the Gang was back together in Cairo. Myrtle was still very close to Margaret Murray and the Petries as well, so she had several avenues to help her get permanent work. She just needed the right project, and she found it—in Abydos with Amice Calverley.

Amice Calverley had been working at Abydos as an artist since January 1928. Even though Myrtle had been in Egypt at the time, having finished the tomb work with Olga at Qau el-Kebir, the two women didn't know each other then, meeting only when Myrtle joined the crew at Abydos in the autumn of 1929. Amice was born in England in April 1896, eight years after Myrtle. Her father Edmund's army service moved the whole family, including her older brother Hugh and younger brother Osbert, to South Africa by 1905. They then moved to Canada, and later, she herself moved to New York. Amice had several years of formal art training at the prestigious Slade School of Fine Art at UCL, along with some years of piano study. In 1922, she moved to England permanently because she had won a scholarship to the Royal College of Music, where she decided she wanted to write an opera. She spent the next four years working on her music and art. Despite her efforts, her opera was not picked up by any performing group, and she was losing hope for her music career.

To make ends meet, she worked at the Ashmolean Museum in Oxford. It was there in 1926 that she met Leonard Woolley, the famous archaeologist who was then in the middle of twelve total seasons at Ur, a biblical site in Mesopotamia. He had also led excavations at the Middle Egypt site of Amarna in 1921–22. As an experienced archaeologist, he instantly recognized Amice's artistic talents and encouraged her to pursue archaeological drawing instead of the opera she kept working on.[12] When her opera failed, she decided to follow his advice. Amice soon started working with Aylward M. Blackman, an Egyptologist at Oxford. He also happened to be working for the Egypt Exploration Society on the Temple of Seti I at Abydos, and he needed a trained artist to copy the art, which was slowly deteriorating on the walls.

Abydos is a hugely significant site for those who study ancient Egypt because it was a necropolis, or cemetery, for the first kings of Egypt as far back as c. 3100 BCE. It later became a pilgrimage destination as the mythical birthplace and burial site of the god of the afterlife, Osiris. There are records of thousands of years of activity on the site, mostly focusing on death and burial, but some having to do with the land of the living. The site and its tombs and temples are now situated near the towns of El Araba El Madfuna and El Balyana, but they are still far from major tourist sites and relatively difficult to get to.

The mortuary temple of Seti I at Abydos is an L-shaped temple, built by Seti I's son, Ramesses II, during the nineteenth dynasty (c. 1303–1213 BCE). Like most other mortuary temples in ancient Egypt, it serves to honor and deify the deceased pharaoh. Past the first pylon, or gateway, into the first court, there are two wells, one on either side of the center pathway, and a stairway that leads to the second court. Beyond the second court are the first, then second, hypostyle halls. The second hypostyle hall—that is, a hall whose roof rests on columns—leads to several more galleries and halls. The most important to the copying project were the seven chapels that honor seven gods, listed in order here as they are on the map, numbered 1 through 7: the deified Seti I, Ptah, Re-Horakhty, Amun-Re, Osiris, Isis, and Horus.[13] As the American Research Center in Egypt describes the chapels:

> These chapels are decorated with scenes of the king offering to the gods and of him receiving the symbols of life and dominion, as well as royal insignia, in return. These scenes would have been complemented by the rituals that would have been performed by priests within the chapels' walls, that served to transform the king into the god of death and resurrection, Osiris.[14]

The Osiris chapel leads to several more chapels for worshipping the god Osiris and the mysteries associated with him. The temple also contains the "Gallery of the Lists," which is now known as the Gallery of the Ancestors, and the famous Abydos King List. Although meant to be a ceremonial and not necessarily true chronology, the list has helped Egyptologists to make sense of the ancestry

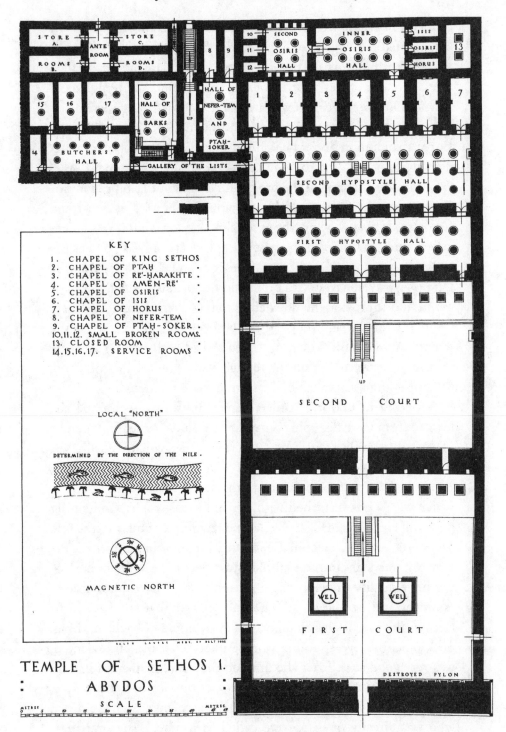

Fig. 6.1: Plate 1A from *The Temple of King Sethos I at Abydos, Volume III* (1938).

of Egypt's earliest kings while noticing who was missing from the list, deemed not worthy of being remembered.

Another building on the large site is the Osireion. Also called the Cenotaph of Seti I, it is located just behind the temple, and it would be sporadically excavated and recorded over several decades, most notably by Margaret Murray in 1902–3. By 1925, the Egypt Exploration Society had hired an engineer and photographer named Herbert Felton to photograph the strange monument. Alan Gardiner, the director of the project for the Egypt Exploration Society, assumed Felton could photograph the temples of Seti I and Ramesses II that were nearby as a quick side job. Felton was an excellent photographer, but his photographs were only as good as the technology he had to work with. The light and shadows within the temples wreaked havoc with production, and, in the end, the photographs didn't provide the fine details that Gardiner and the Society wanted. To make sure they did the best possible job recording the temple, Aylward Blackman had been tasked with finding an artist to help preserve the art on the temple walls. He hired Amice, and, as soon as she was available, she started to do the drawing.

Working in Oxford, Amice began by using a technique she learned from the Epigraphic Survey. She would receive photographs of the temple walls from Egypt and would then collate drawings—that is, she would make line tracings of the photographs. To do this, Amice bent herself for hours at a time over a special tracing board, which was "a box furnished with a ground-glass top . . . containing powerful electric lamps."[15] She used a technique similar to the one Henrietta Swan Leavitt had perfected for the Harvard Observatory to track stars in the night sky just twenty years before. Placing high-quality drawing paper on top of a detailed photograph, Amice would be able to see the lines clearly that she needed to trace in the bright electric light. It meant hours of back-breaking, neck-pinching, eye-straining work. Amice, tenacious and talented, was very good at it. After she finished the detailed tracings in Oxford, they were taken back to Egypt to be completed in the temple, in front of the original art itself. Then, "experts" like Alan Gardiner, who was already on-site, were called in to check the drawings. When Amice and other copyists encountered destruction, either

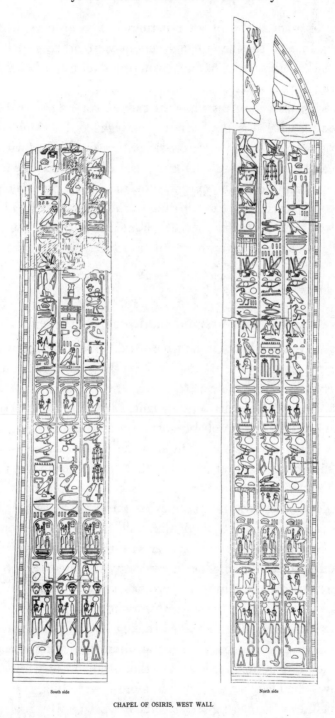

CHAPEL OF OSIRIS, WEST WALL

Fig. 6.2: Detail of plate 8 from *The Temple of King Sethos I at Abydos, Volume I* (1933), showing destruction.

ancient or gradual, they made no attempt to reconstruct what was missing. Instead the incomplete sections were noted, usually with hash marks. They could not and would not venture to guess what had been in that space.

As frequently happens when the careful work of an artist is recognized for what it is, the Society soon realized that Amice would be a major asset if she were on-site. She was familiar with each photo, and with the temple walls themselves, and would do a better job than the piecemeal operation they had set up. She was immediately sent to Abydos for full-time work in January of 1928. Her hand was so accurate that, because of her, the Society expanded its original goal of photographs to one much larger and more ambitious.

Arriving in Abydos

Amice arrived in Abydos in January of 1928. Her main job was producing the copies of the art and script on the walls of the Temple of Seti I. She was now the expert, checking the photographs against her drawings and the art on the walls. Living in South Africa as she did as a child, this probably wasn't her first time visiting Egypt, but it was her first time working there. She did such a good job in what she was given that first year that Alan Gardiner hired her again for the next season, but in her second season she went out there alone. There was little money for the project—as usually was the case with the Society, while they still struggled to get and keep subscribers. Amice also had to deal with the day-to-day demands of running the camp. She had several servants with her who surely kept her company. The most important servant to Amice (and later Myrtle) was Nannie, a Syrian woman who took care of the house and gardens, cooked, and cleaned the dig house. Sardic (his name was most likely Sadiq, but Myrtle transliterated his Arabic name in letters to her parents in this way, so that is how history remembers him) was the head servant and ran almost everything Nannie did not, including managing the several Egyptians working on and around the house and site. Sardic was Egyptian and, even though his family lived nearby, would sleep at the dig house to help keep watch over its inhabitants. Sardic went on all the excursions with Amice and Myrtle and acted as a dragoman for them when they decided to be tourists far from the site. He was also an adviser in most cultural interactions that Amice and Myrtle had with the people who lived nearby.

In the 1928–29 season, when she was the only one working on-site, Amice entertained several visitors. Probably the most important visitor that year was James Breasted, the American Egyptologist from the University of Chicago. He was the founder of the Epigraphic Survey, from which the Seti I project took most of its methods. In that season, he was on a publicity tour with his patron, John D. Rockefeller, Jr. Rockefeller was and remains one of the wealthiest people to have walked the earth, having inherited his money and livelihood from his father, John D. Rockefeller, the builder and owner of Standard Oil in the United States. The Rockefellers wanted to use some of their money for good, and, like Emma Andrews and other wealthy patrons before him, they supported work in the arts, humanities, and social sciences. Egyptology, both then and now, sat at the intersection of these three broad fields. Breasted, in turn, had Junior's ear—and access to his checkbook.

Seeing the opportunity for a new and wealthy patron, Amice gave the men and their entourage a tour of the site and showed them her work. Rockefeller was astounded at Amice's talent in reproducing the painted reliefs of the temple so accurately. With Breasted's encouragement, Rockefeller understood the importance of her work and wanted to make sure it continued beyond the Society's accounts. He negotiated with Alan Gardiner, who was also a good friend of James Breasted's, and the men decided to split the cost of the project between the Epigraphic Survey (that is, Rockefeller) and the Society. On the basis of Amice's work alone, Rockefeller gave £21,000 to the cause in 1929, the equivalent of close to £1 million ($1.12 million) today, thus creating the joint project. The cost wasn't an equal split—Rockefeller was clearly paying the lion's share. He had already been partially funding the Epigraphic Survey in Chicago since 1905 and fully funding Breasted's and the University of Chicago's work since 1919. His father had granted much of the original money to found the University of Chicago itself, so the Rockefellers had a long legacy of partnering with Chicago, and working with the Society was a logical next step.

This kind of financial opportunity is a field-worker's dream. Amice now had a viable budget and could hire at least one other copyist to help her full-time. She was beyond happy, and Mary Jonas commended her, writing, "I congratulate you on the good impression your work must have made on the powers that be to induce such substantial help to be offered."[16] She also cautioned Amice in taking too much American money.

> *I hope that you are sufficiently British to wish your work to be a British undertaking. I do not want the Americans to think that because they are putting down the cash that we are willing to hand over our work (and incidentally workers) to them. Don't you agree with me?*[17]

This must have been the Society's big worry, because Gardiner was adamant, as were Breasted and Rockefeller, that Amice was to remain the director. She had been working as quickly, but as accurately, as she possibly could. But if a skilled photographer couldn't speed up the work, there was no way an artist on her own could do so. There were only a few people who could keep up with the demanding work on-site. Myrtle was known to the Society, and to Gardiner, thanks to her work with Petrie and Olga Tufnell at Qau el-Kebir a couple of years earlier. Her talent was at least equal to that of Amice's, and Gardiner had suggested her. He wrote that she was "a very first-rate draughtswoman ... who has some experience of Egypt and some knowledge of hieroglyphs," so Myrtle was hired.[18] That is how, as Gardiner put it in the introduction to the first volume of copies, "henceforth these two ladies have borne practically the whole brunt of the work ..."[19]

Making Abydos Home

Just six months after her previous, disappointing, trip to Egypt, Myrtle found her way onto the SS *Ranpura* for this next journey, which turned out to be fairly easy and simply delightful. She went straight from the London train to the ship, found her cabin, then booked her seat and table for meals for the trip. She also made sure to book seats at her table for Miss Calverley and her brother, Hugh, who would be joining her on the ship in Marseilles in about a week's time. She was anxious to meet the people whom she would be working with in the isolated site of Abydos for the next several months, but until then, she enjoyed the time to herself.

Relishing her downtime, she would sleep until eight, then dress and have breakfast, choosing from a large menu. She was happy they had real milk on board the ship. It was made from butter, which confused her a little and, as she explained to her parents, they "just reverse the process."[20] She would then walk the deck for exercise. After lunch, she would read her book in the sun for the afternoon and eat dinner at 7:00 or 7:30. When she could, she took excursions. A few days after leaving England, the ship arrived at Gibraltar, where Myrtle enjoyed the "quaint little Spanish town. Lattice windows. Peeps of tiled courtyards & quaint roofs."[21] Their next stop was Marseilles, where the ship remained for almost three days. Myrtle went about town, going to the zoo and taking a tram tour, and finally Amice and Hugh arrived just after lunch on Saturday, October 5.

Myrtle spotted the siblings as they made their way on board the ship. She let them settle into their cabins, then went to greet them. Even though they had never met before, the two women were fast friends. They dispensed with formalities almost immediately. The first day all three of them were together, the women went to town to get Amice's hair cut, then had coffee and pastries before heading out on an adventure to the Château d'If. After a wild boat ride, tossed about by wind and waves that almost made them sick, they made it to the château and "had a splendid view of the bay and town."[22] On the way back, the wind was worse than it had been before, and the women got soaked by the waves splashing over the sides of the boat. Amice's brother, Captain Hugh Calverley, had stayed on the boat to unpack and relax, and he was annoyed he had missed the adventure to the château. Later that day, he talked Myrtle into going to the theater. From the first day, Myrtle was sure that the three of them would "have a very jolly time in camp we have not wasted any time in being polite."[23] They felt like they had known each other for years.

After some sightseeing in Cairo, they arrived at the Egypt Exploration Society camp at El Araba El Madfuna, near Abydos, around the twentieth of October. At Abydos by 1929, the Society had continued to build on the palimpsest of the ancient site. The Society had already built and torn down (or at the very least completely abandoned) at least five dig houses. As vast as the site was, and is, several houses might be in use at the same time. Flinders and Hilda Petrie had the first house built there in 1899, and it was essentially a row of connected huts built out of mud brick, roofed with planks and reeds, with reed mats as doors and the sand of the desert as the floor. Today, that house has become its own tell, a pile of disused mud brick and sherds, waiting to be excavated by some future archaeologist. Some of the bricks from that house were also used later in walkways around the camp and one of the tennis courts. By 1902, that first house was no longer livable, so the Petries built the second house, the one in which Margaret Murray spent her time almost thirty years earlier. The Society built another house in 1908, but it was far too small to be useful to the larger teams they were sending.

The house that Amice and Myrtle lived in had been built around 1907 by Harold Jones for John Garstang's Liverpool group, before Jones left for full-time work with Emma Andrews and Theodore Davis.[24] The Society bought the house in 1909 from Liverpool. It stood one story, consisted of mud brick painted white, with several rooms and a "battlement tower" that was Myrtle's first bedroom there. In its earlier days, the house had a tennis court and miniature golf course nearby, but later expeditions had no time or interest in maintaining either of those amenities.[25] With Garstang as the leader of the expedition that lived in this house first, the golf course comes as no surprise.

The house was theirs to use, but the women had to furnish much of it themselves, which they did with supplies bought in Cairo and shipped in on camelback. The first year Myrtle was there, they brought plates, pots, pans, jugs, slop pails, china, mattresses, pillows, mosquito nets, and, apparently, a lemon squeezer that broke

Fig. 6.3: Abydos dig house, 1928.

in the move from Cairo or in the chaos of unpacking.[26] In an earlier season, Amice had planted a garden, kept by her, Sardic, and mostly Nannie. Once Myrtle arrived, the seeds her parents sent her provided carrots, lettuce, and other fresh produce. Myrtle's room in the tower of the Jones/Garstang house was "so cosy & pretty," she wrote to her mother.[27] She had brought, or made, a tablecloth and curtain for her shelves out of blue and white checked cloth and had grass mats on the floor. They frequently used local artisans for rugs, clothwork, and other items they needed on-site and in the house.

Myrtle didn't last long in the tower room, though, as much as she loved it. Their assistant that first year, Beazley, had not done the work he had promised. Myrtle wrote to her parents that he wasn't good for much but complaining and taking all of the crossword puzzles they sent her. Amice reported to Mary Jonas back in London that "he will not try to learn what is needed for the work & I can't afford too much time checking every tiny detail which is what it comes to—let alone the discomfort of the antagonism to any criticism of the work."[28] Amice later told James Breasted that Beazley was "unable to become efficient in the work and bitterly resented any criticism, and for <u>this</u> reason the situation became impossible. . . ."[29] In the end, his fragile ego forced him out of the work. To the relief of both Myrtle and Amice, he left of his own accord, and Amice didn't have to pay him for the rest of the season. Myrtle then moved down to his newly opened room. It was divided into two spaces, so she had a bedroom and a sitting room. Although it was a much larger room, she missed the privacy and coziness of the tower. Nannie liked that Myrtle was on the main floor now, though, because the stairs had been hard for her to climb several times a day to clean or bring tea.[30] They also had at least one guest room, a dining room, a kitchen, a sitting room, and more.

At the start of their second season, December 1930, Myrtle was excited to go to Luxor again. Both Amice and Myrtle needed to visit Chicago House to learn their "methods & processes."[31] Amice had requested this help so they could make color copies just like the ones Chicago was making at Medinet Habu.[32] The chief artist at Chicago House "very kindly showed us all his methods & gave us quite a lot of useful hints, & we got quite a lot of information about retouching photos so we feel our visit was not a waste of time."[33]

They got to stay in the Chicago House. Built in 1924, the dig house was a large, sprawling institute on the West Bank in Thebes, nestled in farmland and tucked behind the Colossi of Memnon. By 1930, Old Chicago House was too small to fit everyone, and construction of a new one began on the East Bank. The new house, completed by 1931 and moved into by 1932, had seventy rooms and a full staff, including a librarian.[34] Both Old and New Chicago Houses were always busy and bustling, not at all like the rural house at Abydos. Myrtle told her parents that life at Chicago House was "very formal & polite & we are feeling a little overwhelmed . . ."[35] The two women laughed at the metal furniture in their room, painted to look like wood and wicker. "Of course," Myrtle admitted, "it is really excellent for the climate as the white ants cannot eat it; but it is so awful to have it made to so exactly imitate wood, even to grooving & turning . . ."[36] When the women finished their Luxor work, they returned to their small Abydos house. Myrtle wrote to her mother, "We do not at all regret the grandeurs of Chicago house, it is really a branch of the university & not a camp at all . . ." They had clearly become homebodies and preferred their time at Abydos.[37]

Getting to Work

In Egypt, the sun has always brought the new day. Rising deep red in the east, Khepri, Re, Atum—the sun—travels its path across the deep blue sky. The Aten—the light that emanates from the sun—cuts across the cultivation and the Nile, both of which allowed those in the land of the living to prosper in the otherwise harsh desert. The sun's path takes twelve hours of the day. At the end of the long day, the sun dies in the west, ready to rejuvenate through the Amduat, the twelve hours of the night, only to be reborn and rise again the next day.

Each day, Myrtle woke up thinking she knew, in general, what to expect. She was hardly wrong. A typical day for Myrtle and Amice began before the sun had been reborn on the eastern horizon. They were usually up at 5:30, sometimes earlier depending on the heat, for breakfast at the house at 6:00, which Nannie would have ready for them so they could eat quickly. After breakfast, the women would mount their donkeys to make their way across the sand, riding almost a mile, to the chapels in the Temple of Seti I to settle into work by 7:00 A.M. Hunched over drafting tables, they worked carefully, tracing lines on photographs, filling in the blanks, and getting the colors just right. After a few years being stooped over a table, Myrtle finally thought to bring an easel with her from England so she could work standing up when she felt like it. They often worked with bowls of water next to them so they could cool their hot, cramped hands.

At noon, their donkeys were summoned so they could ride back to the house for lunch and rest. By the time they finished eating, it would be too hot to work in the temple for a few hours. There was no point trying, anyway; the temperature could get so high their pencils would smudge. The air inside the temple usually cooled down enough in the afternoons (November through March) and they would return to work around 3:00 and work until dinner, around 6:00 or 7:00. If it was still too hot to be at the temple (April and May) they would take care of tasks around the house, washing clothes, writing letters, paying workers, and, of course, tending to ill or injured patients. Some days they used the engine in the temple to work in the cool of the evening by powering electric light and having their dinner there. Myrtle was a little disconcerted by the evening work, writing to her mother, "Abdullah brought our supper down to the temple & we sat among the columns and eat omeletes [*sic*], bread & butter & chocolate mould. our [*sic*] white robed servants waiting on us like attendant priests. it [*sic*] was a weird scene."[38]

On market days—their usual days off—they would sleep in and have breakfast at 8:00 instead of 6:00. On these days, they would have a lot of time to write letters and do other personal errands. On Fridays, the holy day for Muslims, Amice let the men have an hour to go pray in the morning. They found a rhythm on each day and throughout each season. As Myrtle told her parents, "Every day is perfect, yet every day is different."[39]

In the middle of the first December she spent on-site, they had a day quite unlike any other. They woke up to a real sandstorm. Myrtle couldn't open her windows, not that there was anything to see but driving sand, and there was no way they were going to the temple. So they set about doing their house chores, all the while listening to the wind and sand beat against the shutters. Myrtle called herself the general handyman of the house, so she got to work mending some clothes and bedding. Amice asked her to make a case for a camera lens out of a kid glove. Hugh asked her to help him mount a map. It wasn't an exciting day, and the next day, they were able to go work in the temple.

While the sandstorm was over, its remnants were everywhere. They swept off the surfaces that were covered in sand, which was all of them, and got to work. It was a week until Christmas, so the weather had cooled off enough that the women could take their break after lunch sunbathing on the sand instead of hiding in the shade. As they walked around, looking for a good spot to lie down, Myrtle spotted a strange hole in the sand. They looked at each other—could it be they actually found something? They immediately started removing the sand from the mouth of the hole. They were shocked to find a mud-brick wall inside the cavity. By the time the women had cleared part of the pit's entry, it was time to go back to work. They made a quick rock cairn marker and returned to the temple.

After work, they found Ahmed—he was the first person they thought of. Myrtle knew that Ahmed had been digging at Abydos since he was "big enough to carry a basket," so he would have been the most experienced digger on-site. They took him out to the cairn and showed him where they had dug. Ahmed went inside. After some time—Amice and Myrtle wondered if he'd gotten crushed—he came out, slightly dusty but excited to inform them that there were the remains of a man in the hole. It turned out to be a Roman-era burial, common for the area, but exciting for everyone on-site, especially, wrote Myrtle, for "old" Ahmed. She intimated to her parents that, on top of their copying project, she and Amice might apply for an excavation permit. They didn't.[40]

In their seemingly mundane work, they were rarely short of adventures. When Myrtle arrived back on-site for the beginning of the third season in November 1931, the women set up work in the Amun chapel again as though they had never left. Amice was on a tall scaffold they named "George Rex," and Myrtle was on a shorter one, lower to the ground, who was "just plain George." They had a lot of details to fix in their photograph tracings, and were in the chapel for the next several weeks.

In the monotony of the days, Myrtle wrote to her parents that the sparrows in the Amun chapel were "very chirpy."[41] One day in early December, as they worked over their tables, they got an unplanned break. There was a "terriffic [*sic*] sparrow fight in the temple this morning . . ." Myrtle told her parents that

> *a party of birds who live in Osiris chapel came into Amon's chapel where we are working & said rude things to the sparrows who live there. there <u>was</u> a haroosh you have no idea the noise & commotion 8 small spaggers can make, they completely upset our work for about 10 minutes, we could'nt [sic] hear each other speak. I think Amon's sparrows were victorious & drove the intruders out & possibly continued the battle else where.*[42]

By March, however, Myrtle was firmly on the side of the Osiris sparrows. Amice and Myrtle had tamed the birds with crumbs in the morning after their breakfasts. They brought crumbs most days, but on April 1, 1932, crisis was averted only with Sardic's help. Both Amice and Myrtle had forgotten their crumbs for Mr. and Mrs. S (the sparrows). Mrs. S approached Myrtle by landing on the table that held her paints. She "looked all round for crumbs, she was dreadfully upset when she could not find any & she gave me such a look of reproach that I felt I ought to creep away & hide. . . . Amice was also crumbless. We felt so badly about it that we sent Sardic to see if he could buy a loaf of bread . . ." He did, and when he returned, Mr. and Mrs. S "were overjoyed and had a feast."[43] The copying they did was tedious most days, while at the same time being physically draining, so these bird games kept them busy.

Visitors and Hospital Parades

On top of feeding the birds, Myrtle and Amice entertained several visitors over the years. Sometimes their friends and family came to visit, or they put up scholars from other sites. Other times, it was tourists, cruisers, and strangers. Everyone who came was hosted at the dig house.

The women gladly gave friends and colleagues a place to stay, had special meals cooked, and gave them tours of the temples, the desert, the village, and more. Several Egyptologists came to visit, and Myrtle and Amice were happy to show off their work. The Bruntons, the Newberrys, and Belgian Egyptologist Jean Capart came to visit, and they showed them all of their drawings. A General Wilson and his wife came from Luxor, so they got a picnic, and the women introduced them to sand sloping, which was like sledding but on sand instead of snow.[44]

When Amice was gone in January 1929, a General Gordon and a Major Anderson came to visit. They had been on a steamer voyage up and down the Nile. When their steamer arrived, Myrtle joined them for dinner on the boat, and the next day they came to the site to see the work. The project saw several Chicago visitors over the years, including a few visits from James Breasted, and the artist Nina de Garis Davies from Chicago House also came to do some work with the women in their space, whom they were very happy to have.[45]

Fig. 6.4: Mary Jonas, Myrtle Broome, and Amice Calverley.

Mary Jonas came to visit the women on-site for Christmas 1929 on her first visit to Egypt, ten years after she had taken over from Emily Paterson as the EES General Secretary.[46] She and Amice had been writing back and forth for months, and they continued to do so as part of their jobs with the Society, but they became very close friends during Mary's visit. Mary wrote to Alan Gardiner, confirming everything Amice and Myrtle had written about Beazley: "There are of course frictions & troubles here—& I'm afraid Beazley is by no means a congenial member of the party . . . [Amice] & Miss Broome get on well & are working hard but the men scarcely pull their weight . . ."[47] With evidence mounting against Beazley, Gardiner allowed Amice to choose her own staff from then on. Myrtle and Amice missed Mary once she left, but in the off seasons they often visited the Society offices and were able to stay in touch with her both there and through their letters.

Toward the end of their first season of work together, they

welcomed several important visitors, but maybe none so important as Amice's fiancé. In March of 1930, Myrtle wrote to her parents that they had as visitors a doctor and his wife, and, at the same time, "another doctor who is Miss C's prospective fiancé."[48] But she also noted that Amice was not in a hurry to get married, and "in fact has done her best to avoid it so far."[49] Gardiner, the technical director of the survey and the editor of the published volumes of artwork, was also dreading the prospect. If Amice got married, she would likely move back to England and end her career as the best copyist in Egypt. Myrtle had told her parents that Gardiner had mentioned that, if Amice did get married and did leave, Myrtle would take over being the director of the project. She had run the project herself a time or two while Amice was away in Cairo, but Myrtle didn't know if she could do it on her own, full-time, or if she even wanted to.

It turned out that they shouldn't have worried. No one liked the man. Not even Amice. Myrtle wrote to her parents that even Nannie hated him "with a venom truly oriental, her feelings are shared by Sardic."[50] It was Amice's aunt who was trying to set the two up, as he had money and position, but Amice had been trying to break it off for years. On March 15, Myrtle told her parents that Amice had finally broken up with him for good. Two weeks later, Amice began a letter to Mary Jonas, writing "I got engaged to that man & then found that it was impossible & have broken it off— there was something very queer about the whole thing but I'll tell you when I see you again . . ."[51] Both Amice and Myrtle believed that he had been controlling her through hypnotism. He had been bragging "of being able to control people by hypnotic influence & make them obey him without them knowing anything about it."[52] Amice had to escape to Alexandria in case he came looking for her on-site, because she knew she had to avoid him at all costs. Once the relationship was over, Amice safely returned to Abydos and was very happy to get back to work—even work interrupted.

The tourists who arrived on-site got to be so difficult on Fridays that Myrtle called them "one of the plagues of Egypt," but she wondered if "perhaps they have the same opinion of us."[53] As Cook's steamers came through, everyone was of the opinion that the tourists aboard them were not nice and left nothing of merit in their wake. Not all tourists were nameless, though. In March of 1930, around the same time as her fiancé came to visit, Amice wrote to Mary about the "epidemic of Queens" that they suffered. First, the queen of Romania, then the queen of the Belgians came to visit.[54] In 1933, the king and queen of Italy got a VIP tour, but they were some of the lucky ones.[55]

In 1931, the women decided they would stop welcoming all visitors without question, due to two troublesome groups of visitors. The first group consisted of a Professor Oliver and his wife, her sister, and a friend. Myrtle and Amice didn't know them at all. They were all over the age of sixty-five and had no interest in seeing or learning about the temple, but at the same time they expected to be put up for several days without paying for anything. It was too much work for Nannie and Sardic, and it took resources and time from the women.[56] Their last group of tourist visitors that year had what Myrtle called some "pretty cool cheek." There were four of them asking to be put up for two nights. Amice suggested they should ask at the Antiquities Rest House, but apparently the Antiquities Department didn't allow rest stays for nonarchaeologists. In an attempt to be good hosts, on market day, the women bought chickens, mutton, eggs, tomatoes, lentils, oranges, and more so they could make their stay a comfortable one. The party consisted of "a very dull uninteresting lot of youngish people" who ended up taking rooms away from some of Myrtle and Amice's friends. The situation became very uncomfortable when one of the group

> said to Amice "I suppose you have a hospitality grant" I am afraid we all stared in amazement. & Amice said "Oh no, the society provides us with everything necessary for the work, but all such extras have to come out of my pocket." I dont know exactly what reply they made to that, but the subject was quickly changed.[57]

What did change on-site was that after that, they refused to host people they either didn't know (or weren't famous) or weren't associated with Chicago House, the Society, or other Egyptologists. The women were tired of playing host when their male counterparts on other sites weren't expected to do so.

Flinders Petrie wasn't known for his hospitality. In his auto-biography, he recalled of Abydos that it was "not a happy place as regards the people."[58] Amice and Myrtle had seen evidence of this when they had some issues with certain area residents not wanting them there. As early as 1931, the British Ministry of the Interior was writing to the women and warning them of "a great deal of distress and unemployment in the provinces, and although we hope there will be no troubles or hunger-riots, one cannot be sure of the future."[59] They had some protection from local police, and nothing major happened while they were there.

Memory, however, leaves a long legacy. While Petrie tended not to comment on the social or political issues in Egypt, he frequently told of the problems some of his workers had with theft and dishon-esty. He recollected that one day, sometime in the 1902–3 season,

> one of my men fell ill; I gave an order that he should be sent off at once to his home, but they concealed the case and left him till he was much worse. I then sent him home, by three or four men who carried him. Unhappily he died at home. Then the doctor came down on the family to inquire—this is what an Egyptian dreads more than death itself. He said that unless they paid him five pounds he would record the case as murder, and they had to raise the money.
>
> I reported the matter to Surgeon-Major Gallwey. He or-dered a native inquiry, and they concluded that the man had died from the fall of a wall upon him in his work. I at once requested that the reporters should be prosecuted for per-jury, but nothing was done. Whenever accusations are made against an Egyptian, his only idea is to invent some story which will throw blame on the accuser.[60]

It is interesting to note that he recalled the perceived wrong done to him but not the fact that he didn't offer to help his digger in any way, except to have him sent home. It was very different when women ran sites.

When women were in charge on sites in the early twentieth century, or even if women were simply present on-site, tourists and

Egyptians who lived nearby would often come to them for help
with just about anything, but especially matters of health or injury.
This was clearly a gendered expectation of women who came to
Egypt, and most of the women working in the field at this time
represented an element of care for others. Usually Europeans and
Americans had access to treatment methods that Egyptians did not,
or they brought with them a medicine cabinet full of ointments and
pills that could help better than what was locally available. Going to
a doctor or hospital was often too expensive for them, they had to
travel too far away, they didn't think the doctor could help them, or
they faced a combination of these issues. Sometimes injuries were
sustained during the workday and needed to be treated immediately.
Many times it was a family member of a worker or nearby resident
who needed treatment. Myrtle and Amice continued the tradition
of treating others, and they called theirs the "hospital parade."

Most mornings began with the hospital parade, according to
Myrtle's letters home to her parents. They treated common ailments
of cuts and minor infections, and sometimes had serious burns
to treat. The first patient Myrtle wrote home about visited them
around two weeks after they had arrived at the house in 1929. As
they were off to work early in the morning, a girl of fifteen arrived
with her baby. She needed treatment for a wound on her breast that
was not healing. It looked to Amice and Myrtle that the baby had
bitten the girl while she was feeding, but nothing was done about it.
The cut got infected, and now the young mother was in a lot of pain,
making it hard to feed her baby. Myrtle and Amice saw that this
was beyond their skill level, and they didn't have the supplies to do
the procedure. They thought the infection needed to be lanced and
drained, so they sent her to the hospital, eleven miles away, where
there would be a doctor with the right tools to help her. Myrtle told
her mother that the girl almost cried about going to the doctor—
she was afraid and she probably couldn't afford treatment. It isn't
clear if she got treated by anyone or not, but in the end, it seems, the
infection healed. Later on that same day, a man arrived with a "nasty
cut" on his shin that was five days old. He had been walking around
with it uncovered for that long, and it had gathered dust and flies
and likely an infection. Myrtle washed out the open wound with

"lysol water put hot boracic lint on & bound it up." He came back the next day for another washing and a clean dressing.[61]

Their common treatments included Lysol, which they sometimes diluted and other times applied directly to the infection, and Epsom salts. Lysol had been in use for forty years by this point as an antiseptic liquid, so washing wounds in the disinfectant was a common practice. It worked so well that during the 1918 Spanish flu pandemic, it had been used as a strong antiviral measure. The Epsom salts, Myrtle told her parents, were also available for purchase in the village, but their patients would argue that "what we give them has greater power—so we dole out Epsom & get much credit there by."[62] The women treated men, women, and children of all ages. Theirs may have been the only medical treatment many women in the area received.[63] The ointments, disinfectants, and bandages Myrtle and Amice brought with them and used on their neighbors were not available in Egypt at the time, at least not to Egyptians, so it seemed like they were working some strange magic. When someone would be cured (or successfully treated), family members would come back more often, expecting the same result for other ailments.

Starting the morning with a hospital parade, and continuing a cycle of care for several days or weeks, including the invisible and emotional labor of helping and caring for people, impacted the amount of time they could spend working. Amice and Myrtle worried about their patients and would frequently check up on them. They connected with their patients on such a level that they received gifts and invitations to meals, teas, and weddings. Because of these personal connections, women integrated themselves more into the field than men did. But even in the field, women couldn't escape domestic labor. Margaret Murray had long lines of people waiting for her after her long day of work. She successfully treated the dreaded ophthalmia (eye infection) in almost everyone. Emma Andrews wanted everyone to have the option for treatment, so instead of tending to people herself, she became a patron of a local hospital. Myrtle and Amice, as far as we know, treated everyone so successfully that some of their practices influenced Egyptian doctors.

The Temple of King Sethos I at Abydos: Volumes I–IV

After the first season, 1929–30, Amice and Myrtle both made their way back to Bushey, as though they were sisters going home after a holiday. They were looking forward to relaxing while also getting a little work done. Amice was very welcome at the Broome home and stayed with Myrtle and her parents for several weeks while finishing up some of the drawings from the season. Not very close to her own parents, Amice clearly connected with Ma and Pa Broomie, as she called them, and they shared a fondness for each other.

Despite all the visitors and travel and personal issues, sparrow problems and Egyptian politics, the women were set on their work. Their main goal was to make a complete and accurate copy of the art on the walls, columns, and ceilings of the Temple of Seti I at Abydos. The second season (1930–31) and third season (1931–32) were just as busy with visitors—this time known to either or both women or dignitaries of some kind—and copying. By mid-April 1931, Amice reported to James Breasted at the Institute that the women were "still hard at work on the colour," and, even though they felt in a rush, she thought the plates were "looking rather fine . . ." She continued, explaining, ". . . we have done 6 simple scenes & 1 large scene with the second barque. I hope to get 3 more scenes done before I leave, which I expect will be in the middle of May."[64] She and Myrtle worked, as usual, quickly and accurately.

The first volume of *The Temple of King Sethos I at Abydos* was published in 1933. It was printed in a large quarto format and measured almost two feet long and eighteen inches wide. It contained copies of three of seven chapels that made up the innermost temple: the chapels of Osiris, Isis, and Horus. The second volume comprised the other four chapels: those of Amun-Re, Re-Harakhti, Ptah, and Seti, and was published in 1935.[65] Both of these were very well received, due to both the high publication quality of the color plates and, mostly, the excellent reproductions. Both Alan Gardiner (the Society director of the project, but not the real, on-the-ground director that Amice was) and James Breasted thought that the temple required eight folio volumes of plates, along with several smaller volumes of text, explaining the history, context, and importance of the temple and its art. Whatever the temple may have required, the project never reached its completion.

In December 1935, the Egyptology world learned of the death of James Breasted. His sudden death from a strep infection at the age of seventy would change the landscape—both literally and figuratively—of Egyptology for the rest of the twentieth century. Then, due partly to James's death, the funding from the Rockefeller Foundation dried up, so Myrtle and Amice both left Egypt in 1937. Thanks to Rockefeller's careful budgeting, the project had somehow lasted through the first eight years of the Great Depression, but he just couldn't guarantee the money anymore. To add to the turmoil was the fact that everyone was anticipating another European war. After the 1936–37 season, Myrtle would leave Egypt, never to return. Her father was ill, and her mother needed her help at home. They both died within a few years.

Amice, meanwhile, had very few domestic concerns, so she moved to Toronto and continued working on the drawings for publication. Myrtle helped as she could, and was invaluable as an expert in the color and copy work. The two women visited each other when possible, maintaining their friendship across an ocean. In 1938, the third volume presented the Osiris Complex, which, on the site, is situated directly behind the seven chapels published in the first two volumes. The introduction to this volume noted:

> The execution of the work has, as hitherto, lain almost entirely on the shoulders of Miss Calverley and Miss Broome, of whom the former had, in addition, charge of the entire organization, was responsible for the running of the camp, devised down to the last detail the methods employed and personally carried out nearly all the photography.[66]

After this volume was published, World War II stopped all Egyptology fieldwork. There is little evidence of Myrtle's activities during the war. Amice, on the other hand, became a volunteer for several civil defense organizations. She was commissioned by the Royal Air Force for some detailed photography analysis, and some even say she was a spy in Cairo. Intelligence wouldn't have been out of the ordinary for someone with her experience in the country and who spoke Arabic fairly well, but Amice was in England for much of the war.

Right after the war was over, Rockefeller immediately reinstated all his funding for several projects, including the Epigraphic Survey in Chicago and the Society project for the Seti temple. He gave $17,000 more to the project to complete fourth and fifth volumes of plates. Amice returned to the project and to Egypt, with a new colleague, a Miss Collins, but Myrtle stayed home.

While she worked on the copies for the temple over her final few seasons, Amice also had an idea for a film. She took depictions of ancient life off the walls of the Seti I temple at Abydos and compared them to scenes of real modern life in Egypt. She tried to show how life in Egypt was quaint and provincial, simple and unchanging, almost ancient.

As she worked on the film, in September of 1948, John Wilson, then Associate Director of Chicago's Institute, wrote to Amice in Toronto that she "should clear with the Egyptian Consul the question of your previous film. In the Egyptian state of mind of today, it is important to get from him a full and final approval of the film you have already taken, so that there may be no question about future work."[67] One month later, she and Wilson spoke on the phone, and he took notes about their call. He wrote in his notes that, among other issues, Amice was "very provoked" with the "sniping at her films, with criticism that they are anti-Egyptian.... [S]he never received a written approval from the Egyptian consul in NY, and he is now back in Egypt. I promised her that I would go into writing in approval of her film project if she needed that."[68]

She arrived in Egypt safely for that season in 1948, and wrote as much to the Institute on November 20. John Wilson and others worried about her safety due to growing tensions in Mandate Palestine. But the next correspondence that exists to John Wilson is from Amice on December 22, 1948: "I wish to inform you that there has been some trouble with regard to my work at Abydos and that orders have been issued from the Antiquities Dept via Rachid Nowaer Bey, Chief Inspector of Middle Egypt, and the local Inspector, Aziz Morkos Eff[endi]. to the effect that I am to discontinue working on the Survey of the Temple.... The exact reasons for this action I am not aware of . . ."[69] It had nothing to do with Palestine. Instead, the news had come down from the Antiquities Department on December 18 in a letter that she was only able to read on the following day. In the end, she told John that she understood that "the cause behind this lies in the difficulties recently raised on the subject-matter of the cine-films I took during the past 2 seasons . . ."[70]

Amice was stunned. She explained to the Institute that she had been given permission to make the film and that the Egyptian Consul-General in New York had viewed and censored it, but the problem lay with him: he hadn't censored the film properly. She tried to explain that the project wasn't done yet, and she wanted the chance to finish it.[71] She argued that both the American and British embassies should be helping to get her back into the country to finish both her film and the work on the temple, but each of them disagreed in their own ways, though for similar reasons. The Foreign Office of Britain described it as such in April 1949: "The object of this film—to draw comparisons between ancient and modern rural life—is unfortunately offensive to Egyptian susceptibilities."[72] In the end, she offered to resign to save the expedition's reputation, but her resignation was rejected, at first.

John Wilson responded to Amice's long statement of defense of herself and her project and her request for the Institute to step in. He wrote to her on February 22, 1949:

> We are living in the middle of the 20th Century and not at the beginning of that Century. Egypt is a sovereign nation and has a sovereign right to make and enforce its own rules for international affairs whether those rules conform to the highest moral principles or not. Intervention of any other country into the international affairs of Egypt might be temporarily successful, but it would be followed by such resentment on the part of Egypt that the temporary victory would probably be a long run defeat.[73]

In other words, John could have possibly helped her but chose not to because the Institute still had work to do in Egypt. In the end, after much diplomatic maneuvering, she was denied entry into the country and was forced to work on volume 4 at home. She never went back.

The fourth, and final, volume was finally published in 1958 and presents the second hypostyle hall.[74] The introduction to this last volume talks about the issues that war and personal loss caused for both Myrtle and Amice and how the volume was delayed because of them. There was no mention of the difficulties with the film. One Miss Winifred Needler of the Royal Ontario Museum in Toronto, where Amice now lived and worked, made a "special visit to Abydos in the spring of 1956 to check certain details which needed confirmation."[75] There was anticipation of at least two more volumes, with Amice working on volume 5, "made possible by the continued generosity of Mr. Rockefeller."[76]

Amice died in Toronto in 1959, and efforts to continue publishing any more of these huge, and hugely expensive, volumes died with her. Currently only the four volumes exist. Most Egyptologists agree it would be impossible today to continue to publish any drawings, partly because of the expense, but mostly because they were the "most magnificent produced by the Society" due to the expertise and talent of Amice and Myrtle.[77]

There is some evidence that the fifth volume made it to the proof stage, meaning that there are, or were, actual printed pages that were sent out to several different scholars in the hopes that someone could work on the volume. In December of 1964, Herbert Fairman reported to the Institute that all materials were in the hands of the press and that he expected the proofs very soon.[78] By February 1966, all photographic work was completed and the proofs were picked up at Lime Street Station in Liverpool that March. It isn't clear what happened, but the proofs sat on one desk after another, with complaints of busyness and lack of time by several people, including T. G. H. James and Harry Smith. By the end of 1971, the project was dropped. No more volumes were ever produced.[79]

Myrtle died in 1978, having lived the rest of her years in England, quietly. There was no mention of Myrtle in the Egyptological community when she died, but Amice received a four-page obituary in the *Journal of Egyptian Archaeology*, thanks mostly to her cousin who wrote it.[80]

"Farewell to Seti I, Abydos"

Caroline Ransom Williams arrived at Abydos with Dr. Harold Nelson on January 26, 1936. She had been told about what the young women working for Chicago House and the Society had done with the Temple of Seti I using the methods she had developed ten years earlier. She was happy to get to meet the women working on this important project. She got the feeling Miss Broome thought she was too old to be there, so she shared the story of how in 1925 she had brought her own mother, who was seventy-nine at the time, with her to Egypt. She smiled as she recounted the adventures they had had back then. Myrtle seemed comforted by the stories, and even told her own parents "so you see there is still time for you."[81] Amice knew who Caroline was, and what she had done for the Epigraphic Survey; Myrtle never really remembered her name, but that was okay. Caroline was impressed by their skill and promised them she would purchase both of their volumes for her already massive Egyptology library back in Toledo, Ohio.

At Christmastime the following season, Amice knew it was their last for the foreseeable future, so she penned a poem to say goodbye. Like Amice's heart, it was full of sadness, but also hope. For most of the previous ten years they had lived at and with and in Abydos. Amice wanted to leave a door open, for Seti to return to her.

> Seti, the Beloved of Ptah,
> It's ten long years we've lived together
> And now I'm leaving you for ever—
> Shall I see you where you are
> (In Osiris' kingdom) when I'm dead?
> And will you know that you were wed
> To a last and foreign wife,
> Who gave you ten years of her life?
> —Or is all thought of life too far
> Departed, Seti-Mer-n-Ptah?
>
> Mer-n-Ptah and Men-Maat-Rē,
> Did your Ka partake each day

Of our small lunch, and think how strange
The offerings were? May happy the change,
Both in the food and in the priests,
Delighted you; for your stone feasts
Must have got very dull and trying
After three thousand years of drying!
And perhaps a little breath
Of life is pleasant after death?

And when I thought myself alone,
And filled your silent Halls with song,
Did your royal shadow walk among
The echoes?—which were caught and thrown
As though the gods upon the wall
Played with the sound, as with a ball
Until, so joyous was the ringing,
I caught again my voice while singing
And sang in canon!
    Surely then your ghost came near,
    Listening unseen that you might hear
    The curious praises that I sing
    To you, Beloved-of-Ptah, the King?

And now it seems I'll come no more,
Nor hymn your beauty as I draw—
Forsaking you, and sun, and sand,
For a grey and chilly land—
But is the Under-World so far
From England, Seti-Mer-n-Ptah?
Could you not come and take a look
At your great temple in our book,
And see again your wife one day
—In England—Seti-Mer-Maat-Rē? [82]

7

Caroline Ransom Williams

She is certainly an example to us of enthusiasm and application and will be of the greatest value to the work. I am delighted to have her here and expect to learn a great deal from her.

—Harold Nelson to James Breasted, December 3, 1926

In the autumn of 1910, Caroline Louise Ransom walked through New York's leafy Central Park. It was a warm day in early October, but she was glad there was finally relief from the rain. She was trying to figure out the quickest way from her new rooms in the Beresford building at 81st Street and Central Park West to her new job on the east side of the park at Fifth Avenue, between 79th and 85th Streets: the Metropolitan Museum of Art. Yesterday, she had tried entering the park at 79th Street, right in front of the American Museum of Natural History, taking the smaller sidewalks through the park. The quiet that enveloped her as soon as she crossed into the park, where she was surrounded by trees and grass and birds, made her feel like she wasn't even in the city, but the smaller sidewalks that wound through the park could be confusing. She eventually found her way to the museum, but she wanted a quicker path. Today, she walked along the brand-new transverse road that went straight across the park from West 79th Street and came out at Fifth Avenue on the east side of the park and the south side of the museum. Getting there couldn't have been easier for her that day. Getting to that point in her career had been a bit tougher.

As Caroline walked through the front doors of the museum at the Fifth Avenue entrance, she entered the cavernous, classical-style Great Hall. Just twenty years after Amelia Edwards and Kate Bradbury had visited, the museum had changed a lot. It had gone from the not-quite-large-enough building with a red brick façade and banded-granite pointed arches in 1890 to one with several extensions faced with limestone in 1910. In the early days, the Great Hall not only welcomed visitors but also housed a number of classical statues, which made it seem even more crowded. The growing collection was just what Caroline was there to help with.[1]

She was on her way to work in the relatively new Egyptian Art Department under the leadership of the previous curator of the Boston Museum of Fine Arts, Albert Lythgoe. The department was in the process of moving into the newly built Wing E, thanks to the money and leadership of banking giant J. P. Morgan.[2] She looked straight ahead as she entered the Great Hall and could see down the corridor, just to the right of the staircase, where the Egyptian collection had been displayed for the last six years.[3] There were still a few pieces in there, but most of it was now in the much larger space to the north of the hall. As she stood there, she looked around at all the people streaming through the doors, on their way to see priceless pieces of art. She wondered if she could even make a dent in this world. All she knew for certain was that she wanted to do more research where her expertise lay—Egyptian art—and this job would let her do that. Caroline took a deep breath and, quickly and confidently, headed through the passage that would take her to her new life.[4]

Almost forty years old but relatively new to the field, Caroline had applied for the assistant curator job earlier that year by simply writing a letter to Albert Lythgoe in late March. She told him that she was tired of her heavy teaching load and administrative duties. Just five years after earning her doctoral degree, she had become associate professor and chair of the Department of the History of Art and Classical Archaeology at the women's college in Bryn Mawr, Pennsylvania. She liked her department and the work she was doing, but she wanted more time for her own academic work. She told him that she was also thinking about caring for her aging mother and needed time to do that, too. In the return post, much to her surprise and delight, he offered her a position as assistant curator. This really should have come as no surprise to her. She was one of only a few people in the United States, not to mention the rest of the world, that had her academic pedigree and expertise.

There was a lot for her to give up at Bryn Mawr, but she was excited about the new opportunity in New York. There was also the matter of Grant Williams. What would she do about Grant? The real estate developer from her hometown of Toledo, Ohio, had been trying to marry her for, oh, she couldn't remember how long. She had put him off for years, but she knew she just had to try this first. Studious and fiercely independent, she felt she needed to prove, to herself, to Grant, to everyone, that she could run a curatorial department and write worthwhile scholarship.

In the six brief years Caroline worked at the Metropolitan Museum as a full-time assistant curator, alongside Lythgoe and other assistant curators Herbert Winlock and Arthur Mace, she published eleven articles, countless museum pamphlets, and a book. She acquired thousands of objects from Egypt and rebuilt an entire tomb bought and sent from Egypt, brick by brick, near the entrance to Wing E. Even though she was an *assistant* curator, she was arguably responsible for keeping the Egyptian Art Department afloat when Albert Lythgoe was gone for months at a time on excavation; he

Fig. 7.1: Caroline Ransom, c. 1908.

usually brought Herbert and Arthur along. To this end, she was responsible for all correspondence coming through the department, as well as all labels for objects and figuring out their displays. Because of this, any Egyptologist working with or for the museum would have known her and worked with her, from the time of Emma Andrews. Caroline quickly became a central figure in early American Egyptology, and her work is still visible at the museum in the Tomb of Perneb, other objects she curated, and the articles she published.

It isn't clear why—possibly because of budget cuts due to World War I—but in late May 1916, Caroline's job at the museum ended. She agreed to marry Grant Williams in June of that same year, which meant she and her mother would have to move back to Toledo. Despite the fact that her domestic duties doubled overnight, caring for both her mother and her husband, Caroline continued with a few odd academic jobs in New York, Chicago, Ann Arbor, and Toledo. Grant made enough money for the three of them, so Caroline didn't have to work, but she wanted to stay involved in the professional community she helped to build. Like the way pigments on a temple wall fade over time, Caroline, this onetime cornerstone of the Egyptian Art Department, eventually disappeared from view.

Caroline Ransom was the culmination of all the women who came before her and whose stories lead to this point in time. She traveled; she was in the field; she was university educated; she taught, copied, and wrote; she was a museum curator at the center of a vast professional network. Her successful career was the legacy of all the women who had developed Egyptology as a professional pursuit for other women. Ransom left Bryn Mawr in 1910, before she could establish a visible academic lineage. She left the Metropolitan Museum of Art in 1916, before she could be promoted. She left New York for the last time in 1930, before she was truly done with her work. However, the books and articles she published on dozens of artifacts in the collection of the Egyptian Art Department at the Metropolitan Museum of Art and the New-York Historical Society introduced thousands of people to their priceless collections.

Her connections to other women, both the few who are well-known and the majority who are virtually unknown, demonstrate just how intertwined their lives and work were, and how they each made it possible for others like them to maintain their careers in what was, and often is still, a man's world. By building upon the work of previous generations, these women were living out the dreams of those who came before.

The Lake Erie Seminary and a Grand Tour

Caroline was born in Toledo, Ohio, on February 24, 1872, to middle-class parents who were prominent in their community. Her mother, Ella Agnes Randolph, as most women of her socioeconomic class did at the time, stayed at home while her father, John Ransom, sold dental and other surgical instruments.[5] Caroline went to a coeducational primary and secondary school, because Toledo was a larger city, and girls in late-nineteenth century American cities were often educated in public schools. Her parents made sure that she received a solid college preparatory education. In 1890, when she was eighteen, she attended Lake Erie Seminary (now Lake Erie College), a women's college in Painesville, Ohio, about 150 miles from Toledo. It was the sister institution to Mount Holyoke Seminary in Massachusetts, on whose model Lake Erie was based.

At first, and when Caroline attended the leafy campus in 1890, the curriculum was focused on the liberal arts and had a heavy emphasis on domestic training for women. Knowing she was being funneled into a position she didn't want quite yet—or maybe ever—Caroline left Lake Erie after a semester.[6] She then accompanied her aunt, Louise Fitz-Randolph, who was professor of art history at Mount Holyoke, on a Grand Tour of Europe for the next two years. It is probable that Caroline had heard of Amelia and Kate from her aunt Louise, who must have met them when they were in South Hadley, Massachusetts, at the end of January 1890. Maybe she wrote to her niece, who she knew wanted to know more about Egypt and art history, urging Caroline to see this knowledgeable woman speak. So, it is possible that Caroline attended Amelia Edwards's lecture in Toledo in February of 1890, or perhaps the lecture in Cleveland.

When she left for the Grand Tour, Caroline was eighteen, and according to her passport application, she was five feet four inches tall with blue eyes (and glasses) and a fair complexion. She was also ready for a little adventure outside her comfort zone. Even before Lucie Duff Gordon's travels in the mid-nineteenth century, the Grand Tour was a popular rite of passage for well-to-do Europeans. For Americans of higher status, this didn't become an expectation until the late nineteenth and early twentieth centuries. Young people, both men and women, typically visited London, Paris, Venice, and Rome, with a number of small towns in between. Often, especially around the 1890s, the trips would extend into Egypt. If you claimed to have gone on a Grand Tour but said you didn't go to Egypt, people would wonder if you went anywhere at all.[7] Other than her passport application and some things she mentioned in a letter to a later mentor, James Breasted, there are scant details on where Caroline and her aunt went. It is clear that they did go to Egypt for a brief period, and the trip, maybe combined with Amelia's lectures, inspired her to study the ancient world and its art. When they returned home after almost two years abroad, Caroline stayed in South Hadley to study. Not wanting her to be too far from home, her parents may have let her stay there due to her aunt Louise being at Mount Holyoke.

In 1896, she completed her BA in art history, graduating Phi Beta Kappa from Mount Holyoke at the age of twenty-four. She had been active in campus groups, was the editor of the campus newspaper, *The Mount Holyoke,* and served on the executive committee of her class (1895–96).[8] After graduation, she moved back to Ohio to teach part-time at Lake Erie Seminary. Over the next few years of teaching, Caroline realized that in order to teach the way she wanted to, and the way she thought her students deserved, she needed to better understand the ancient Egyptian civilization and the scripts they used.

By the time she had formulated a plan, it was the end of January 1898. Caroline looked out her window at the start of a frigid Toledo Monday. The snow that had fallen before Christmas was still piled up where it had been shoveled off the walk. The next day wouldn't bring any reprieve. February 1 would be the coldest day of the whole winter. She tried to warm her chilled fingers as she put the finishing touches on what she thought might be the most important letter of her life, so she could get it in that day's post.

She was writing a letter to America's first university-trained Egyptologist, James Henry Breasted, brand-new assistant professor of Egyptology and assistant director of the Haskell Museum at the new University of Chicago. She expressed to him that she wanted to begin "such studies as will best fit me for original investigation in regards to the development of Ancient Art."[9] Her interest in Egyptian art, she wrote,

> *began with a general course in Art History, taken in the Spring of 1890 [at Lake Erie College]. I then went abroad for two years and besides study of the collections of Egyptian antiquities in the British Museum, the Louvre, the Museums of Berlin and Turin, I had the great privilege and pleasure of journeying to the First Cataract in Egypt and of spending several weeks in Cairo. In 1896, during my senior year in college [at Mount Holyoke], I again gave particular attention to Art History, beginning with Egyptian Art.*[10]

Her main aim, she stated in the letter, was to study classical archaeology and take a minor in Egyptology. The only place in the United States at the time that had anything like what she would need was Chicago, which was about 250 miles from her home.

Her letter to Breasted arrived as planned. Unfortunately, the fellowship application and all her letters of recommendation that were sent to college president William Rainey Harper never did. They were somehow misplaced—by either the university or the post, we will never know. In the end, through the intervention of Miss Mary Evans, the principal at Lake Erie Seminary, and James Breasted, Caroline Ransom was accepted to the program. She also received the fellowship she had applied for. This was the beginning of her long career in art history and Egyptology and her decades-long connection to the University of Chicago. It was also the beginning of her lifelong friendship with James Breasted. For her, James began as a supportive mentor and then went seamlessly from being her instructor to being a friend and colleague. He had a clear and deep respect for her, and she brought an intelligent, confident viewpoint in most matters that he always took to heart.

Chicago

Caroline arrived at the University of Chicago on the first of October 1898, after an academic summer probably spent in Berlin.[11] While at the university in the then-suburban Hyde Park district of Chicago, she studied mostly under Frank Tarbell in classical archaeology, but it is clear that a lot of her interest was in Egyptian archaeology and art. She completed her master's degree in classical archaeology and Egyptology in 1900 after two years of study. After that, James did for her what he would have for any of his exceptional male students. He encouraged her to go to the University of Berlin to study with his mentor, Adolf Erman, the well-known Egyptologist who had trained James. She gladly went and was in Berlin for the next three years. It was there that she undertook four semesters at the University of Berlin and worked in the Egyptian department at the Berlin Museum.

It was German custom to welcome students into your home, and the Ermans' home was always warm and inviting. While Caroline was the only woman in the group, she was always included at the "long supper table with its beer glasses, its plates of rye bread, cold sliced meats and sausages, and the games after supper in the garden below."[12] She and the Erman family soon developed a warm friendship. She often went on outdoor excursions with the family on Sundays, rowing in the Havel River or hiking through the hills, being pulled along by their black, curly-haired dog as it chased rabbits.[13]

During this time, she also traveled throughout Europe and the Middle East, including excursions to Crete and elsewhere in Greece, and again Egypt. She also visited the archaeological sites of Delphi and Troy. She shared her experiences and research with her aunt Louise, who then used Caroline's work in her classes and other presentations.[14] She didn't seem to write much to James Breasted during her three years in Berlin, save for a few letters early on, in which she asked James and Frances when they would arrive in the city and where they would like to meet for a visit.[15]

Caroline reluctantly returned to Chicago from Berlin in 1903. But she was ready to complete work on her PhD in history of art and Egyptology. Fresh from her training under Erman, she finished her degree in 1905, becoming the first American woman to earn the distinction.[16] Her dissertation, "Studies in Ancient Furniture," was published as a well-illustrated volume that same year by the University of Chicago Press, for which her parents paid the cost.[17] Her training and expertise were unmatched at the time, regardless of gender. There was no one in Egyptology in the United States with her academic pedigree, her skill level, or her scholarly connections.

Caroline was immediately offered a position as assistant professor in the department of History of Art and of Classical Archaeology at Bryn Mawr College in Pennsylvania, which she accepted. She taught at least five classes per year in Egyptian art and art history, on top of heavy administrative duties, but her focus always shifted to her research. To this end, in August of 1908, Caroline visited Chicago, both to see the Breasteds—including their eleven-year-old son Charles, of whom she was quite fond—and to work a bit in the collections they had at her alma mater. She was planning a sabbatical trip to Egypt for the spring of 1909 and was preparing for the research time. Surely she talked to her friend and mentor about her upcoming trip, and the two made plans so she would get the most out of her time in Egypt. Caroline had a few aims for the trip. She needed photographs for lantern slides, so she could show her students the places she was teaching them about. In addition, she wanted and needed to go there as a professional scholar so she could make those important professional connections. Her mother and aunt were joining her for the journey, so she also simply needed a vacation from the overwhelming duties she had taken on at Bryn Mawr.

Much like other trips to Egypt that women before her took, Caroline's time there was certainly the catalyst for a complete shift in her career and life's work. The three women arrived in Alexandria on February 8, and from there they sailed up the Nile as far as the Second Cataract. Caroline had wanted to go farther, into Sudan, as far as Khartoum, but they simply couldn't spare the time. When they were in Cairo, together they visited the west side of the Nile to see pyramids, from Abu Roash at the northern end down to Lisht, which marks the southern end of the pyramid field.

The three women also stayed for several weeks in Luxor, where they met with Albert Lythgoe, who had only been at the Metropolitan Museum for a few years after leaving his post at the Boston Museum of Fine Arts. Caroline may have met Albert before this trip—there weren't many Egyptologists in the United States at the time, and neither Boston nor New York City was that far from Bryn Mawr. It was probably here that Caroline got to know Albert and some of his other museum staff well, because he invited the whole group to the Kharga Oasis, about two hundred miles east of Luxor. There, they stayed with the Metropolitan camp during excavations. It may have been in Kharga that Albert told Caroline about the work needing to be done at the museum. Caroline didn't remark much about her time with the crew from the museum, but she told Frances Breasted that she was ready to get home and out of the coming summer heat of Egypt; the women left Egypt in June.

She accomplished her goal of getting photographs for slides. She took over 400 with her Kodak camera and more than 150 with a camera that produced five-by-seven-inch images. She also bought some slides in Egypt for her collection and borrowed slides from other scholars. In the end, she came home with over 800 lantern slides for her classes.[18] She obviously had the tools to spend the foreseeable future teaching. Her time in Egypt, much as it did for Amelia Edwards, Maggie Benson, and Emma Andrews, got Caroline thinking about taking her career in a different direction.

In early 1910, she had completed her sabbatical and had been back in Bryn Mawr for some months. By this time, Caroline had become the chair of her department, and her research had all but come to a standstill. She sat at her desk, looking around at the papers strewn all over it. None of them were even hers. They all belonged to students, and she still needed to grade them. She loved her students—connecting with them, mentoring them, and watching them learn about the topics she was an expert in. There was one student in particular who had caught her attention. Mary Hamilton Swindler's future was extremely promising, and Caroline wanted to be a mentor to her. At the same time, Caroline hated the fact that there were so many different things to do in her job—teach classes, advise students, attend meetings, administer the department—that she felt she couldn't get really good at any one thing. She just didn't have the time to do it all. On top of all of that, she was also caring for her aging mother, and she longed to do full-time research again.

After Albert Lythgoe offered her the job at the Metropolitan Museum as assistant curator, there were salary and situational negotiations to work out. She didn't want to make less money than she would have at Bryn Mawr, who had offered her about a 40 percent raise in salary, from $2,500 to $3,500, trying to keep her there.[19] The museum offered her only $2,000 at first. In the end, they negotiated for a salary that was amenable to both of them, but it isn't clear what her pay was. She later told James Breasted that she would be glad to be freed of the institutional financial worries that Bryn Mawr had, because the museum had the "means to look after its work without straits."[20] Before taking up her position in October 1910, she wanted to travel to Berlin for the summer to study hieroglyphs again with Erman. Her mother became suddenly ill, so they had to stay in Pennsylvania, where she was able to study the scripts on her own. In September, Caroline had a chance to visit the collections at the Reef, the home of Theodore Davis and Emma Andrews. It isn't clear if they were there when she went, but the pair didn't leave Newport for Egypt until the end of October that year, so this may have been the first time she made their acquaintance. After a well-deserved break during her relatively slow summer, she arrived at the museum on Fifth Avenue in October ready for work.

New York

The Beresford today is a famous historic building at 211 Central Park West in Manhattan. Constructed in 1929, it was placed on the National Register for Historic Places as part of the Central Park West Historic District in 1982. Some of its more well-known residents have included Helen Gurley Brown, Glenn Close, John McEnroe, and Jerry Seinfeld. Its apartments sell for between $2.5 million and $20 million today. The Hotel Beresford that Caroline Ransom and her mother lived in from 1910 to 1917 was a very different place than the current building. The hotel was demolished on that same spot in 1928.

Prime real estate today, the Hotel Beresford into which Caroline and Ella moved was built as an apartment-hotel building, which were popular in the early twentieth century for those who didn't want to deal with housekeeping, usually unmarried women or childless couples. There were no kitchens in the apartments, which rented for about $100 to $150 per month, so meals were meant to be taken in the dining room and cost $7 per person, per week.[21] The dining room on the seventh floor of the Beresford had broad views of the park, and Caroline loved that she could go home to meet her mother for lunch without depending on the subway or taxis.[22]

In the autumn of 1910, Caroline fell right into the rhythm of museum work. She didn't have to start there until ten, so she could get in at least ninety minutes of her own study and research in the morning at home, when she was at her most productive. She would then walk to the museum through the park to work for a few hours before returning home to eat lunch with her mother. Then she would go back to the museum and work until around 5:00 or 6:00 P.M. At first she had really no museum tasks to do, so she spent her time studying and giving her time "wholly to work that counts intellectually" in order to be ready to take on the "considerable responsibility and routine work" that would be her job while Albert Lythgoe was in the field. Caroline enjoyed working on the museum team with Lythgoe, who she thought was "ideal to work with" because he let her have quite a bit of autonomy.[23]

Due to the ebb and flow of excavation and museum work at the time, Ransom was also given four to six weeks of leave in the summer for her own research interests and language training as well as weekly time to take care of her mother.[24] Once they had finished arranging the Egyptian Art Department, it officially opened in November 1911 with Ransom's accompanying handbook as a guide. Less than two months later, Lythgoe, Herbert Winlock, and Arthur Mace all left for the field, leaving Caroline virtually alone to run the department.[25] Albert and his crew were often in Egypt and Europe for more than half the year, from December to July, as was customary, excavating sites, disbursing finds, and meeting colleagues.

Caroline effectively took on the curatorial role for most of the year when personnel decisions needed to be made, letters written, and exhibits organized. As she explained in a letter to Breasted, once the others were in the field, the research time she was able to carve out from administrative work was "largely given to selected objects, or single large tasks" for the museum.[26] In addition, Lythgoe continued to send hundreds of boxes of artifacts from Egypt back to her at the museum throughout each season. These finds, along with periodic donations and loans, formed the foundation of the museum's Egyptian collections.[27] In this, Caroline was not unlike a number of other administrative women who stayed behind in the domestic museum spaces while their male counterparts were out in the field, like Margaret Murray did for Flinders Petrie at University College London. Importantly, once Lythgoe left for the winter, everyone who needed to work with him and the growing collections would have known and needed to work with Caroline. Like Kate Bradbury and Emily Paterson, Caroline was, by default, the central disciplinary gatekeeper for one of the nation's preeminent institutions.

As she grew in her professional stature and expertise, she was often busy with publications, such as a number of short articles and handbooks guiding visitors through the collections.[28] Many of these were in-depth analyses on several of the objects, such as the stela of a Middle Kingdom official named Mentuwoser, her first publication of a hieroglyphic translation of and commentary on an object.[29] The stela of Mentuwoser is from the twelfth dynasty (c. 1944 BCE), and was probably found at Abydos. A finely carved and painted rectangular stone, it shows Mentuwoser at his funeral banquet. The museum was given the piece in 1912 by the wealthy philanthropist Edward S. Harkness as a gift after he bought it from New York–based antiquities dealer Dikran G. Kelekian.[30] Other pieces came in that year, such as the masterfully carved Stela of Senu, a New Kingdom royal scribe, but Caroline chose the Mentuwoser piece to research, translate, and describe in fine detail. She wrote to Breasted that "the publication is intended primarily to make the stela known to Egyptologists, [but] I have had to consider the fact that it is to be sold at the Museum entrance" and so she wrote for the public, as well.[31] Her small books sold well at the museum, and her research reached countless visitors. Part of her work as a curator was to bring a larger audience to the growing collections and to establish the museum itself as a center of Egyptology research and preservation in the eyes of public visitors.

After this important stela was published, one of Caroline's biggest responsibilities was the acquisition, organization, unpacking, and installation within the museum of the mastaba tomb of Perneb from Saqqara, Egypt, in 1913.[32] Perneb lived in the fifth dynasty (around 2650 BCE), and his tomb states that he was a high official in the house of the pharaoh, who would have been either Djedkare Isesi or Unas (at the end of the fifth dynasty). He was in a high enough position to be buried at Saqqara, near Memphis, which was then the capital of Egypt. Over the course of millennia, sand covered several tombs, and stones were taken from other mastaba tombs to be repurposed for structures in the nearby villages (even as late as the 1840s and 1850s); Perneb's tomb remained undisturbed until 1907.[33] The tomb was inadvertently uncovered that year by British Egyptologist Edward Quibell and his diggers while attempting to retrieve painted walls from a different tomb.

The mastaba tomb of Perneb was then purchased for the museum by Edward Harkness and had to be boxed and moved. In total, the structure comprised 601 boxes of blocks, which took two months to move from the site to New York. It was Caroline who received and accessioned all of the boxes from the tomb upon their arrival at the museum because she was at home, in New York, and not in Egypt.

Then the assistant curator had a brand-new problem on her hands: preservation. Egyptian limestone contains certain salts that are dormant in the dry desert air but will cause major issues for stone and painted surfaces in relatively humid climates such as New York's. There were a number of options Caroline could have chosen to protect the delicate artwork. The most effective method, soaking each stone in water until the salts had essentially dissolved, was also the most destructive. All of the painted surfaces would have been ruined. So instead, she chose to seal the stone—Lythgoe later called it "bottling up"—by covering it with a varnish-like substance. They had to do this for every single block, and the method locked out any other substances that could get in. The work was time consuming, but by May of 1914, Caroline was happy to report to Lythgoe that the stones were preserved and reconstruction work was ready to begin.[34] During the entire process, Caroline and her team were given temporary use of a basement room for prep and storage, while much of the rest of the Egyptian collection was moved out of the way so that there would be room to build the tomb. The gallery on the northern end of the Fifth Avenue hall was prepped for installation, which began in August 1914 and was finished by early 1916.[35]

When the tomb was completed, Caroline stood back and admired the work. They had actually reconstructed a tomb indoors. People had doubted her. If she was honest with herself, she had doubted it could be done, too. In the end, though, they had done it. In a short piece on January 30, the *New York Times* reported "Perneb's Gay Tomb Ready for Visitors."[36] Caroline and her team were ready for visitors, as well. The grand opening of the tomb for the public was on February 3, 1916.[37] From the time the display was available, it became the main focus of the Egyptian collection, and remains one of the most popular exhibits at the Metropolitan Museum of Art. Visitors clamored for the first, and at that time the only, display of its kind outside of Egypt. Ransom was rightfully proud of her work and wrote to Breasted about the opening day:

> *The opening of Perneb's tomb took place with great éclat and the interest of the public has not yet subsided. . . . People were formed in line two abreast all the way back to the Fifth Avenue entrance to get into the chambers. Glass positions electrically lighted illustrate the former position and the taking down of the tomb. There are two cases of the objects found in the course of the excavations including the greater part of Perneb's skull. A model of the entire tomb makes clear the position of the burial chamber.*[38]

Caroline had spearheaded this initiative and produced, for those visiting the museum, a guidebook for the exhibit. It was published in a first edition of twenty-five hundred copies at around the same time as her scholarly history of the tomb, and, she told Breasted:

*It is only a popular thing, but in a way I think such pieces of writ-
ing are a more responsible undertaking than a scientific work. If
you make mistakes in writing for your fellow Egyptologists, they
soon set you straight, but the public is so trusting and rarely goes
into the more technical books!*[39]

Caroline was doing what so many other women had done—she
used her scholarly influence to pioneer a new method in educating
the public. She had developed, with the help of several departments,
the museum's methodology in displaying a fully articulated tomb. It
should be done carefully, accurately, with an accompanying booklet
whose aim was to educate and bring in visitors. At the time, all
other collections in the United States looked to the Metropolitan
Museum as an example. The public handbook was in fact so well-
written and popular with visitors that Breasted used it in Chicago to
persuade the Field Museum to install their own mastaba chambers.[40]

Albert Lythgoe and Caroline jointly wrote the book. The first
half was Albert's part. He wrote about the process of uncovering
the tomb and moving it to New York. Caroline opened her half of
the book by informing readers and museum patrons that Perneb
had a family who loved him and would visit this tomb. They would
bring offerings and continue to honor his life and mourn him. Caroline then invited modern visitors to step into the place of Perneb's
family. Upon approaching the tomb, they would find "a startling
reminder of the appearance of the departed nobleman as they had
often seen him in life, issuing, staff in hand, from the door of his
house."[41] The features that were portrayed on his likeness, "while
not a detailed portrait, were strongly reminiscent of the proud and
noble countenance of the deceased grandee."[42] But, as she continued, visitors could be sure they were seeing "typical" Egyptian figures from which scholars could learn a lot about the Fifth Dynasty
in which he lived. She described in detail what the hieroglyphs said
about Perneb and his family, but told readers that the scenes were
incomplete because the tomb itself was never fully finished. As the
leading scholar of Perneb's tomb, Caroline had closely studied every
surface with a magnifying glass in order to understand the various
steps the original artists followed to get the colorful tomb in order.

Her fascination was with the use of the ancient pigment Egyptian blue throughout the tomb, demonstrating, as she argued, that "far from being crude and all too simple, as a superficial acquaintance might suggest, these painted reliefs reveal vividly conceived scenes, a facile technic, and a sophisticated color scheme," as well as a long development of religious artwork and superior talent.[43]

Caroline was an art historian and museum curator whose expertise was decorative elements and scripts, so the opportunity to design and install such an exhibit was a perfect job for her. Further, because she was the main curator in charge of the conservation, organization, and installation of the tomb, she had the most in-depth knowledge of these particular elements. In archaeology, this is not the exciting fieldwork of *National Geographic* specials. It *is*, however, the necessary academic work that needs to be done in order to further the historical narrative. In addition, at this time in her life, it was the only work she could have done. She was a woman in the field of Egyptology and, despite her outstanding qualifications, she had her home life to consider. Largely due to caring for her aging mother, her prospects for going to the excavation site—especially from the United States—were not good in most years.

Caroline's written work was useful to the museum, and patrons liked it, so Albert asked her to write two more public guidebooks

Fig. 7.2: Entrance to the Tomb of Perneb as it currently stands.

for their other sets of mastaba reliefs, which she did.[44] In a second book about the tomb, *The Decoration of the Tomb of Per-Neb*, finally published in 1932 (under her married name of Ransom Williams), Ransom analyzed the techniques and color conventions of the wall paintings in the tomb, and thereby of the Old Kingdom; it became a useful reference work and is still used today.[45] These books, and the public reception of them, made both the Metropolitan Museum and Caroline herself arbiters of the public knowledge the audience would receive as they wandered through the displays. Caroline arguably had a much larger influence than excavators would have had on what the public saw of Egyptology and what they thought about the objects. Most museumgoers weren't reading site reports.

While she was busy with research and publication, Caroline was the main liaison between the absent curator and the activities at the museum. In one of several long letters to Albert, who was in Thebes (Luxor) at the time, she detailed a number of things that had happened during his absence. She opened the letter telling him that she had "so much to relate that I think I will confine myself to those things which you ought to perhaps hear before you return."[46] She had been working under the supervision of Edward Robinson, the director of the museum, while Albert was away and it seemed that he wrote more letters to the director than he did to Caroline. It is likely that Robinson was supposed to share the letters with his assistant curator to avoid writing duplicate letters. Whatever the case, Caroline reported on personnel news such as vacation plans and who was writing which articles about which objects.

Caroline supervised two curatorial assistants, Bernice Cartland and a Miss McCann, who were both busy writing exhibition reports.[47] She also organized and opened new exhibits, such as the month-long show she had arranged in the Recent Accessions Room that displayed Egyptian furniture and musical instruments. She wrote the accompanying article for this exhibit as well.[48] She also had to deal with personnel and process problems. One striking example was Mr. Kent, the photographer at the museum, who had changed the process by which pieces could be photographed, probably without consulting the curators. The new process took longer, the photos were smaller, and fine details were not visible. He may have done this prudently, to save money, but Caroline didn't like it and didn't agree with him. To circumvent the new process, she told Albert to have everything photographed in the field, as it would be cheaper and easier, and the photos would be of better quality.

On top of these duties, Caroline also had inherited a network of correspondents during Albert's absence that she quickly made her own. She was writing letters to dozens of Egyptologists and archaeologists needing information and collaboration with the museum. Albert sent a number of people to her who had private collections that needed to be assessed for importance and monetary value. One of them was a major benefactor and trustee of the museum since 1888 and its president since 1904, the wealthy banker J. P. Morgan. In the spring of 1912, Morgan had a head of a Greek statue that needed an appraisal, so Caroline arranged for a meeting between him and the "head in the Classical section of the museum," which had just been established in 1910.[49]

Other patrons were just as important. By the time they left Egypt for good in 1914, Theodore Davis had created a massive personal collection of art and antiquities, as had Emma Andrews. Caroline met with Theo and Emma and went to their home in Rhode Island a few times to see and secure a number of pieces, ensuring a good relationship between the wealthy couple and the museum.[50] Upon Theo's death in 1915, his will bequeathed to the museum the portion of his collection that wasn't already there. Emma Andrews did the same when she died in 1922.

Edward Harkness, the wealthy philanthropist whose money had funded the excavation, purchase, move, and conservation of the Tomb of Perneb and several other objects, consulted with Caroline about possibly funding more excavations and museum projects. In the end, she and Robinson, the museum director, could not agree on what the building needed or how to use space.[51] Harkness also asked Caroline about a few pieces that he wanted to purchase and loan to the museum, and she reported to Albert that the purchases were successful.[52] Caroline was also a personal friend of Mary Emma Harkness, Edward's wife, so she enjoyed some connections that many curators might not have, but it is unclear if she used that friendship for garnering more donations.

The letters between the curator at home and the curator in the field in the early days of the Egyptian Art Department clearly demonstrate the important discipline- and institution-building work that women like Caroline did in this period. She held the department together while the head curator was gone. More than that, she actively built up the collections within the department on her own, reporting to Albert in a few long missives to the field about the tasks she had completed. Like Kate Bradbury and Emily Paterson, Caroline was needed "at home," which meant in the home institutions, so they rarely made it to the field. In this way, in a brief six years essentially at the helm, she had made the museum one of the best and most important Egyptian collections outside of Egypt. In that time, she had also situated herself at the center of a professional Egyptological network, and she was able to wield that influence wherever she went.

Marriage and Toledo

By 1916, World War I was raging in Europe, and, even though the United States had not yet become directly involved, the museum's donors were tightening their purse strings. Budgets were cut, excavation seasons were canceled (due also to safety), and Caroline ultimately left the museum as a full-time employee. Possibly as an outcome of this change in her position, or perhaps the cause of it, she finally agreed to marry Grant Williams. The couple were wed on June 28, 1916, in Mercer, Pennsylvania; the bride was forty-four years old, and the groom was fifty-one. It was the first marriage for both of them. She changed her name to Caroline Ransom Williams and began to sign her letters not as Dr. Ransom but as Mrs. Grant Williams, or Caroline R. Williams, in accordance with the traditions at the time. She and her mother moved to Toledo with Williams, into another apartment-hotel, the Chesbrough Dwellings in Toledo's West End. While she yearned to start work in the first "really commodious and healthful study" she had had since her faculty office at Bryn Mawr, she was constantly delayed.[53]

Having taken so much time away from work, she worried she was beginning to disappear from the discipline. Her colleagues were worried, too. In response to her wedding announcement, Alan Gardiner of the Egypt Exploration Fund wrote to her that he "supposed that [she] would not give up Egyptology altogether!"[54] She wouldn't be, because, as she told Gardiner, she had just taken on a new, large project with the New-York Historical Society (NYHS).[55] She was lucky. She wrote to Breasted that her "husband is unselfishly interested in my plans and encourages me to take any opportunity for congenial work that comes my way."[56] So, she continued to work for the museum by commuting to New York a few times a year for several weeks at a time. Toledo was on a main railroad line, and the journey, though long, was easy.

Much like other women had to do at the time, she began to piece small part-time jobs together in addition to her work at the Metropolitan Museum, to make ends meet. She taught a number of courses at the University of Michigan and a few in Chicago, where she was also busy with research. She catalogued the Egyptian collections at the Cleveland Museum of Art, the Detroit Museum of Art, and the Drexel Collection in Minnesota.[57] The tasks themselves would keep her connected to the discipline, and her productivity remained relatively steady thanks to her continued association to these collections. Not one to be relegated to the margins, Caroline used her position as the core of the vibrant scholarly network that she had established at the museum to remain in the discipline and to continue to position herself as essential in a science where the immediate aftermath of marriage, for a woman, was usually expulsion.

Not long after the Perneb display opened in 1916, James Breasted came upon the Abbott Collection at the NYHS. The collection, the same one that Kate Bradbury wrote needed its own museum, contained around one thousand objects and was named for British physician and antiquities collector Henry Abbott.[58] It was the first Egyptian antiquities collection owned by an institution in the United States.[59] While it contained many important objects, it had been virtually untouched by academics and sat, decidedly unorganized, in the NYHS for over fifty years. More than twenty-five years after Kate had remarked on the collection, James Breasted saw the same old catalogue in December of 1916, which Abbott himself had put together. He immediately wrote to Caroline that "the unpublished things there made my mouth water. There is a chance for a large and beautiful monograph on these things."[60] Caroline would be perfect to catalogue, organize, and publish the collection, and Albert Lythgoe agreed.

Caroline, as a woman, commanded a lower salary than a man would, despite her unmatched expertise. She was without a doubt the most well-qualified scholar of any gender to do it. In January of 1917, she responded with thanks to her former mentor for recommending her for the job. She wrote, "If I undertake it I shall endeavor to endure to the end!"[61] And she did. The Society announced her involvement in April 1917, believing it would take "a year or so" for her to do the "exhaustive scientific catalogue . . . to replace the catalogue made by Dr. Abbott at the time the Society secured his collection, which is still in use."[62] In the end, it seems, it took seven years to complete a partial catalogue of jewelry and get it published.[63]

The project took so long to complete mainly because she was commuting a very long distance by train, she had other paying jobs, and was responsible for domestic tasks. She was unable to have access to the pieces all the time, which meant that she could not properly study or organize them. Caroline did as she always did—she worked quickly, but carefully, when she was in New York, and many times she was able to get photographs of particular objects to take back to Toledo with her. In Toledo, she was still caring for her mother and husband, and, unlike her male counterparts in Egyptology and museum work, many of whom had wives to take care of things in the home and family, Caroline was dealing with the double bind of domestic and professional duties at the same time. It is possible that someone without these concerns could have done the job more quickly, but no one else could have done it better.

At a few points over those seven years, she tried to use her considerable influence to hand the catalogue over to other scholars to give them some professional experience, but to little avail.[64] By 1922, she wished to take a break from the cataloguing project, which had already been going on for close to six years. To the NYHS, she suggested that Nathaniel J. Reich should take her place.

He was an Egyptologist working in Austria-Hungary until the end of World War I. Caroline, along with other Egyptologists in the United States, tried to get Reich work so he could emigrate and remain a vital part of the discipline.[65] She also tried to get him some work in Cleveland. Simply put: neither museum could afford to hire a man to do the work they paid a woman, Caroline, to do. Due to the gender salary expectations at the time, the collections where Caroline tried to find him work would have had to pay him much more than they were paying their star scholar; such an arrangement was not tenable. In fact, by 1927, the postwar situation in Europe had turned so dire that both James and Caroline tried to find paying jobs for many of their German colleagues. Despite the fact that there were so many Egyptologists they knew both in the United States and across Europe, there were not enough jobs and not enough funding to hire them.[66]

As she researched the collection, she came across a curious document. In late November of 1920, she wrote to James in Chicago about "the medical papyrus of the Smith collection" owned by the NYHS, which she did not have the time to translate and publish.[67] She further wrote to him:

> . . . I feel that it is imperative, if possible, to get work started soon on that medical papyrus by a competent authority, whose name on the title-page would carry conviction that the papyrus had been well handled. I am authorized by a sub-committee of the Executive Committee to ask you whether you would care to prepare the publication and would have time for it. The papyrus is probably the most valuable one owned by the Society and I am ready to waive my interest in it, in the hope that it may be published sooner and better than I could do it.[68]

In the end, James agreed, and by 1930 it was published as *The Edwin Smith Surgical Papyrus*, in two volumes.[69] It was not that she thought her friend could use the experience, but she knew how important the papyrus would be to Egyptology and wished to have it published as soon as possible. Caroline definitely had the expertise, she just did not have the time, so she used her influence to complete the work. She also helped James in editing his translations, marking up his page proofs, and communicating with the NYHS about the progress of his work to a degree that she was almost like a research assistant.[70] While he acknowledged her in the volume, very few scholars note that Caroline was the one who brought the papyrus to light in the first place and pushed its publication.

Caroline had no choice but to continue and finish the Abbott cataloguing work. When her part was completed, the catalogue was well-received among Egyptologists and jewelry historians, and it is used by scholars who study the collections today. Even though she did not complete the whole catalogue, her work began the long and difficult task. Again, as a woman in the field, she used her experience as an institution-building curator and laid the foundation for the cataloguing and academic study of the Abbott Collection and other small collections in the Midwestern United States.

The Epigraphic Survey

In the 1926–27 field season, at the personal invitation of James Breasted, Caroline finally went with the University of Chicago's Epigraphic Survey to work on Medinet Habu near Luxor.[71] What is now called Old Chicago House was still new on the West Bank and still in the process of being upgraded, with a new library and furniture being installed. It was crowded before the season even started, and Assistant Director Harold Nelson wrote to James that in 1926 he would have "eleven people here next week with only ten beds in which to put them.... Only this time they are, unfortunately, not all men."[72] "Unfortunately" here didn't mean that Harold thought it was bad to have women on-site—far from it—but just that he couldn't fit everyone in the house who needed to be there. In the end, he accommodated Caroline and her mother but couldn't fit Grant or Louise Fitz-Randolph, so they stayed home.[73] Caroline and Ella arrived at the beginning of December that year, and she was eager to begin her work on the inscriptions that she had been summoned for, specifically, in Medinet Habu.

Two days after Caroline arrived with her mother, Harold Nelson wrote to James that she was already hard at work on the reliefs.

Fig. 7.3: Old Chicago House, 1926, with the Colossi of Memnon just behind the house, and the Nile flowing beyond.

He continued, reporting that "she is certainly an example to us of enthusiasm and application and will be of the greatest value to the work. I am delighted to have her here and expect to learn a great deal from her."[74] Their photographer, John Hartman, became ill and died just a few days later that December. His cause of death was possible liver lesions due to drinking Nile water instead of bottled Evian water, which he told Nelson he didn't care for. It was devastating to his wife and daughter, and a blow to the Survey. They needed to find someone to replace him quickly. Hartman's death also left an opportunity to reevaluate their process for reproducing the art on the temple walls.

Their artist at the time was Alfred Bollacher, but James was interested to see how Caroline worked with him, thinking that with an expert like her on-site, "her suggestions and observations on the relief material will be very useful and give us more assurance on the character of Bollacher's work than we have had hitherto."[75] While the Epigraphic Survey had been James's brainchild since 1905, it had only been in operation for two years by this point. Caroline's thorough assessment found that the copying process currently used

by the survey simply wouldn't make for the most accurate reproductions. Caroline reworked the entire process, with the help of
Epigraphic Survey staff William Edgerton and John Wilson. They
enlarged the images being produced, changed the photographic
processes, and had more than one epigrapher do the final collation
(checking of the copies against the original art).[76]

The first step is to produce a large-format black-and-white photograph with a camera positioned directly parallel to the surface
being captured. An artist then mounts the photograph to the wall
itself and pencils in all the visible carved details and those that aren't
visible on the photograph. It is a completely noninvasive system. No
tracing paper or plastic is ever attached to the fragile walls. Back
at the Chicago House or back home in the summer, the artist then
inks lines on the photograph, helping to create a three-dimensional
image on the paper. After inking, the photographic image is dissolved, leaving just the ink drawing. The collation process then begins, where the ink drawing, or blueprint, is cut into smaller pieces
and taken back to the original wall. Here, at least two epigraphers

Fig. 7.4: Caroline Ransom
Williams on a ladder at
Medinet Habu, 1926–27
season.

correct and refine the image itself. The artist then returns to the wall
to review the corrections and record color.[77] This is the process that
Myrtle Broome and Amice Calverley would use in their work at
Abydos, after learning it from the Epigraphic Survey.

Caroline took almost no money for her work that year. She
would only accept travel and other expenses, no salary. She was
also the last woman to work as an Egyptologist on the Epigraphic
Survey for almost fifty years. The Survey's directors after James and
Harold didn't think women had a place on-site.[78]

She returned to Toledo with her mother in April of 1927 to a
lot of attention. The *Toledo Times* published a story entitled "Mrs.
Grant Williams Returns from a Six Months Visit to Egypt."[79] The
article was complimentary of her work as a "well known" Egyptologist, but focused mostly on the fact that she had arrived back in time
to host a tea party for the president of Mount Holyoke College.

After a winter that she felt revived her not only physically but
also academically, she was ready to work. She took a position at the
University of Michigan as a special lecturer for the 1927–28 academic year, combining that with some part-time work for the Toledo Museum of Art, starting in 1928. On hearing this news, James
wrote her a congratulatory letter, but he also lamented her absence
from Chicago House that next year. The rest of the letter was full
of worry about funding, the state of the field, and promise for the
future. He wrote to Caroline, fretting that some Egyptology vacan-
cies wouldn't be filled at institutions like Johns Hopkins or Harvard,
and he was worried about the future of the discipline. He wrote:

> *There is a desperate need that a large and statesmanlike program
> of the development of Oriental science, both in education and in
> research, should be drafted by some one and brought to the notice
> of those who have the means to alter this situation and who might
> lay down a permanent foundation on which Oriental science of
> the future could build. The specific point I have in mind is this:
> if such a program could be carried out and such a dream be made
> practically possible, what share in it do you think your interests,
> your capabilities, and your family responsibilities might lead you
> or permit you to undertake? There is an appalling lack of trained*

people for assuming these new responsibilities, and I earnestly
hope that you may be able to share in this future development of
which I am now dreaming.[80]

James was always thinking big in terms of the discipline of
Egyptology, so requests like this from him were normal. He realized
that Caroline's expertise was irreplaceable, even with all the trained
men around. And even with all the trained men he knew, and the
ones he trained, he sought out Caroline explicitly for "such a program" that could have been life-changing. It never came to pass.

She kept working. Her reproduction was so accurate and James's
respect for her leadership and talent so high that every year after
that he continued to ask her to join them in the field. While the
field was important to her, personally, and she excelled in copy work
professionally, it never became a main part of her career. This is
likely because her time was split across multiple jobs and caring
for her mother and husband. She preferred the research but liked
museum work the least. Still, museum work paid the best, and so
she took jobs in that part of the discipline. By 1930, she was done
teaching and instead doing museum work full-time, earning a combined monthly salary from the Metropolitan Museum of Art and
the Toledo Museum of Art, where she was honorary curator of
Egyptian Art until 1951, of around $500 (the equivalent of $9,000
in 2023).[81] That is to say, she did not really need extra money.

Ella Randolph Ransom, Caroline's mother, died in 1933 at the
age of eighty-five after two decades of declining health and Caroline's almost full-time support and care. In 1934, Caroline also
lamented the deaths of well-known Egyptologists Thomas Eric
Peet in February and Frank Griffith in March. She grieved the early
death of Albert Lythgoe in January of that year more than she could
express. After all the sorrow, Caroline wrote to James that she was
ready to get back to some Egyptological work.[82]

In 1935, she went out to Egypt for the last time. She had plans
to work with the Art Institute of Chicago, not on the Epigraphic
Survey but on the Coffin Texts project in Cairo.[83] James had invited
her to work a bit in Cairo and at the Institute's Memphis House in
Saqqara. She was also planning to work with Gustave Jéquier on

reliefs found in Saqqara, so her time in Egypt at the age of sixty-three would be jam-packed with activity.[84]

She also wanted to join the crew of the Metropolitan Museum's Egyptian Expedition, operating near Luxor. She was already in Egypt, and she hoped to go into the field one more time. To this end, Caroline wrote to her former colleague Herbert Winlock, who was now the curator at the museum, to see if she could join the expedition. Ambrose Lansing, associate curator at the museum, responded to her that she would be very useful in answering the question of color usage on small fragments from a Ramesside temple from the previous season.[85] He offered her a small room in the Expedition House in Luxor, and she wrote back that she would love to take it. Because of impending war in Europe, the season was tentative, but by late October she was cleared to go.

Caroline must have arrived in Egypt with the Metropolitan group in late November because they all sailed on the SS *Exeter* on November 12.[86] It is hard to determine exactly what she did there, however. By December 3, she was in Saqqara at the Chicago Memphis House. In the middle of that morning, the site field director Prentice Duell sent for the crew working in the tomb of Mereruka and asked them to return to the house. As everyone piled into the car, they wondered about the situation. There must have been some grave reason for Duell to ask everyone to leave their work and come home. The worst case Caroline herself imagined on the ride back was that England had declared war on Italy and they would all have to leave at once. Others agreed with her—it must have been war. When, instead, she heard that her friend James Breasted had died the day before, she considered this news much worse.[87] She sent a telegram of condolence right away, and the following day she sent a letter to Charles Breasted about the sudden death of his father.

James had been returning to the United States from a long tour of his sites in Egypt and Palestine, and he caught a cold on the ship. This was a normal occurrence for most travelers. But James also contracted a strep infection that may have been made worse by latent malaria in his system from years before. In New York, a team of doctors treated him and were able to get rid of the malaria; however, without antibiotics, they could not effectively treat the strep infection and were unable to save him.[88]

It's hard to figure out exactly what Caroline did during the rest of this trip, as there is no record of her working for Chicago during that season. She mourned her friend of almost forty years. They had worked closely together on several projects, having a mutual respect and affection for one another. She was either working on Old Kingdom material for the Metropolitan Museum, doing her own research on Old Kingdom material from Saqqara (which is the location of the tomb of Mereruka), or she was consulting with the Chicago team on an entirely different project.[89] It is clear that she was at Memphis House because James had invited her to stay there for some period of time.

Later during that field season, Caroline finally made it to Abydos. She had wanted to visit the site the last time she had been in Egypt, almost a decade earlier, but hadn't been able to go. When she went in the winter of 1935–36, she was delighted (as much as the serious Caroline could be) to see in person the work of Amice Calverley and Myrtle Broome at the Temple of Seti I.[90] She was impressed with their work and loved seeing two young women successfully running a site.

Home for Good

When she returned home to Toledo after the season, in the spring of 1936, she continued her part-time jobs at various institutions, including the universities of Michigan and Chicago, but she was sixty-four years old and tired. She missed her mother, and she missed her friends. Soon, she shifted her focus to the Toledo Museum of Art and a few other small projects she had been wanting to find the time for. In the summer of 1937, she received an honorary degree from the University of Toledo for her work in Egyptology and archaeology.[91] Next to her photo, the *Toledo Blade* ran an article claiming that "many Toledoans for the first time were made aware of her accomplishments as a student of the ancient civilizations" largely because she was "long a fugitive from the spotlight of lay acclaim . . ."[92] The tone of surprise throughout the piece was palpable through the page. Toledo had had an Egyptological celebrity in their midst the whole time.

Her Egyptological library, which she mentioned frequently to James Breasted throughout their letters, was the subject of a newspaper article a few years earlier, in 1933.[93] Caroline had detailed to Breasted how she had been growing the collection one treasured acquisition at a time. Throughout her home, she had several heavy, rare, and expensive books that were difficult to get by 1933, and which are impossible to get today. The room she called her study was a long, narrow space that would have been dark but for the windows on one end that let in sunlight. The walls were lined with books from the floor to the high ceilings. On the desk, pushed against one wall, was a typewriter with a specialized set of keys so she could continue transcribing ancient scripts into Latin letters. Next to the typewriter was a small limestone artifact from Egypt, dating back to the earliest days of the Old Kingdom. Turning around and opening the closet door, visitors would be overwhelmed by the collection of thousands of lantern slides she had amassed over the years.

Working within her renowned library, Caroline continued to publish short pieces of scholarship as well as reviews. Caroline also continued working with the Metropolitan Museum of Art in New York intermittently until her husband died on Christmas Eve, 1942, at the age of seventy-seven.[94] From that point on, her friend Katharine Reusch became a steady companion, and her work slowed down.

In 1943 Caroline gave her "small collection of Egyptian antiquities" to her alma mater, Mount Holyoke College. According to the acquisition records at the Mount Holyoke Art Museum, the 1943 donation consisted of approximately sixteen small scarabs that were from the collection of her aunt, Professor Louise Fitz-Randolph. In 1944, she gave a sixteenth-century print of the Pantheon in Rome to the Mount Holyoke Museum, too. Louise had been donating objects to Mount Holyoke since 1902, and her estate had continued to gift the museum as late as 2013. Because Mount Holyoke holds some of her aunt's papers, it is possible that some of Caroline's papers went to her alma mater as well, but there is no substantial collection there. Much like Caroline's labor had done her whole career, her book collection served as the linchpin for several major institutional libraries. Some of it went to the library of the Egyptian Art Department at the Metropolitan Museum of Art in 1943 and later. The Toledo Museum of Art also received quite a few of her books. It is unclear where the rest of her slides, her typewriter, and her other books may have gone.

The End

Saturday, January 26, 1952, was a clear and warm day in Cairo. The morning was quiet, especially in the areas of the city frequented by tourists, much to the relief of journalist Ernie Hill. The *Chicago Daily News* reporter and his wife were guests at the storied Shepheard's Hotel, near the Azbakiya Gardens in central Cairo. News was quickly spreading to the city about a firefight between British troops and Egyptian police forces in what became known as the Battle of Ismailia, a town founded near the Sinai Peninsula during the building of the Suez Canal to house workers. The previous day, British forces had demanded that Egyptian police hand over their weapons and leave the governorate building in Ismailia, but they refused. The ensuing battle saw thirteen British troops killed and twenty-two wounded, in contrast to the fifty-six Egyptian police officers killed and seventy-three wounded. After more than a century of violent colonization by the British, Egyptians that January day were worn out and angry. Tensions rose quickly.

By early afternoon, news of the battle had spread widely. There were fires raging in other parts of town, but the Azbakiya Gardens were still relatively quiet. Guests at Shepheard's were shuffled away from street-facing windows as the shutters were closed and secured. Ernie Hill and his wife waited in the opulent lobby of the hotel, decorated in an ancient Egyptian–inspired theme, as angry crowds gathered out on the street. He recalled that "the hotel became a gloomy place inside when the lights went out about 2:30pm."[95] Management had already extinguished a fire in the hotel's garden when gasoline-soaked rags were thrown into the building, catching rugs and furniture on fire and causing flames more than twenty feet high. While trying to escape, Ernie heard yelling and gunshots outside in the street. Using wet handkerchiefs over their mouths to keep out the smoke, Ernie, his wife, and other guests were led by Maya Medwar, an Egyptian actress who had also been a guest at Shepheard's, "out into the side garden between Shepheard's and Cook's Travel Agency next door."[96]

When they arrived outside, the scene was equally as ominous. Thousands were in the streets—Ernie called them a "snarling mob"—and they had to find a way to safety. Not sure what to do, Maya sprang into action. She grabbed both of the Hills by the hand and, yelling in Arabic the whole way, led them to a garage down the street, where they waited for a cab to get to the Heliopolis Palace Hotel, out in what was then the suburbs of Cairo. Most of the Shepheard's guests went there, as did guests from the Metropolitan and the Victoria, both of which were also burned down.

Egyptians chose Shepheard's and other European-run hotels because they saw the hotels as symbols of foreign powers in Egypt. By burning down the concrete reminders of more than a century of exploitation, they were burning Europeans—especially the British—out of Egypt. By 11:00 P.M. that Black Saturday, hotels, movie theaters, clubs, coffee shops, bars, and restaurants had burned. Corporate offices had been destroyed. Department stores and other shops were gone. Twenty-six people died, and over five hundred suffered injuries. The Egyptian Museum had been spared, as had neighborhoods without foreigners in them. While there was some movement toward strengthening British forces in Egypt at that time, in the end, it was the Egyptian military who settled the uprising. After centuries of outside influence and over a hundred years of Western colonial power, Egypt was finally able to declare independence. Within the next year, General Mohamed Naguib was installed as the first president of an independent Egypt, and all foreign interests were kicked out of the country—especially the Egyptologists.

Caroline couldn't believe the news that January morning. She read the headlines on the front page of the *Toledo Blade* as she and Katharine ate breakfast: "Martial Law Clamped on Egypt; Anti-British Hordes Riot in Cairo"; "Property Losses Run into Millions;

20 Killed, 80 Hurt."⁹⁷ Shepheard's? Burned? She thought back to her first trip to Egypt with her aunt Louise and how they had enjoyed tea on Shepheard's terrace while watching the camel caravan pass by on the street below. She had been back several times. Upheaval in Egypt? Caroline knew there were political issues in Egypt, but she couldn't believe it had gotten as bad as Black Saturday. She couldn't bring herself to believe the news. She put the paper down on the table and tried to take a deep breath. She wasn't feeling well that day, but maybe it was just worry over Egypt.

She didn't last the week.

Caroline Ransom Williams died February 1, 1952, after a very short but acute case of myocarditis. She was eulogized in the *Toledo Blade* as "Dr. Williams, Woman Distinguished as Egyptologist."⁹⁸ As important as she was to the field, there are no other obituaries, eloges, or memorials of Caroline Louise Ransom Williams around the time of her death or in the years after it. Her name did not appear in any of the journals she wrote diligently for, nor did remembrances materialize from any of the institutions she gave her time and expertise to or from any of the colleagues she left behind, except one. Caroline's friend Barbara Grace Spayd wrote to Ambrose Lansing, by then the Curator of the Egyptian Art Department at the Metropolitan Museum, of her passing. She asked for some bibliographic notes about her friend, and he must have sent them, because an article appeared in the June 1952 edition of the *University of Chicago Magazine*.⁹⁹ Caroline did pass away after many of her contemporaries were already gone, but it seems that memories of her life and work went with the passing of those who knew her.

Caroline Louise Ransom Williams is the culmination of all the women in this book who came before her. She was educated at a university and earned her PhD. She taught at the highest levels of academia before moving into the curatorial world, where she flourished. She worked in the field and as a mentor. She published dozens of pieces of academic writing. Like most of the women in this book, had she been a man, we would know so much more about her.

Caroline's contributions to and impact on the fields of Egyptology, museum curation, and language study were critical to each discipline. The esteem in which the men she worked with held her demonstrated her unmatched abilities. Her life also fits into the large group of women professional scientists who lost (and continue to lose) their careers because of the difficulties of balancing the physical and emotional burdens of home with the pressures and deadlines of academia. Academic institutions largely lacked the infrastructure for understanding that scientists sometimes must be able to care for families while participating in a professional capacity. Caroline's colleagues continued to include her in their pursuits and plans because of her expertise, but these plans were too far from home for her to commit to them. Despite her hard work, she was one of many women who followed the same path as her male colleagues but did not receive credit for her accomplishments.

Epilogue

What dominates the view from the East Bank to the West Bank of the Nile River in Luxor, other than the river, is the pyramidal peak that is familiar to the countless generations of people who have lived here. It has been called Ta Dehent, meaning "the Peak"; Meretseger, after the cobra-headed goddess who watches over the Valley of the Kings and the Theban necropolis; and now El Qurn, which means "the Horn."

There is nothing about the view that would be familiar to Jenny Lane or Nettie Gourlay except for this peak, towering over the hills and mountains that form it. Even the flow of the Nile has changed since the building of the Aswan High Dam in the 1960s. The West Bank, the realm of the ancient dead yet always full of life, now boasts a bustling and vibrant community. The tour buses, taxis, motorbikes, and cars dominate the roads as they move alongside donkeys and horses pulling carts of sugarcane, bananas, and dates.

Wandering down the sloping sidewalk on the East Bank, I head down to an area that is lower than street level. This was the ancient quay where millions of Egyptians had moored their boats. Now, it holds shops and restaurants where people gather to enjoy the evening with friends and families. Here was where Amelia first caught sight of the French House, where Emma would have alighted to meet friends for tea, and where Caroline caught a ferry to reach Chicago House. You can still get a boat from here. Today, the ferries go back and forth across the river with some regularity. The expert felucca captains will sail you all over the area, gliding on the water either with or against the current, using the wind to fill their sails.

Looking to the West Bank across the wide expanse of water, you can almost make out some of the taller monuments, like the Colossi of Memnon, whose now blank faces have looked out over this river valley since around 1350 BCE. Greek and Roman tourists were as familiar with these monuments as they were with some of the tombs in the Valley of the Kings, just behind them. Now, tourists from all over the world flock to see these statues of Amenhotep III, if only briefly. Then they head across the road to the *taftish*, the Antiquities Inspectorate office, to get their site tickets for the day.

Amenhotep III's likenesses stand well within the plain that used to flood each year, and there is still rich farmland all around them. Just a few meters behind Amenhotep III is the desert. The contrast between the desert and the sown earth is still stark, almost shocking to the senses. How could such rich life-giving soil touch the dry and barren desert? How could such a vast and ancient necropolis sit well within a vibrant city?

Just on the edge of the desert and the arable land on the West Bank, within view of Amenhotep III's statues, is a popular hotel among both tourists and archaeologists. Everyone who visits finds great food and refreshing drinks, along with friendly faces, after a long day of sightseeing or working. Called Marsam Hotel today, it is still known as Sheikh's to many visitors. The building has been run as a hotel since around 1939 or 1940, when Sheikh Ali Abd el Rasul bought the land and some of the architectural elements of Old Chicago House from the University of Chicago. To the east, the porch view overlooks the same fields Caroline Ransom Williams would have seen, stretching to the Colossi and on to the Nile. To the west, the walk to Medinet Habu, the mortuary temple of Ramesses III, is only about ten minutes. Each day of the season, this is where Caroline helped to develop the Chicago House Method.

The worlds into which each of these women walked were very different from the worlds they left behind. In many ways, they dismantled parts of the discipline that would see them fail, at worst, and fade into the background, at best. For a majority of these women, they not only benefitted from these institutions that, in the end, erased them and Egyptians they worked beside, they also helped to strengthen their foundations. They left their marks when and where they could and changed the ways in which the discipline of Egyptology operated.

Like their lives, the West Bank has changed a lot in the last 150 years. There are now cars, ticket offices, restaurants, workshops, tour buses, and asphalt. All of this is to serve visitors to Egypt who flock to the West Bank each year to visit the Valley of the Kings.

Driving up to the Valley of the Kings today is a wholly different experience from what Emma Andrews would have had when she rode in on her donkey chair. Where the rocky floor of the desert wadi used to welcome visitors and where clumps of Cook's tourists had blocked the archaeologists' work, the space has now been fully modernized. The asphalt parking lot is usually full of buses and taxis, and the line of visitors waiting for tickets into the valley itself, then choosing up to three tombs per ticket, stretches far back into the lot. The tomb of Tutankhamun has been one of the most popular tickets—an expensive, separate one—since it opened to regular tourists in 1927. The valley didn't even get regular electricity until the 1970s, with guards preferring to use mirrors to reflect and guide the abundant sunlight into the reaches of the decorated sepulchers. There are some tombs that still eschew electric light for this ancient technique.

On this particular day, I had brought my friend Dr. Julia Troche with me to the Kings' Valley. Following in the footsteps of Emma Andrews, we decided to climb up to KV 43 to see the view that Emma had while she was enjoying lunch with Theo while at the same time trying to convince him not to go back into the tomb too soon. It would have been a steep climb for their party over uneven, rocky ground. It would have been slippery, so their diggers probably helped them up. Reaching the top is still a challenge, but thankfully there are steps today. The large plateau at the top of the precipitous climb offers a shady respite, even in the hottest parts of the day. We sat up there for a while. Just below us was a sweeping vista of the mountains, a bird's-eye view of the trails people have walked for over three thousand years, and clear sight down to several tomb entrances. It's obvious why this was a favorite lunch spot.

It's also obvious why these women came here in the first place.

They hoped to heal their hearts and bodies, and they ended up making a legacy for themselves, for the women who came after them, and for the discipline of Egyptology—as problematic as it is. They were as complex as the landscape we watched, its colors changing, now in the light, now in the shadows. They were forces of nature, like the breeze that blew around us, slowly changing the contours of the desert. They changed the contours of science, making those around them reckon with their presence, and their absence. They deserve a reckoning, these women in the Valley of the Kings.

Acknowledgments

No project, even a single-author book, is truly done alone. I found many of the women in these pages first in project acknowledgments or as last names, mentioned once, in the hundreds of pages of work their male counterparts did. Then I met them in the archives. Understanding networks of influence begins, I think, in such places.

First, thanks go to my agent, Sarah Levitt. I've thanked you a million times for your support, encouragement, and the opportunity to tell these stories to people. Thank you. Again. Also to the entire team at St. Martin's Press, especially my editor Michael Flamini, Claire Cheek, Katie Bassal, Sara Beth Haring, and the copy editor, designers, and marketing staff. Thank you for your patience and for helping me make this a story that people will hopefully want to read over and over.

To the amazing people who helped me discover these women in hard-to-find spaces, I couldn't have gotten so much background information without you. Librarians are and always have been huge helps to me. Jeanna Purses, director of the Lincoln Library at Lake Erie College, thank you for correcting my early information on Caroline Ransom and sending images from your archives. Thanks to the Failsworth Historical Society, especially Richard Unwin, Christine Herd, and Les Garner for their generosity in sharing Mr. Unwin's book about Kate Bradbury's home, Riversvale Hall. Amanda Quink of the Preservation Society of Newport County sent several images and pieces of information about Theodore Davis's and Emma Andrews's mansion, the Reef. Ingrid Peters from the Newport Historical Society also guided me to important answers about these Americans. Sarah Ketchley at the University of

Washington, and director of the Emma B. Andrews Diary Project, has done amazing work on the digitization of Emma's diaries. She shared typewritten text from the diaries with me and guided me through Emma's words. Gayle Harmon-Herbert at the Toledo Lucas County Public Library answered the phone when I called asking for possible newspaper articles. Thank you for taking the time to find them, turn them into photos, and send them to me. Julie McMaster, the archivist at the Toledo Museum of Art, helped me work through several questions about Caroline Ransom. It was a joy to meet you in person and have a wonderful long chat about her. Dominique Navarro of the Epigraphic Survey and Emily Teeter of the Institute for the Study of Ancient Cultures (ISAC, formerly the Oriental Institute) at the University of Chicago also chatted with me about Caroline and her impact on Egyptology and shared several resources I didn't know about. Anne Flannery, also at the ISAC, has always been generous with her time and knowledge, allowing me to see decades of correspondence at short notice. Many of these experts answered random emails or phone calls from me, and each of them, without exception, was enthusiastic about helping me. Thank you.

In England, I'm always welcomed by Carl Graves and Stephanie Boonstra of the Egypt Exploration Society (EES). Even during train strikes, they get to the office to let me in and show me the most amazing resources. Francisco Bosche-Puche and Elizabeth Fleming at the Griffith Institute always pull what I ask for, and more, and are always founts of information for me that lead me in new and exciting directions. Chris Naunton, former EES director and current director of the Robert Anderson Trust, has heard too much about this project already but always has something good to add or a new direction to send me. Special thanks go to the family of Mary Jonas, specifically Merial Thurstan and Michael Jonas, for sharing more detail about the life of their great-aunt and photos that I had never seen before. I hope you like the cover! The story of these women has been made so much richer by all of you. Thank you.

Trips to Egypt are the best when you're with wonderful people. Dr. Anne Austin and Dr. Julia Troche were both there at the same time I was, for different reasons. Even though we all live within a one-hundred-mile radius of each other in Missouri, it was a great time to get the band back together. Thank you for coming with me on some adventures and sharing yours with me!

Trying to navigate the field, on the ground or within the Ministry of Antiquities, without experts is difficult. There are so many wonderful people to thank. I am really lucky that Mary Sadek is at the Cairo office of the American Research Center in Egypt (ARCE). She and ARCE supported my access to sites. Dr. Bahaa Gaber, General Director of the Antiquities Inspectorate of Western Luxor, thank you for being generous with tea and advice on how to see the Kings' Valley at its best. Thanks also to Dr. Ali Reda Mohamed, director of the Valley of the Kings, for tea and a wonderful chat on the terrace. Mr. Hussein Fawzy Zaki gave us an unparalleled tour of the valley and a few tombs we were lucky enough to get into. Thank you. Finally, our driver, Mr. Ahmed Saleh, whose family roots go so far back in Luxor there is no one who knows the area better, thank you for safely and efficiently driving us, and for showing us great coffee shops.

None of this travel would have been possible without the financial support of the History and Political Science Department at Missouri S&T, especially the Lawrence Christensen Memorial Fellowship and the University of Missouri System Research Board.

How do you thank the people who have supported you day in and day out? Each and every one of the people here, and those whom I haven't listed, have given me nonstop encouragement, excitement, and confidence to move into a kind of writing I wasn't sure I could do. In no particular order, a million thanks to: Mike Bruening for listening to me talk about this for months; John McManus for being more excited about this than I was and for all of your advice; Joy Lisi Rankin for helping me celebrate every little and big milestone in both writing and running, and for reading every word of this manuscript more than once; Luca Rankin for being the youngest reader of the manuscript and giving me the confidence to know that there are people of all ages who will be inspired by these stories; Claire Thornhill, Tom Aldred, and the boys for making London home; Leila McNeill and Anna Reser for encouraging me to talk more about some of these women in *Lady Science;* the best

Zoom-based writing group to ever exist, Lydia Pyne, Elaine Ayers, Eddie Guimont, Alison Laurence, Anna Toledano, and Ada Link; the best and most inappropriate friends who keep me going on the daily, Shannon Fogg, Kris Swenson, Audra Merfeld-Langston, and Kate Drowne; Stacy Davidson, Lisa Haney, Anne Austin, Julia Troche, Sara Orel, Rozanne Klinzing, and Clara McCafferty-Wright for being the coolest ARCE chapter board; Katherine Pandora, Sarah Naramore, Sarah Pickman, Sarah Qidwai, Cornelia Lambert, Michael Robinson, Alex Ratowt, Julie Jonsson, Dan Reardon, Lisa Deluca, Kevin Edwards, Marikay Asberry, Samantha Boon, Amanda Byrne, and Beth Dare for all being there in different but significant ways throughout this project. I know I have forgotten several people, but do know that I appreciate you.

Finally, to my family. My parents have been gone for several years, but they always believed in me; Mel Holbrook, thank you for still believing in me today. Thank you to Mary Ellen Noonan, my godmother, who quietly buys all my books, hearts all my posts, and comes to all my online talks: half a continent away, I see you! My siblings who always toast my success, when it happens. My husband, Dan, and my son, Miles, have to hear me talk about all the women in this book, and they might know just as much about them as I do. Thank you for always being there to listen and for being my biggest fans. It is to them that I dedicate this book and paraphrase Flinders Petrie's (in)famous dedication to his wife, Hilda, from 1932.

Notes

Prologue

1. Lucie Duff Gordon to Alexander Duff Gordon, 26 February 1864, in *Lady Duff Gordon's Letters from Egypt,* rev. ed. by Janet Ross (London: R. Brimley Johnson, 1902), 122.
2. Quoted in Jason Thompson, *Wonderful Things: A History of Egyptology, Volume 1: From Antiquity to 1881* (Cairo: AUC Press, 2015), 98.
3. David Gange, *Dialogues with the Dead: Egyptology in British Culture and Religion, 1822–1922* (Oxford: Oxford University Press, 2013).

1. Amelia Edwards and Marianne Brocklehurst

1. Amelia Edwards, *A Thousand Miles Up the Nile* (London: Longmans, Green, 1877), 454.
2. Joan Rees, *Amelia Edwards: Traveller, Novelist, and Egyptologist* (London: Rubicon Press, 1998), 34, 33.
3. Richard Morris, "The Victorian 'Change of Air' as medical and social construction," *Journal of Tourism History* 10:1 (2018), 49–65.
4. Brenda Moon, *More Usefully Employed: Amelia B. Edwards, Writer, Traveller and Campaigner for Ancient Egypt* (London: Egypt Exploration Society, 2006), 93–94.
5. England, Marriage Register, October 10, 1832, Manchester.
6. 1841 England Census, Lancashire, Manchester, Hulme, District 30.
7. 1861 England Census, Lancashire, Chorlton upon Medlock, District 21.
8. 1871 England Census, Lancashire, Chorlton on Medlock, District 21.
9. The 1871 census shows a maid, Sophia Agars, thirty-eight years old, living with Lucy. This could be S.
10. Amelia Edwards, *Untrodden Peaks and Unfrequented Valleys: A Midsummer Ramble in the Dolomites* (London: Longmans, Green, 1873), 319–22.
11. Moon, *More Usefully Employed,* 93–94.
12. Gerald N. Wachs Collection of Nineteenth Century English Poetry,

University of Chicago Special Collections, https://uchicagoscrc
.tumblr.com/post/163264111572/association-copies-ephemera-in
-the-gerald-n.

13. Moon, *More Usefully Employed*, 93.

14. Baptism records indicate that she was baptized in June 1833. Marriage records to William Norton Western in 1885 say she was fifty years old at the time.

15. Moon, *More Usefully Employed*, 112–13.

16. "Lane, Jenny," Griffith Institute, University of Oxford, http://archive
.griffith.ox.ac.uk/index.php/lane-jenny (accessed July 17, 2020).

17. Jenny Lane diaries, J. Lane MSS 1, J. Lane MSS 2, J. Lane MSS 3, Griffith Institute, University of Oxford.

18. Marianne Brocklehurst, *Miss Brocklehurst on the Nile* (Macclesfield: Millrace, 2004), 11.

19. Jean Bray, *The Lady of Sudeley* (Ebrington: Long Barn Books, 2000), 9; Margaret Serpico, *Beyond Beauty: Transforming the Body in Ancient Egypt* (London: Two Temple Place, 2016).

20. Bray, *The Lady of Sudeley*, 32.

21. Bray, *The Lady of Sudeley*, 88.

22. Moon, *More Usefully Employed*, 119.

23. Jenny Lane diaries, J. Lane MSS 1 first half, 4 September 1873 to 24 March 1874, Griffith Institute, University of Oxford, 29 November 1873, 76.

24. Jenny Lane diaries, J. Lane MSS 1 first half, 4 September 1873 to 24 March 1874, Griffith Institute, University of Oxford, 29 November 1873, 76.

25. Jenny Lane diaries, J. Lane MSS 1 first half, 4 September 1873 to 24 March 1874, Griffith Institute, University of Oxford, 30 November 1873, 78.

26. Karl Baedeker, ed., *Egypt: Handbook for Travellers* (Leipsic: Karl Baedeker, 1898), 28.

27. Baedeker's *Egypt* (1898), 28.

28. Brocklehurst, *Miss Brocklehurst on the Nile*, 12.

29. Peter Lyth, "Carry On Up the Nile: The Tourist Gaze and the British Experience of Egypt, 1818–1932," in *The British Abroad Since the Eighteenth Century, Volume 1: Travellers and Tourists*, eds. Martin Farr and Xavier Guégan (London: Palgrave Macmillan, 2013), 176–93.

30. Edwards says that it was the twenty-ninth, Lane's journals mark the date as the thirtieth.

31. Edwards, *A Thousand Miles*, 20.

32. Jenny Lane diaries, J. Lane MSS 1 first half, 4 September 1873 to 24 March 1874, Griffith Institute, University of Oxford, 10 December 1873, 84–85.

33. Jenny Lane diaries, J. Lane MSS 1 first half, 4 September 1873 to 24 March 1874, Griffith Institute, University of Oxford, 3 December 1873, 80.

34. Jenny Lane diaries, J. Lane MSS 1 first half, 4 September 1873 to 24 March 1874, Griffith Institute, University of Oxford, 8 December 1873, 87.

35. Edwards, *A Thousand Miles,* 28.

36. Jenny Lane diaries, J. Lane MSS 1 first half, 4 September 1873 to 24 March 1874, Griffith Institute, University of Oxford, 5–6 December 1873, 81–83.

37. Jenny Lane diaries, J. Lane MSS 1 first half, 4 September 1873 to 24 March 1874, Griffith Institute, University of Oxford, 11 December 1873, 85–86.

38. Edwards, *A Thousand Miles,* 31.

39. Edwards, *A Thousand Miles,* 30.

40. Jenny Lane diaries, J. Lane MSS 1 first half, 4 September 1873 to 24 March 1874, Griffith Institute, University of Oxford, 12 December 1873, 87.

41. Jenny Lane diaries, J. Lane MSS 1 first half, 4 September 1873 to 24 March 1874, Griffith Institute, University of Oxford, 13 December 1873, 88; Edwards, *A Thousand Miles,* 60.

42. Edwards, *A Thousand Miles,* 58–61.

43. Edwards, *A Thousand Miles,* 60.

44. Edwards, *A Thousand Miles,* 449–50.

45. Edwards, *A Thousand Miles,* 450.

46. Brocklehurst, *Miss Brocklehurst on the Nile,* 107–16.

47. Brocklehurst, *Miss Brocklehurst on the Nile,* 109.

48. Brocklehurst, *Miss Brocklehurst on the Nile,* 109.

49. Brocklehurst, *Miss Brocklehurst on the Nile,* 113.

50. Brocklehurst, *Miss Brocklehurst on the Nile,* 115.

51. Brocklehurst, *Miss Brocklehurst on the Nile,* 115–16.

52. Edwards, *A Thousand Miles,* 466.

53. Edwards, *A Thousand Miles,* 466.

54. Edwards, *A Thousand Miles,* 466.

55. Jenny Lane diaries, J. Lane MSS 2 Journal 2, 1 May to 29 June 1874, Griffith Institute, University of Oxford, 6 May 1874, 4.

56. Jenny Lane diaries, J. Lane MSS 2 Journal 2, 1 May to 29 June 1874, Griffith Institute, University of Oxford, 19 May 1874, 23.

57. Jenny Lane diaries, J. Lane MSS 3 Journal 3, 26 February to 6 March 1876, Griffith Institute, University of Oxford.

58. Photograph album, J. Lane MSS 4, Griffith Institute, University of Oxford.

59. Thelma Whistow, *Marianne Brocklehurst: Benefactor, Explorer, Artist;*

Her Life and Times 1832–1898 (Macclesfield: Macclesfield Museums Trust, 2004); Serpico, *Beyond Beauty*, 72–73; Rosalie David, *The Macclesfield Collection of Egyptian Antiquities* (Warminster: Aris & Phillips, 1980).

60. Brocklehurst, *Miss Brocklehurst on the Nile*, 117.

61. Edwards, *A Thousand Miles*, 70.

62. Moon, *More Usefully Employed*, 149.

63. Edwards, *A Thousand Miles*, 8.

64. Edwards, *A Thousand Miles*, 13.

65. Moon, *More Usefully Employed*, 153–57.

66. Moon, *More Usefully Employed*, 160.

67. Moon, *More Usefully Employed*, 161; Morris Bierbrier, *Who Was Who in Egyptology*, 5th rev. ed. (London: Egypt Exploration Society, 2019), 374.

68. Moon, *More Usefully Employed*, 162.

69. *The Academy* (June 19, 1880); Moon, *More Usefully Employed*, 165.

70. Moon, *More Usefully Employed*, 169–70.

71. Moon, *More Usefully Employed*, 171.

72. Serpico, *Beyond Beauty*, 71.

73. Donald Malcolm Reid, "The Urabi Revolution and the British Conquest, 1879–1882," in *The Cambridge History of Egypt*, vol. 2, ed. M. W. Daly (Cambridge: Cambridge University Press, 1999), 217–38.

74. John M. Adams, *The Millionaire and the Mummies: Theodore Davis's Gilded Age in the Valley of the Kings* (New York: St. Martin's Press, 2013), 31.

75. Jason Thompson, *Wonderful Things: A History of Egyptology, Volume 2: The Golden Age: 1881–1914* (Cairo: AUC Press, 2015), 14.

76. Thompson, *Wonderful Things: The Golden Age*, 15.

77. John Gardner Wilkinson, *Murray's Handbook for Travellers Egypt: Including Descriptions of the Course of the Nile to the Second Cataract, Alexandria, Cairo, the Pyramids, and Thebes, the Overland Transit to India, the Peninsula of Mount Sinai, the Oases, &c.; Condensed from "Modern Egypt and Thebes"* (London: John Murray, 1867).

78. E. Naville, *The Store-City of Pithom and the Route of the Exodus* (London: Egypt Exploration Fund, 1885).

79. W. M. F. Petrie, *The Pyramids and Temples of Gizeh* (London: Field and Tuer, 1883).

80. W. M. F. Petrie, *Tanis. Part I: 1883–4, Second Memoir of the Egypt Exploration Fund* (London: Trübner & Co., 1885).

81. Thompson, *Wonderful Things: The Golden Age*, 18.

82. Petrie, *Tanis. Part I: 1883–4*; W. M. F. Petrie, *Tanis. Part II: Nebesheh and Defenneh, Fourth Memoir of the Egypt Exploration Fund* (London: Trübner & Co., 1888).

83. W. M. F. Petrie, *Racial Photographs from the Egyptian Monuments* (London: R. C. Murray, 1887); Kathleen Sheppard, "Flinders Petrie and Eugenics at UCL," *Bulletin of the History of Archaeology* 20, no. 1 (2010): 16–29.

84. Moon, *More Usefully Employed*, 214.

85. "List of Excavations in Egypt by the British 1880–1980," Artefacts of Excavation, British Excavations in Egypt 1880–1980, The Griffith Institute, University of Oxford, https://egyptartefacts.griffith.ox.ac.uk /excavations-index.

86. Moon, *More Usefully Employed*, 219.

87. Moon, *More Usefully Employed*, 219, 238.

88. Moon, *More Usefully Employed*, 220.

89. Moon, *More Usefully Employed*, 233.

90. Moon, *More Usefully Employed*, 234.

91. Amelia Edwards, *Pharaohs, Fellahs and Explorers* (London: Osgood, McIlvaine, 1891).

92. Edwards, *Pharaohs, Fellahs and Explorers*, vi.

93. A. H. Sayce, "*Pharaohs, Fellahs and Explorers*. By Amelia B. Edwards," *The Academy* (February 13, 1892), 163.

94. Sayce, "*Pharaohs, Fellahs and Explorers*. By Amelia B. Edwards," 164.

95. Quoted in Rosalind Janssen, *The First Hundred Years: Egyptology at University College London, 1892–1992* (London: UCL Press, 1992), 2; also Margaret Drower, *Flinders Petrie: A Life in Archaeology* (Madison: University of Wisconsin Press, 1985), 200.

96. Joan Rees, *Women on the Nile: Writings of Harriet Martineau, Florence Nightingale, and Amelia Edwards* (London: Stacey International, 2008), 101.

97. Janssen, *First Hundred Years*, 2.

98. Janssen, *First Hundred Years*, 2.

99. Quoted in Janssen, *First Hundred Years*, 3.

100. Janssen, *First Hundred Years*, 3.

101. Brocklehurst to Newberry, 5 April 1896, NEWB2/106, Griffith Institute, University of Oxford.

2. Maggie Benson and Nettie Gourlay

1. Amara Thornton, *Archaeologists in Print: Publishing for the People* (London: UCL Press, 2018), 69–70.

2. A. C. Benson, *Life and Letters of Maggie Benson* (London: John Murray, 1917), 118.

3. Simon Goldhill, *A Very Queer Family Indeed: Sex, Religion, and the Bensons in Victorian Britain* (Chicago: University of Chicago Press, 2016).

4. Rodney Bolt, *As Good as God, as Clever as the Devil: The Impossible Life of Mary Benson* (London: Atlantic Books, 2011).

5. Benson, *Life and Letters*, 3–4.

6. Benson, *Life and Letters*, 4.

7. Benson, *Life and Letters*, 50.

8. Benson, *Life and Letters*, 248.

9. Emma Andrews Diaries, January 11, 1890. Egyptian Art Department, Metropolitan Museum of Art, New York City, 38.

10. Benson to her mother, 11 March 1894, in *Life and Letters*, 177.

11. Benson to her mother, 11 March 1894, in *Life and Letters*, 178.

12. Baedeker's *Egypt* (1892), 101–2.

13. E. F. Benson, *Our Family Affairs* (London: George H. Doran, 1921), 312–13.

14. Margaret Benson and Janet Gourlay, *The Temple of Mut in Asher* (London: John Murray, 1899), 8.

15. Betsy M. Bryan, "The Temple of Mut: New Evidence on Hatshepsut's Building Activity," in *Hatshepsut: From Queen to Pharaoh*, ed. Catharine H. Roehrig (New York: The Metropolitan Museum of Art, 2005), 181–83; Kara Cooney, *The Woman Who Would Be King: Hatshepsut's Rise to Power in Ancient Egypt* (New York: Crown Publishers, 2014).

16. Benson and Gourlay, *The Temple of Mut*, 10.

17. Auguste Mariette, *Karnak: Étude Topographique et Archéologique* (Leipzig: J. C. Hinrichs, 1875).

18. Benson to her mother, 2 January 1895, in *Life and Letters*, 190.

19. Benson to her mother, 2 January 1895, in *Life and Letters*, 190.

20. Benson and Gourlay, *The Temple of Mut*, 26.

21. Benson, *Our Family Affairs*, 313–14.

22. Benson and Gourlay, *The Temple of Mut*, 14. Five pence is equal to around £6.62 today, or around $9. But purchasing power has changed quite a bit in the last century.

23. Benson to her mother, 2 January 1895, *Life and Letters*, 190.

24. Benson and Gourlay, *The Temple of Mut*, 25.

25. Benson and Gourlay, *The Temple of Mut*, 31.

26. Benson and Gourlay, *The Temple of Mut*, 32–33, 189–90.

27. Benson and Gourlay, *The Temple of Mut*, 32.

28. Benson to her father, 13 February 1895, in *Life and Letters*, 192–93.

29. Benson and Gourlay, *The Temple of Mut*, 35. The statue's number at the Egyptian Museum in Cairo is CG 566.

30. Benson to her mother, 2 January 1895, in *Life and Letters*, 191.

31. Fred Benson to his mother, in *Life and Letters*, 201.

32. Passenger list for Cook's Nile Service, P.S. *Tewfik*, Black Box 1, Thomas Cook Archives, formerly in the Thomas Cook corporate offices, Peterborough, UK.

33. Benson, *Life and Letters*, 420.

34. Kathleen Sheppard, "'Constant Companions' and 'Intimate Friends': The Lives and Careers of Maggie Benson and Nettie Gourlay," *Lady Science* (June 2019), https://www.ladyscience.com/constant -companions-and-intimate-friends/no57?rq=sheppard.
35. Benson to her mother, 18 May 1896, in *Life and Letters,* 206–7.
36. Benson to her mother, 20 February 1896, in *Life and Letters,* 203.
37. See Sheppard, "'Constant Companions' and 'Intimate Friends.'"
38. Benson and Gourlay, *The Temple of Mut,* 38–39.
39. Benson to her mother, 14 February 1896, in *Life and Letters,* 202.
40. Benson and Gourlay, *The Temple of Mut,* 237.
41. Benson to Gourlay, 10 August 1896, in *Life and Letters,* 216.
42. Benson to Gourlay, 28 August 1896, in *Life and Letters,* 220.
43. Benson, *Life and Letters,* 144.
44. Benson to Gourlay, 28 August 1896, in *Life and Letters,* 221.
45. Gourlay to Newberry, 18 June 1896, NEWB2/317, Griffith Institute, University of Oxford.
46. Gourlay to Newberry, 16 November 1896, NEWB2/317, Griffith Institute, University of Oxford.
47. Gourlay to Newberry, 12 December 1898, NEWB2/317, Griffith Institute, University of Oxford.
48. William H. Peck, "E. F. Benson in Egypt," http://williamhpeck.org/e _f_benson_in_egypt.
49. Benson and Gourlay, *The Temple of Mut,* 64.
50. Benson and Gourlay, *The Temple of Mut,* 65, 357.
51. Benson and Gourlay, *The Temple of Mut,* 63.
52. Benson and Gourlay, *The Temple of Mut,* 21.
53. Benson and Gourlay, *The Temple of Mut,* 21.
54. Baedeker's *Egypt* (1898), 225; Peck, "E. F. Benson in Egypt."
55. Gourlay to Newberry, 13 December 1900, NEWB2/317, Griffith Institute, University of Oxford.
56. Benson, *Life and Letters,* 391.
57. Benson and Gourlay, *The Temple of Mut,* 402.
58. Bertha Porter and Rosalind L. B. Moss, *Topographical Bibliography of Ancient Egyptian Hieroglyphic Texts, Reliefs, and Paintings, II: Theban Temples,* 2nd ed. (Oxford: Clarendon Press, 1972), 259–61.

3. Emma Andrews

1. Adams, *Millionaire and the Mummies,* 233.
2. Percy Newberry, *The Amherst Papyri: Being an Account of the Egyptian Papyri in the Collection of Lord Amherst of Hackney* (London: Bernard Quaritch, 1899); Percy Newberry, *The Life of Rekhmara: Vezir of Upper Egypt Under Thothmes III and Amenhetep II (circa B.C. 1471–1448)* (London: A. Constable, 1900).

3. Andrews to Newberry, 24 August 1900, NEWB2/019/3/2, Griffith Institute, University of Oxford.

4. Andrews to Newberry, 18 September 1900, NEWB2/019/3/3, Griffith Institute, University of Oxford.

5. Adams, *Millionaire and the Mummies,* 30–33.

6. "Queer Compact Entered Into by a Couple, One of Whom Is Dead," *Cincinnati Enquirer,* August 29, 1897, 1.

7. "Queer Compact Entered Into by a Couple, One of Whom Is Dead," *Cincinnati Enquirer,* August 29, 1897, 1.

8. Ruth Ellen Patton Totten, *The Button Box: A Daughter's Loving Memoir of Mrs. George S. Patton* (Columbia: University of Missouri Press, 2011), 32.

9. Chris Naunton, *Searching for the Lost Tombs of Egypt* (London: Thames and Hudson, 2018), 57–90.

10. ARCE, "Development of Tombs in the Valley of the Kings," https://thebanmappingproject.com/articles/development-tombs-valley-kings.

11. The typewritten copies of her diaries are available in physical form in the Metropolitan Museum of Art's Egyptian Art Department archives. They are available online at the American Philosophical Society. Sarah Ketchley's team at the University of Washington has transcribed them for an online digital project called the Emma B. Andrews Diary Project, http://www.emmabandrews.org/project/ (visited September 28, 2023). See also Sarah Ketchley, "Witnessing the 'Golden Age': The Diaries of Mrs. Emma B. Andrews," *Kmt, Modern Journal of Ancient Egypt* 31:4 (2020–21): 32–43.

12. Andrews Diaries, December 12, 1889.

13. Andrews Diaries, December 12, 1889.

14. Lyth, "Carry On Up the Nile," 184.

15. Passenger List P.S. "Sethi" Leaving Cairo February 7th 1890 with Private Party, Black Box 2, Thomas Cook Archives, formerly in the Thomas Cook corporate offices, Peterborough, UK.

16. Andrews Diaries, December 29, 1889.

17. Adams, *Millionaire and the Mummies,* 51. Emma was likely on the boat, too, but she didn't mention his evening visit; Carter had recorded it in his journal. Nicolas Reeves and John H. Taylor, *Howard Carter Before Tutankhamun* (New York: Harry Abrams, 1993), 55.

18. Robb de P. Tytus, *A Preliminary Report on the Re-excavation of the Palace of Amenhetep III* (New York: The Winthrop Press, 1903).

19. Percy Newberry, *Scarabs: An Introduction to the Study of Egyptian Seals and Signet Rings* (London: Archibald Constable, 1906), iii.

20. Earl E. Elder, *Vindicating a Vision: The Story of the American Mission in Egypt, 1854–1954* (Philadelphia: The United Presbyterian Board of Foreign Missions, 1958).

21. Andrews Diaries, February 3, 1902.

22. See, for example, Andrew Porter, ed., *The Imperial Horizons of British Protestant Missions, 1880–1914* (Grand Rapids, MI: Wm. B. Eerdmans, 2003).

23. Andrews Diaries, February 3, 1902.

24. Theodore M. Davis, *The Tomb of Iouiya and Touiyou* (London: Archibald Constable & Co., 1907), xxv.

25. Davis, *Tomb of Iouiya and Touiyou,* xxv.

26. Joseph Lindon Smith, *Tombs, Temples & Ancient Art,* ed. Corinna Lindon Smith (Norman: University of Oklahoma Press, 1956), 27.

27. Smith, *Tombs, Temples & Ancient Art,* 27; Andrews Diaries; Davis, *Tomb of Iouiya and Touiyou.*

28. Davis, *Tomb of Iouiya and Touiyou,* xxvi.

29. Andrews Diaries, February 12, 1905.

30. Smith, *Tombs, Temples & Ancient Art,* 27–30.

31. Cars probably hadn't been introduced as far south as Luxor in 1905, as they had just arrived in Egypt in 1904. By the end of 1905, there were about 160 cars total in Egypt (Samir Raafat, "A History of Motoring in Egypt," *Egyptian Gazette* [March 2, 1997]).

32. Andrews Diaries, February 13, 1905.

33. Davis, *Tomb of Iouiya and Touiyou,* xxviii.

34. Smith, *Tombs, Temples & Ancient Art,* 33.

35. Smith, *Tombs, Temples & Ancient Art,* 35–36.

36. Andrews Diaries, February 13, 1905.

37. Toby Wilkinson and Julian Platt, *Aristocrats and Archaeologists: An Edwardian Journey on the Nile* (Cairo: AUC Press, 2017).

38. Gaston Maspero, *Guide to the Cairo Museum,* trans. J. E. and A. A. Quibell (Cairo: IFAO Institute, 1908), 496–97.

39. Maspero, *Guide to the Cairo Museum,* 497.

40. Andrews Diaries, February 8, 1906.

41. Andrews Diaries, February 8, 1906.

42. Accession number 12.183.5, not on public view.

43. Andrews Diaries, January 12, 1907.

44. Theodore Davis, "The Finding of the Tomb of Queen Tiyi," in *The Tomb of Queen Tiyi* (London: Constable and Co., 1910), 1.

45. Davis, "Finding of the Tomb of Queen Tiyi," 2.

46. Andrews Diaries, January 9, 1907.

47. Andrews Diaries, January 9, 1907.

48. Nicholas Reeves and Richard H. Wilkinson, *The Complete Valley of the Kings: Tombs and Treasures of Egypt's Greatest Pharaohs* (London: Thames and Hudson, 1996), 150.

49. Gaston Maspero, *Egypt: Ancient Sites and Modern Scenes,* trans. Elizabeth Lee (London: Unwin, 1910), 5.

50. Smith, *Tombs, Temples & Ancient Art,* 55–57.

51. Andrews Diaries, January 19, 1907.

52. Reeves and Wilkinson, *Complete Valley of the Kings,* 119–20.

53. Andrews Diaries, January 25, 1907.

54. Reeves and Wilkinson, *Complete Valley of the Kings,* 120.

55. G. Elliot Smith, "A Note on the Estimate of the Age Attained by the Person Whose Skeleton Was Found in the Tomb," in Davis, *Tomb of Queen Tiyi,* xxiii–xxiv.

56. Reeves and Wilkinson, *Complete Valley of the Kings,* 78.

57. Adams, *Millionaire and the Mummies,* 126–32, and Smith, *Tombs, Temples & Ancient Art,* for example.

58. Andrews Diaries, December 24, 1911.

59. Andrews Diaries, May 29, 1912.

60. Theodore Davis, *The Tombs of Harmhabi and Touatânkhamanou* (London: Constable and Co., 1912), 3.

61. Adams, *Millionaire and the Mummies,* 301–2.

62. Contract between Newberry and Davis to purchase the *Bedauin,* NEWB1/06, Griffith Institute, University of Oxford. Conversion done on the Bank of England inflation calculator, https://www.bankofengland.co.uk/monetary-policy/inflation/inflation-calculator (accessed September 23, 2023).

63. Elder, *Vindicating a Vision,* 137–38.

64. Elder, *Vindicating a Vision,* 133.

4. Margaret Alice Murray

1. For further reading about Margaret Murray, see Kathleen Sheppard, *The Life of Margaret Alice Murray: A Woman's Work in Archaeology* (Lanham, MD: Lexington Books, 2013).

2. Margaret A. Murray, *The Osireion at Abydos* (London: Bernard Quaritch, 1904), 3.

3. "Professor Flinders Petrie on Egyptology," *The Times* (London), January 16, 1893, 8.

4. Adolf Erman, *Egyptian Grammar,* trans. James Breasted (London: Williams and Norgate, 1894).

5. Janssen, *First Hundred Years,* 13.

6. Guy Brunton, Margaret Murray, and Flinders Petrie, *Lahun: The Treasure* (London: British School of Archaeology in Egypt, 1920).

7. Winifred Brunton, *Kings and Queens of Ancient Egypt* (London: Hodder and Stoughton, 1926).

8. Margaret Murray, "Queen Hatshepsut," in Brunton, *Kings and Queens of Ancient Egypt,* 53–66; Margaret Murray, "Sety I," in Brunton, *Kings and Queens of Ancient Egypt,* 119–32.

9. Barry Kemp, "Abydos," in *Excavating Egypt: The Egypt Exploration Society 1882–1982,* ed. T. G. H. James (Chicago: University of Chicago Press, 1992), 85.

10. Raymond O. Faulkner, *A Concise Dictionary of Middle Egyptian* (Oxford: Griffith Institute, 1962), 12.

11. *The Weekly Weather Report of the Meteorological Office for the Year 1908,* vol. 25, new series (London: Darling & Son, 1909), 129–50, https://digital.nmla.metoffice.gov.uk/IO_b5263ea3–90d4–419e-bd2e-c5a76f9414b5/ (accessed July 7, 2022).

12. See also Kathleen Sheppard, "Between Spectacle and Science: Margaret Murray and the Tomb of the Two Brothers," *Science in Context* 25:4 (2012): 525–49.

13. Samuel J. M. M. Alberti, *Nature and Culture: Objects, Disciplines and the Manchester Museum* (Manchester: Manchester University Press, 2009), 124–26.

14. Margaret A. Murray, *The Tomb of the Two Brothers* (Manchester: Sherratt & Hughes, 1910), 8.

15. Rosalie David, *The Two Brothers: Death and Afterlife in Middle Kingdom Egypt* (Bolton: Rutherford, 2007), 2.

16. Murray, *Tomb of the Two Brothers,* 32.

17. "The Mummy of Khnumu Nekht of the XII Dynasty (About 2500 BC)," *Manchester Guardian,* May 7, 1908.

18. "Khnumu Nekht," *Manchester Evening Chronicle,* May 8, 1908.

19. Murray, *Tomb of the Two Brothers,* 7.

20. David, *The Two Brothers;* Campbell Price, "Interpreting the 'Two Brothers' at Manchester Museum: Science, Knowledge and Display," *Archaeologies* 19 (2023): 104–28, https://doi.org/10.1007/s11759-023-09475-4.

21. Margaret Murray, *The Witch-Cult in Western Europe: A Study in Anthropology* (Oxford: Oxford University Press, 1921).

22. Margaret Murray, *My First Hundred Years* (London: William Kimber, 1963), 166.

5. Kate Griffith and Emily Paterson

1. Kate Bradbury to Jane Bradbury, 4 July 1878, RH MS 965, Box 3, Folder 10, Grant-Bradbury Family papers, Kenneth Spencer Research Library, University of Kansas.

2. Richard Unwin, *Riversvale Hall: The Story of a Victorian Country House* (Failsworth: Failsworth Historical Society, 2011).

3. Patterson, E Miss, 11 July 1888, Private Statement Copy, Amelia Edwards, Archives of the Egypt Exploration Society.

4. Patterson, E Miss, 11 July 1888, Private Statement Copy, Amelia Edwards, Archives of the Egypt Exploration Society.

5. Patterson, E Miss, 11 July 1888, Private Statement Copy, Amelia Edwards, Archives of the Egypt Exploration Society.

6. Diarmid A. Finnegan, *The Voice of Science: British Scientists on the Lecture Circuit in Gilded Age America* (Pittsburgh: University of Pittsburgh Press, 2021).

7. Margaret C. Jones, *The Adventurous Life of Amelia B. Edwards: Egyptologist, Novelist, Activist* (London: Bloomsbury Academic, 2022), 133.

8. Rev. William Copley Winslow, Letter to Amelia Edwards, April 28, 1889, Lucy Gura Archive of the Egypt Exploration Society, EES. II.d.233.

9. Quoted in Moon, *More Usefully Employed*, 221.

10. Jones, *Adventurous Life of Amelia B. Edwards*, 134.

11. Roberta Muñoz, "Amelia Edwards in America—A Quiet Revolution in Archaeological Science," *Bulletin of the History of Archaeology* 27, no. 1 (December 28, 2017): DOI: 10.5334/bha-598.

12. Kate Bradbury's Journal, vol. 1, Griffith K. MSS. 17.58, 6, Griffith Institute, University of Oxford.

13. Kate Bradbury's Journal, vol. 1, Griffith K. MSS. 17.58, 6, Griffith Institute, University of Oxford.

14. Kate Bradbury's Journal, vol. 1, Griffith K. MSS. 17.58, 10, Griffith Institute, University of Oxford.

15. Kate Bradbury's Journal, vol. 1, Griffith K. MSS. 17.58, 14, Griffith Institute, University of Oxford.

16. Kate Bradbury's Journal, vol. 1, Griffith K. MSS. 17.58, 11–12, Griffith Institute, University of Oxford.

17. Kate Bradbury's Journal, vol. 1, Griffith K. MSS. 17.58, 12, Griffith Institute, University of Oxford.

18. Moon, *More Usefully Employed*, 224.

19. Anonymous, "Buried Cities: An Interesting Lecture by Miss Amelia B. Edwards," *Brooklyn Daily Eagle,* November 8, 1889.

20. Kate Bradbury's Journal, vol. 1, Griffith K. MSS. 17.58, 29, Griffith Institute, University of Oxford.

21. Kate Bradbury's Journal, vol. 1, Griffith K. MSS. 17.58, 88, Griffith Institute, University of Oxford.

22. Kate Bradbury's Journal, vol. 2, Griffith K. MSS. 17.58, 152, Griffith Institute, University of Oxford.

23. Kate Bradbury's Journal, vol. 2, Griffith K. MSS. 17.58, 166–67, Griffith Institute, University of Oxford.

24. Kate Bradbury's Journal, vol. 2, Griffith K. MSS. 17.58, 265, Griffith Institute, University of Oxford.

25. Kate Bradbury's Journal, vol. 2, Griffith K. MSS. 17.58, 270, Griffith Institute, University of Oxford.

26. Kate Bradbury's Journal, vol. 2, Griffith K. MSS. 17.58, 341, Griffith Institute, University of Oxford.

27. Finnegan, *Voice of Science.*

28. Muñoz, "Amelia Edwards in America."

29. Muñoz, "Amelia Edwards in America."

30. Jones, *Adventurous Life of Amelia B. Edwards,* 160.

31. EES.XII.e.21, Archives of the Egypt Exploration Society.

32. EES.XII.e.24, Archives of the Egypt Exploration Society.

33. Moon, *More Usefully Employed,* 240.

34. Jones, *Adventurous Life of Amelia B. Edwards,* 163.

35. Moon, *More Usefully Employed,* 242.

36. Jones, *Adventurous Life of Amelia B. Edwards,* 163.

37. Bradbury to Newberry, 22 May 1892, NEWB2/096 Griffith Institute, University of Oxford.

38. Bradbury to Newberry, 7 July 1892, NEWB2/096 Griffith Institute, University of Oxford.

39. EES.II.b.59, Archives of the Egypt Exploration Society.

40. EES.II.b.60, Archives of the Egypt Exploration Society.

41. William Copley Winslow, *The Truth about the Egypt Exploration Fund* (Boston, 1903).

42. Kate Bradbury to Jane Bradbury, 4 July 1878, Grant-Bradbury Family papers, RH MS 965, Box 3, Folder 10, Kenneth Spencer Research Library, University of Kansas.

43. Kate Bradbury to Jane Bradbury, 4 July 1878, Grant-Bradbury Family papers, RH MS 965, Box 3, Folder 10, Kenneth Spencer Research Library, University of Kansas.

44. "in a state of undress"; she likely meant this figuratively and literally.

45. Kate Bradbury to Jane Bradbury, 8 October 1878, Grant-Bradbury Family papers, RH MS 965, Box 3, Folder 10, Kenneth Spencer Research Library, University of Kansas.

46. Kate Bradbury to Aunt Mary Bradbury, 19 October 1896, Grant-Bradbury Family papers, RH MS 965, Box 3, Folder 12, Kenneth Spencer Research Library, University of Kansas.

47. Kate Bradbury to Aunt Mary Bradbury, 19 October 1896, Grant-Bradbury Family papers, RH MS 965, Box 3, Folder 12, Kenneth Spencer Research Library, University of Kansas.

48. Kate Bradbury to Aunt Mary Bradbury, 19 October 1896, Grant-Bradbury Family papers, RH MS 965, Box 3, Folder 12, Kenneth Spencer Research Library, University of Kansas.

49. Alfred Wiedemann, *The Ancient Egyptian Doctrine of the Immortality of the Soul,* trans. Kate Bradbury Griffith (London: H. Grevel & Co., 1895); Alfred Wiedemann, *Religion of the Ancient Egyptians,* trans. Kate Bradbury Griffith (London: H. Grevel & Co., 1897).

50. Emily Paterson Lecture Book, 1902–1908, Archives of the Egypt Exploration Society.

51. Alice Stevenson, *Scattered Finds: Archaeology, Egyptology and Museums* (London: UCL Press, 2019), 50.

52. "Notes and News," *Journal of Egyptian Archaeology,* 3. no. 2/3 (April–July 1916), 139–40, on p. 140.

53. Paterson to Gardiner, 29 January 1915, EES.XIV.c.3(1), Archives of the Egypt Exploration Society.

54. Paterson to Gardiner, 29 January 1915, EES.XIV.c.3(1), Archives of the Egypt Exploration Society.

55. Paterson to Gardiner, 29 January 1915, EES.XIV.c.3(2), Archives of the Egypt Exploration Society.

56. "Valley of the Tombs: Lord Carnarvon to Speak at Meeting Next Thursday," *The Times,* January 5, 1923, 10.

57. Mary C. Jonas to Newberry, 4 January 1923, NEWB2/419 26/60, Griffith Institute, University of Oxford.

58. Mary C. Jonas to Newberry, 5 January 1923, NEWB2/419 26/58, Griffith Institute, University of Oxford.

59. 16.X.1932, Folder: Paterson, Miss E. Archives of Egypt Exploration Society.

60. Julia Webb-Harvey, "Many Years of Devoted Friendship," https://museumofcornishlife.co.uk/2022/02/01/many-years-of-devoted-friendship/ (accessed December 14, 2022).

61. Mary C. Jonas to Paterson, 3 October 1928, Folder: Paterson, Miss E. Archives of Egypt Exploration Society.

62. Paterson to Robert Mond, 15 September 1931, Folder: Paterson, Miss E. Archives of Egypt Exploration Society.

63. Robert Mond to Paterson, 16 September 1931, Folder: Paterson, Miss E. Archives of Egypt Exploration Society.

64. Margaret Taylor to Mary C. Jonas, 10 September 1947, Folder: Paterson, Miss E. Archives of Egypt Exploration Society.

65. Museum of Cornish Life, "Many Years of Devoted Friendship," February 1, 2022, https://museumofcornishlife.co.uk/2022/02/01/many-years-of-devoted-friendship/ (accessed March 2, 2023); Museum of Cornish Life, "Under the Eaves: The Egyptian Collection," February 8, 2021, https://museumofcornishlife.co.uk/2021/02/08/under-the-eaves-the-egyptian-collection/ (accessed March 2, 2023).

66. Egypt Exploration Society, *Annual Report 1947,* 7.

6. Myrtle Broome and Amice Calverley

1. Myrtle Broome, Letter 34, October 25, 1929, Broome MSS, Myrtle Florence Broome Collection, Griffith Institute, University of Oxford.

2. Myrtle Broome, Letter 34, October 25, 1929, Broome MSS, Myrtle

Florence Broome Collection, Griffith Institute, University of Oxford.

3. Broome MSS, Myrtle Florence Broome Collection, Griffith Institute, University of Oxford.

4. Lee Young, *An Artist in Abydos: The Life and Letters of Myrtle Broome* (Cairo: AUC Press, 2021), 5.

5. John D. M. Green and Ros Henry, eds., *Olga Tufnell's "Perfect Journey": Letters and Photographs of an Archaeologist in the Levant and Mediterranean* (London: UCL Press, 2021).

6. Olga also wrote letters home over the course of her time in Egypt and her work in Palestine.

7. W. M. F. Petrie, *Antaeopolis: The Tombs of Qau* (London: British School of Archaeology in Egypt, 1930).

8. The name changed in April 2023 due to the colonial implications of the term "oriental." The term suggests the study of objects, not peoples or cultures, and the name was changed to reflect the shift.

9. W. Raymond Johnson and J. Brett McClain, "The Epigraphic Survey, 1924–2019," in *Discovering New Pasts: The OI at 100*, ed. Theo van den Hout (Chicago: University of Chicago Press, 2019): 191–95.

10. Christina Riggs, *Photographing Tutankhamun: Archaeology, Ancient Egypt, and the Archive* (London: Routledge, 2018).

11. Myrtle Broome, Letter 11, 26 December 1927, Broome MSS, Myrtle Florence Broome Collection, Griffith Institute, University of Oxford.

12. Barbara Lesko, "Amice Mary Calverley, 1896–1959," in *Breaking Ground: Women in Old World Archaeology*, Brown University online project, https://www.brown.edu/Research/Breaking_Ground/bios/Caverley_Amice%20Mary.pdf.

13. "The Temple of Seti I in Abydos," American Research Center in Egypt, https://www.arce.org/temple-seti-i-abydos (accessed September 26, 2023).

14. "The Temple of Seti I in Abydos," American Research Center in Egypt, https://www.arce.org/temple-seti-i-abydos (accessed September 26, 2023).

15. Alan H. Gardiner, ed., *The Temple of King Sethos I at Abydos, Volume I: The Chapels of Osiris, Isis and Horus*, copied by Amice M. Calverley, with the assistance of Myrtle F. Broome (London: Egypt Exploration Society and Chicago: The Oriental Institute, 1933), vii.

16. Mary Jonas to Amice Calverley, 29 April 1929, Papers relating to Miss Calverley, her work at Abydos and its suspension mostly pre-1949, Archives of Egypt Exploration Society.

17. Mary Jonas to Amice Calverley, 29 April 1929, Papers relating to Miss Calverley, her work at Abydos and its suspension mostly pre-1949, Archives of Egypt Exploration Society.

18. Alan Gardiner, "Report and plans for the season, 1929–1930," AB.-COR, Papers relating to Miss Calverley, her work at Abydos and its suspension mostly pre-1949, Archives of Egypt Exploration Society; Gardiner, *Temple of King Sethos I, Volume I*, vii.

19. Gardiner, *Temple of King Sethos I, Volume I*, vii.

20. Myrtle Broome, Letter 24, 30 September 1929, Broome MSS, Myrtle Florence Broome Collection, Griffith Institute, University of Oxford.

21. Myrtle Broome, Letter 25, 1 October 1929, Broome MSS, Myrtle Florence Broome Collection, Griffith Institute, University of Oxford.

22. Myrtle Broome, Letter 27, 5 October 1929, Broome MSS, Myrtle Florence Broome Collection, Griffith Institute, University of Oxford.

23. Myrtle Broome, Letter 27, 5 October 1929, Broome MSS, Myrtle Florence Broome Collection, Griffith Institute, University of Oxford.

24. Kemp, "Abydos," 86.

25. Kemp, "Abydos," 86.

26. Myrtle Broome, Letter 33, 21 October 1929, Broome MSS, Myrtle Florence Broome Collection, Griffith Institute, University of Oxford.

27. Myrtle Broome, Letter 33, 21 October 1929, Broome MSS, Myrtle Florence Broome Collection, Griffith Institute, University of Oxford.

28. Calverley to Jonas, n.d. (c. 1930), AB.COR, Papers relating to Miss Calverley, her work at Abydos and its suspension mostly pre-1949, Archives of Egypt Exploration Society.

29. Calverley to James Breasted, July 28 1930, Folder 5, Calverley, Amice 1930, Directors Correspondence, Box 085, 1009.2, Archives of the Institute for the Study of Ancient Cultures, Chicago.

30. Myrtle Broome, Letter 55A, 20 January 1930, Broome MSS, Myrtle Florence Broome Collection, Griffith Institute, University of Oxford.

31. Myrtle Broome, Letter 95, 8 December 1930, Broome MSS, Myrtle Florence Broome Collection, Griffith Institute, University of Oxford.

32. Breasted to Calverley, September 10, 1930, Folder 5, Calverley, Amice 1930, Directors Correspondence, Box 085, 1009.2, Archives of the Institute for the Study of Ancient Cultures, Chicago.

33. Myrtle Broome, Letter 96, 13 December 1930, Broome MSS, Myrtle Florence Broome Collection, Griffith Institute, University of Oxford.

34. W. R. Johnson, "Chapter 1—The Epigraphic Survey," in Krisztián Vértes, ed. *Digital Epigraphy*, 2nd edition, August 15, 2018, https://www.digital-epigraphy.com/publications/digital-epigraphy-second-edition-by-krisztian-vertes-and-the-epigraphic-survey/chapter-1-the-epigraphic-survey.

35. Myrtle Broome, Letter 95, 8 December 1930, Broome MSS, Myrtle Florence Broome Collection, Griffith Institute, University of Oxford.

36. Myrtle Broome, Letter 96, 13 December 1930, Broome MSS, Myrtle Florence Broome Collection, Griffith Institute, University of Oxford.

37. Myrtle Broome, Letter 96, 13 December 1930, Broome MSS, Myrtle Florence Broome Collection, Griffith Institute, University of Oxford.

38. Myrtle Broome, Letter 36, 30 October 1929, Broome MSS, Myrtle Florence Broome Collection, Griffith Institute, University of Oxford.

39. Myrtle Broome, Letter 40, 16 November 1929, Broome MSS, Myrtle Florence Broome Collection, Griffith Institute, University of Oxford.

40. Myrtle Broome, Letter 48, 16 December 1929, Broome MSS, Myrtle Florence Broome Collection, Griffith Institute, University of Oxford.

41. Myrtle Broome, Letter 146, 13 November 1931, Broome MSS, Myrtle Florence Broome Collection, Griffith Institute, University of Oxford.

42. Myrtle Broome, Letter 152, 4 December 1931, Broome MSS, Myrtle Florence Broome Collection, Griffith Institute, University of Oxford.

43. Myrtle Broome, Letter 185, 1 April [1932], Broome MSS, Myrtle Florence Broome Collection, Griffith Institute, University of Oxford.

44. Myrtle Broome, Letter 60, <2 February 1930>, Broome MSS, Myrtle Florence Broome Collection, Griffith Institute, University of Oxford.

45. Myrtle Broome, Letter 106, 16 January [1931], Broome MSS, Myrtle Florence Broome Collection, Griffith Institute, University of Oxford.

46. Myrtle Broome, Letters 49–50, 25–29 December 1929, Broome MSS, Myrtle Florence Broome Collection, Griffith Institute, University of Oxford.

47. Mary Jonas to Alan Gardiner, 27 December 1929, AB.COR, Abydos Sethos I, Archives of Egypt Exploration Society.

48. Myrtle Broome, Letter 68, 4 March 1930, Broome MSS, Myrtle Florence Broome Collection, Griffith Institute, University of Oxford.

49. Myrtle Broome, Letter 68, 4 March 1930, Broome MSS, Myrtle Florence Broome Collection, Griffith Institute, University of Oxford.

50. Myrtle Broome, Letter 69, 5 March 1930, Broome MSS, Myrtle Florence Broome Collection, Griffith Institute, University of Oxford.

51. Amice Calverley to Mary Jonas, 30 March 1930, AB.COR, Papers relating to Miss Calverley, her work at Abydos and its suspension mostly pre-1949, Archives of Egypt Exploration Society.

52. Myrtle Broome, Letter 72, <15 March 1930>, Broome MSS, Myrtle Florence Broome Collection, Griffith Institute, University of Oxford.

53. Myrtle Broome, Letter 51B, 2 January 1930, Broome MSS, Myrtle Florence Broome Collection, Griffith Institute, University of Oxford.

54. Amice Calverley to Mary Jonas, 30 March 1930, AB.COR, Papers relating to Miss Calverley, her work at Abydos and its suspension mostly pre-1949, Archives of Egypt Exploration Society.

55. Myrtle Broome, Letter 74, 19 March 1930; Letter 219, 3 March 1933, Broome MSS, Myrtle Florence Broome Collection, Griffith Institute, University of Oxford.

56. Myrtle Broome, Letter 115, 17 February 1931, Broome MSS, Myrtle Florence Broome Collection, Griffith Institute, University of Oxford.

57. Myrtle Broome, Letter 117, 22 February 1931, Broome MSS, Myrtle Florence Broome Collection, Griffith Institute, University of Oxford.

58. W. M. F. Petrie, *70 Years in Archaeology* (London: Low, Marston & Co., 1931), 199.

59. R. M. Graves to Calverley, 16 October 1931, Folder 001, Calverley, Amice 1931, Directors Correspondence Box 097, 1009.4, Archives of the Institute for the Study of Ancient Cultures, Chicago.

60. Petrie, *70 Years in Archaeology,* 200–201.

61. Myrtle Broome, Letter 34, 25 October 1929, Broome MSS, Myrtle Florence Broome Collection, Griffith Institute, University of Oxford.

62. Myrtle Broome, Letter 34, 25 October 1929, Broome MSS, Myrtle Florence Broome Collection, Griffith Institute, University of Oxford.

63. Susan Biddle has done an amazing job of summarizing and explaining many of these treatments here: https://blog.griffith.ox.ac.uk/doctors -parades/.

64. Amice Calverley to James Breasted, 17 April 1931, Folder 001, Calverley, Amice 1931. Directors Correspondence Box 097, 1009.4, Archives of the Institute for the Study of Ancient Cultures.

65. Alan H. Gardiner, ed., *The Temple of King Sethos I at Abydos, Volume II*: *The Chapels of Amen-Re', Re'-Harakhti, Ptah, and King Sethos,* copied by Amice M. Calverley, with the assistance of Myrtle F. Broome (London: Egypt Exploration Society and Chicago: The Oriental Institute, 1935).

66. Alan H. Gardiner, ed., "Introduction," *The Temple of King Sethos I at Abydos, Volume III: The Osiris Complex,* copied by Amice M. Calverley, with the assistance of Myrtle F. Broome (London: Egypt Exploration Society and Chicago: The Oriental Institute, 1938), vii.

67. John Wilson to Amice Calverley, 28 September 1948, Archives of the Institute for the Study of Ancient Cultures, Directors Correspondence Box 227, 1007.2, Folder 004.

68. John Wilson and Amice Calverley phone conversation notes, 27 October 1948, Archives of the Institute for the Study of Ancient Cultures, Directors Correspondence Box 227, 1007.2, Folder 004.

69. Amice Calverley to Thorkild Jacobsen, 22 December 1948, Archives of the Institute for the Study of Ancient Cultures, Directors Correspondence Box 227, 1007.2, Folder 004.

70. Amice Calverley to Thorkild Jacobsen, 22 December 1948, Archives of the Institute for the Study of Ancient Cultures, Directors Correspondence Box 227, 1007.2, Folder 004.

71. Amice Calverley, "Statement of the Action Taken to Remove the Embargo on the Abydos Work, and the Reasons for the Delays in Getting Any Decision on the Matter," February 8, 1949. Folder 18, Archives of

the Institute for the Study of Ancient Cultures, Directors Correspondence, 1949, Box 232 1007.3.

72. Quoted in Young, *An Artist in Abydos,* 215.

73. John Wilson to Amice Calverley, 22 February 1949, Folder 18 Directors Correspondence, 1949, Box 232 1007.3, Archives of the Institute for the Study of Ancient Cultures, Chicago.

74. Alan Gardiner, ed., *The Temple of King Sethos I at Abydos, Volume IV: The Second Hypostyle Hall,* copied by Amice M. Calverley, with the assistance of Myrtle F. Broome (London: Egypt Exploration Society and Chicago: The Oriental Institute, 1958).

75. Alan Gardiner, "Introduction," *The Temple of King Sethos I at Abydos, Volume IV,* vii.

76. Gardiner, "Introduction," *Temple of King Sethos I at Abydos, Volume IV,* vii.

77. T. G. H. James, "The Archaeological Survey," in T. G. H. James, *Excavating in Egypt: The Egypt Exploration Society, 1882–1982* (Chicago: University of Chicago Press, 1982), 155.

78. Fairman to Adams, 29 December 1964, AB.ST COR. Archives of the Egypt Exploration Society.

79. AB.ST COR. Archives of the Egypt Exploration Society.

80. Janet Leveson Gower, "Amice Mary Calverley," *Journal of Egyptian Archaeology* 45 (1959): 85–87.

81. Myrtle Broome, Letter 367, 28 January 1936, Broome MSS, Myrtle Florence Broome Collection, Griffith Institute, University of Oxford.

82. Amice Calverley, Farewell to Seti I, Abydos, Christmas, 1936, AB.-COR Abydos Sethos I, Archives of the Egypt Exploration Society.

7. Caroline Ransom Williams

1. Winifred E. Howe, *A History of the Metropolitan Museum of Art with a Chapter on the Early Institutions of Art in New York* (New York: Metropolitan Museum of Art, 1913), 229.

2. Howe, *History of the Metropolitan Museum of Art,* 309.

3. "The New Egyptian Galleries," *The Metropolitan Museum of Art Bulletin* 6, no. 11 (November 1911), 203–5.

4. Derek Strahan, "Grand Staircase, Metropolitan Museum of Art, New York City," Metropolitan Museum of Art, June 24, 2020, https://lostnewengland.com/tag/metropolitan-museum-of-art/; Logan Ward, "Museum Orientalism: East versus West in US American Museum Administration and Space, 1870–1910; Part One," *The Coalition of Master's Scholars on Material Culture,* October 7, 2021, https://cmsmc.org/publications/museum-orientalism-2.

5. According to the 1880 and 1900 US Censuses.

6. Archives of the Lake Erie College, personal communication with Jeanna Purses, director of the Lincoln Library.

7. See Lisa Colletta, ed., *The Legacy of the Grand Tour: New Essays on Travel, Literature, and Culture* (Lanham, MD: Rowman & Littlefield: 2015), especially Elisabetta Marino, "Three British Women Travelers in Egypt: Sophia Lane Poole, Lucie Duff Gordon, and Emmeline Lott," 51–70.

8. Llamarada, *Mount Holyoke Yearbook, Class of 1897*, 22.

9. Caroline Ransom to James Breasted, 31 January 1898, originals in Archives of the Institute for the Study of Ancient Cultures, Chicago, published in Kathleen L. Sheppard, ed., *"My Dear Miss Ransom . . .": Letters Between Caroline Ransom Williams and James Henry Breasted, 1898–1935* (Oxford: Archaeopress, 2018), 14.

10. Caroline Ransom to James Henry Breasted, 31 January 1898, in Sheppard, *"My Dear Miss Ransom . . . ,"* 14–15.

11. Caroline Ransom to James Breasted, 6 April 1898, in Sheppard, *"My Dear Miss Ransom . . . ,"* 16.

12. Caroline Ransom to Ludlow Bull, 10 April 1938. Archives, Institute for the Study of Ancient Cultures, 2.

13. Caroline Ransom to Ludlow Bull, 10 April 1938. Archives, Institute for the Study of Ancient Cultures, 3.

14. Robert Herbert, "History of Art at Mount Holyoke," unpublished manuscript, 52–53.

15. Caroline Ransom to James and Frances Breasted, 6 May 1900, in Sheppard, *"My Dear Miss Ransom . . . ,"* 16–17.

16. Sheppard, "Biographical Introduction," in *"My Dear Miss Ransom . . . ,"* 9.

17. Caroline L. Ransom, *Studies in Ancient Furniture: Couches and Beds of the Greeks, Etruscans, and Romans* (Chicago: Chicago University Press, 1905).

18. The Bryn Mawr College Egyptology Association, "Magic Lantern Slide Digitization Project," https://brynmawrcollegeegyptologyassoc iation.digital.brynmawr.edu/ongoing-project/.

19. In today's dollars, this would have been an increase from $72,600 to $101,642. The MMA initially offered her only $58,000.

20. Caroline Ransom to James Breasted, 12 May 1910, in Sheppard, *"My Dear Miss Ransom . . ."*

21. Christopher Gray, "Streetscapes: The Beresford, the San Remo, the Majestic, the El Dorado, the Century; Namesake Precursors of Central Park West's Towers," *New York Times*, September 14, 1997.

22. Caroline Ransom to James Breasted, 16 October 1910, in Sheppard, *"My Dear Miss Ransom . . . ,"* 33.

23. Caroline Ransom to James Breasted, 16 October 1910, in Sheppard, *"My Dear Miss Ransom . . . ,"* 32.

24. Caroline Ransom to James Breasted, 16 October 1910, in Sheppard, *"My Dear Miss Ransom . . . ,"* 33.

25. Caroline Ransom, *A Handbook of the Egyptian Rooms, Metropolitan Museum of Art* (New York: MMA, 1911); Caroline Ransom to James Breasted, 19 November 1911, in Sheppard, *"My Dear Miss Ransom . . . ,"* 38–39.

26. Caroline Ransom Williams to James Breasted, 25 January 1917, in Sheppard, *"My Dear Miss Ransom . . . ,"* 88–89.

27. Adams, *Millionaire and the Mummies,* 313–14.

28. Ransom, *A Handbook of the Egyptian Rooms* (1911); Caroline Ransom, "The Value of Photographs and Transparencies as Adjuncts to Museum Exhibits," *Metropolitan Museum of Art Bulletin* 7, no. 7 (1912): 132–34; Caroline Ransom, "Egyptian Furniture and Musical Instruments," *MMAB* 8, no. 4 (1913): 72–79; Caroline Ransom, "A Model of the Mastaba-Tomb of Userkaf-Ankh," *MMAB* 8, no. 6 (1913), 125–30; Caroline Ransom, "Nubian Objects Acquired by the Egyptian Department," *MMAB* 8, no. 9 (1913): 200–208; Caroline Ransom, "The Stela of Menthu-Weser," *MMAB* 8, no. 10 (1913): 213, 216–18; Caroline Ransom, "A Late Egyptian Sarcophagus," *MMAB* 9, no. 5 (1914): 112–20; Caroline Ransom, "Pots with Hieratic Inscriptions, *MMAB* 9, no. 11 (1914): 236–43; Caroline Ransom, "A Commemorative Scarab of Thutmose III," *MMAB* 10, no. 3 (1915): 46–47; Caroline Ransom, "Heart Scarab of Queen Amenardis," *MMAB* 10, no. 6 (1915): 116–17; Caroline Ransom, "Three Sets of Egyptian Gold Pendants," *MMAB* 10, no. 6 (1915): 117–20.

29. Caroline Ransom, *The Stela of Menthu-Weser* (New York: MMA, 1913). The stela is on display at the MMA in Gallery 110 (http://www.metmuseum.org/collection/the-collection-online/search/544320, accessed May 30, 2018). Today, the name is transliterated "Mentuwoser," but Ransom's book is titled with the old transliteration.

30. Ransom, *Stela of Menthu-Weser,* 5.

31. Caroline Ransom to James Breasted, 2 May 1913, in Sheppard, *"My Dear Miss Ransom . . . ,"* 58.

32. Albert Lythgoe and Caroline Ransom, *The Tomb of Perneb: With Illustrations* (New York: MMA, 1916).

33. Albert Lythgoe, "The History of the Tomb and the Principal Features of Its Construction," in Lythgoe and Ransom, *Tomb of Perneb,* 24–27.

34. Caroline Ransom to Albert Lythgoe, 7 May 1914, Archives of the Egyptian Art Department, MMA.

35. Lythgoe, "History of the Tomb," 40–42.

36. "Perneb's Gay Tomb Ready for Visitors," *New York Times,* January 30, 1916, 13.

37. Lythgoe, "History of the Tomb," 38–45.

38. Caroline Ransom to James Breasted, 7 February 1916, in Sheppard, *"My Dear Miss Ransom . . . ,"* 73.

39. Caroline Ransom to James Breasted, 18 January 1916, in Sheppard, *"My Dear Miss Ransom . . . ,"* 71.

40. James Breasted to Caroline Ransom, 10 February 1916, in Sheppard, *"My Dear Miss Ransom . . . ,"* 74.

41. Caroline Ransom, "A Study of the Decorative and Inscriptional Features of the Tomb," in Lythgoe and Ransom, *Tomb of Perneb,* 49.

42. Ransom, "Study of the Decorative and Inscriptional Features," 49.

43. Ransom, "Study of the Decorative and Inscriptional Features," 79.

44. Caroline Ransom, "A Model of the Mastaba-Tomb of Userkaf-Ankh," *MMAB* 8, no. 6 (1913): 125–30.

45. Caroline Ransom Williams, *The Decoration of the Tomb of Per-Neb: The Technique and the Color Conventions* (New York: MMA, 1932). After Ransom married Grant Williams in mid-1916, she changed her name to Caroline Ransom Williams. I will use her published name in citations and the name she herself used at any given time in the text.

46. Caroline Ransom to Albert Lythgoe, 7 April 1913, Williams, Carolyn [*sic*] L. Ransom 1909–1917, Egyptian Art Department Archives, Metropolitan Museum of Art.

47. Caroline Ransom to Albert Lythgoe, 28 March 1914, Williams, Carolyn [*sic*] L. Ransom 1909–1917, Egyptian Art Department Archives, Metropolitan Museum of Art.

48. Ransom, "Egyptian Furniture and Musical Instruments."

49. Albert Lythgoe to Caroline Ransom, 3 January 1912, Williams, Carolyn [*sic*] L. Ransom 1909–1917, Egyptian Art Department Archives, Metropolitan Museum of Art.

50. Caroline Ransom to James Breasted, 16 October 1910, in Sheppard, *"My Dear Miss Ransom . . . ,"* 33–34.

51. Caroline Ransom to Albert Lythgoe, 28 March 1914 and 11 April 1914, Williams, Carolyn [*sic*] L. Ransom 1909–1917, Egyptian Art Department Archives, Metropolitan Museum of Art.

52. Caroline Ransom to Albert Lythgoe, 28 March 1914, Williams, Carolyn [*sic*] L. Ransom 1909–1917, Egyptian Art Department Archives, Metropolitan Museum of Art.

53. Caroline Ransom to James Breasted, 2 September 1916, in Sheppard, *"My Dear Miss Ransom . . . ,"* 81–82.

54. Caroline Ransom Williams to Alan Gardiner, 19 July 1917, Gardiner MSS, 370.21–1, Griffith Institute, University of Oxford.

55. Caroline Ransom Williams to Alan Gardiner, 19 July 1917, Gardiner MSS, 370.21–1, Griffith Institute, University of Oxford.

56. Caroline Ransom Williams to James Breasted, 2 December 1916, in Sheppard, *"My Dear Miss Ransom . . . ,"* 85.

57. Dominique Navarro, "America's First Woman Egyptologist— Caroline Ransom Williams," *Digital Epigraphy: An Epigraphic Survey,* https://www.digital-epigraphy.com/reading/americas-first-woman -egyptologist-caroline-ransom-williams (accessed August 12, 2021).

58. Caroline Ransom Williams, "The Abbott Collection," *New-York Historical Society Quarterly Bulletin* 1, no. 2 (1917): 34–37.

59. In 1937, the Brooklyn Museum took it on loan; they purchased it from the NYHS in 1948.

60. James Breasted to Caroline Ransom Williams, 21 December 1916, in Sheppard, *"My Dear Miss Ransom . . . ,"* 86.

61. Caroline Ransom Williams to James Breasted, 16 January 1917, in Sheppard, *"My Dear Miss Ransom . . . ,"* 87.

62. "Notes: The Abbott Collection of Egyptian Antiquities," *New-York Historical Society Quarterly Bulletin* 1, no. 2 (1917): 12.

63. Caroline Ransom Williams, *The New-York Historical Society Catalogue of Egyptian Antiquities, Numbers 1–160: Gold and Silver Jewelry and Related Objects* (New York: NYHS, 1924).

64. Caroline Ransom Williams to James Breasted, 9 December 1921, in Sheppard, *"My Dear Miss Ransom . . . ,"* 125–26.

65. Caroline Ransom Williams to James Breasted, 9 February 1922, in Sheppard, *"My Dear Miss Ransom . . . ,"* 133–35.

66. Caroline Ransom Williams to James Breasted, 29 August 1926, in Sheppard, *"My Dear Miss Ransom . . . ,"* 183–86.

67. Caroline Ransom Williams to James Breasted, 22 November 1920, in Sheppard, *"My Dear Miss Ransom . . . ,"* 101–2.

68. Caroline Ransom Williams to James Breasted, 22 November 1920, in Sheppard, *"My Dear Miss Ransom . . . ,"* 102–3.

69. James Breasted, *The Edwin Smith Surgical Papyrus: Hieroglyphic Transliteration, Translation, and Commentary,* 2 vols. (Chicago: University of Chicago Press, 1930).

70. See James Breasted to Caroline Ransom Williams, 2 April 1930, in Sheppard, *"My Dear Miss Ransom . . . ,"* 215.

71. The Epigraphic Survey, *Medinet Habu, Volume I: Earlier Historical Records of Ramses III* (Chicago: University of Chicago Press, 1930).

72. Harold Nelson to James Breasted, 5 October 1926, Director's Correspondence, 1926, Nelson, Archives of the Institute for the Study of Ancient Cultures, Chicago.

73. Harold Nelson to James Breasted, 14 October 1926, Director's Correspondence, 1926, Nelson, Archives of the Institute for the Study of Ancient Cultures, Chicago.

74. Harold Nelson to James Breasted, 3 December 1926, Director's Correspondence, 1926, Nelson, Archives of the Institute for the Study of Ancient Cultures, Chicago.

75. James Breasted to Harold Nelson, 26 October 1926, Director's Correspondence, 1926, Nelson, Archives of the Institute for the Study of Ancient Cultures, Chicago.

76. Charles Nims, "The Publications of the Epigraphic Survey," *Oriental*

Institute 1973–1974 Annual Report (Chicago: Oriental Institute, 1974), 9; James Breasted, *The Oriental Institute*, The University of Chicago Survey, vol. 12 (Chicago: University of Chicago Press, 1933), 72.

77. Johnson, "Chapter 1—The Epigraphic Survey," https://www.digital -epigraphy.com/publications/digital-epigraphy-second-edition -by-krisztian-vertes-and-the-epigraphic-survey/chapter-1-the -epigraphic-survey.

78. Lesko, "Amice Mary Calverley," 5.

79. "Mrs. Grant Williams Returns from a Six Months Visit to Egypt," *Toledo Times*, April 29, 1927.

80. James Breasted to Caroline Ransom Williams, 27 July 1927, in Sheppard, *"My Dear Miss Ransom . . . ,"* 190–91.

81. Navarro, "America's First Woman Egyptologist."

82. Caroline Ransom Williams to James Breasted, 4 April 1934, in Sheppard, *"My Dear Miss Ransom . . . ,"* 243–44.

83. Sheppard, "Biographical Introduction," 12.

84. Caroline Ransom Williams to Ambrose Lansing, 12 September 1935, Williams, Carolyn [*sic*] Ransom 1931–1936, Archives of the Egyptian Art Department, Metropolitan Museum of Art.

85. Ambrose Lansing to Caroline Ransom Williams, 9 September 1935, Williams, Carolyn [*sic*] Ransom 1931–1936, Archives of the Egyptian Art Department, Metropolitan Museum of Art.

86. Ambrose Lansing to Caroline Ransom Williams, 25 October 1935, Williams, Carolyn [*sic*] Ransom 1931–1936 folder, Archives of the Egyptian Art Department, Metropolitan Museum of Art; Caroline Ransom Williams to Ambrose Lansing, 28 October 1935, Williams, Carolyn [*sic*] Ransom 1931–1936 folder, Archives of the Egyptian Art Department, Metropolitan Museum of Art.

87. Caroline Ransom Williams to Charles Breasted, 4 December 1935, in Sheppard, *"My Dear Miss Ransom . . . ,"* 280–81.

88. Jeffrey Abt, *American Egyptologist: The Life of James Henry Breasted and the Creation of His Oriental Institute* (Chicago: University of Chicago Press, 2011), 390.

89. Emily Teeter, pers. comm.

90. Caroline Ransom Williams to Alan Gardiner, 30 July 1936, Gardiner MSS, 370.1, Griffith Institute, University of Oxford.

91. "Toledo U. Confers Honorary Degrees," *Toledo Blade*, June 15, 1937.

92. "Honorary Degree Reveals Toledoan's Accomplishments," *Toledo Blade*, June 15, 1937.

93. Ethel Lewis, "Library on Egyptology Bares Secrets of Ancient Pharaohs in Toledo Home," *Toledo Times*, May 21, 1933.

94. Sheppard, "Epilogue," in *"My Dear Miss Ransom . . . ,"* 282.

95. Associated Press Staff, "Shepheard's Hotel Is Reported Ruined," *New York Times*, January 27, 1952, 1.

96. Associated Press Staff, "Shepheard's Hotel Is Reported Ruined."

97. *Toledo Sunday Blade*, January 27, 1952, 1.

98. *Toledo Blade*, February 2, 1952.

99. Barbara Grace Spayd, "Caroline Louise Ransom Williams, AM '00, PhD '05," *University of Chicago Magazine* (June 1952).

Image Permissions

Figure 1.1: Pearson, G. "The French House, Luxor" (1890). Rice University. https://hdl.handle.net/1911/21420. Public domain.

Figure 1.2: From *Pharaohs, Fellahs and Explorers* (1891). Public domain.

Figure 1.3: SC/LY/SP/ABE/524/Renshaw. Courtesy of the Principal and Fellows of Somerville College, Oxford.

Figure 1.4: J. Lane MSS 6. © Griffith Institute, University of Oxford.

Figure 1.5: Macclesfield Silk Heritage Trust.

Figure 2.1: From, *Life and Letters of Maggie Benson* (1917), p. 150. Public domain.

Figure 2.2: The Miriam and Ira D. Wallach Division of Art, Prints and Photographs: Print Collection, The New York Public Library. "E. F. Benson, author of 'The Relentless City' [from Harper's Weekly]." New York Public Library Digital Collections. Accessed May 18, 2023. https://digitalcollections.nypl.org/items/510d47dc-8fbc-a3d9-e040-e00a18064a99. Public domain.

Figure 2.3: From *The Temple of Mut in Asher* (1899), plate V. Public domain.

Figure 2.4: From *Life and Letters of Maggie Benson* (1917), p. 376. Public domain.

Figure 3.1: Theodore M. Davis Collection, Bequest of Theodore M. Davis, 1915. https://www.metmuseum.org/art/collection/search/544825. Public domain.

Figure 3.2: Lyon Archives photo 142. Courtesy of the Harvard Museum of the Ancient Near East.

Figure 3.3: The Miriam and Ira D. Wallach Division of Art, Prints and Photographs: Photography Collection, The New York Public Library Digital Collections. Accessed February 21, 2023. https://digitalcollections.nypl.org/items/510d47d9-60e8-a3d9-e040-e00a18064a99. Public Domain.

Figure 3.4: MS 3196, Box 360/Print 25. Reproduced with the permission of the Library of Birmingham.

Figure 3.5: American Philosophical Society, Creative Commons Attribution 4.0 License.

Figure 3.6: Egyptian Art Archives, The Metropolitan Museum of Art.

Figure 4.1: Petrie Journal 1901–1902, Petrie MSS 1.20, p. 3. © Griffith Institute, University of Oxford.

Figure 4.2: NPG x42538. Photographer is Lafayette, Ltd. © National Portrait Gallery, London.

Figure 4.3: Manchester Museum Archives. Courtesy of the Manchester Museum.

Figure 5.1: Courtesy of the Historic England West Listing team.

Figure 5.2: Griffith MSS 23.2 © Griffith Institute, University of Oxford.

Figure 5.3: SC/LY/SP/ABE/421. Courtesy of the Principal and Fellows of Somerville College, Oxford.

Figure 5.4: Photograph no.3 from Griffith MSS 17.58 "Photograph of Professor & Mrs. Kate Griffith." © Griffith Institute, University of Oxford.

Figure 6.1: Courtesy of the Institute for the Study of Ancient Cultures of the University of Chicago.

Figure 6.2: Courtesy of the Institute for the Study of Ancient Cultures of the University of Chicago.

Figure 6.3: Courtesy of The Egypt Exploration Society.

Figure 6.4: Courtesy of The Egypt Exploration Society.

Figure 7.1: Bryn Mawr College Yearbook. Public domain.

Figure 7.2: Metropolitan Museum of Art, https://www.metmuseum.org/art/collection/search/543937. Public domain.

Figure 7.3: Epigraphic Survey Negative 16278. Courtesy of the Institute for the Study of Ancient Cultures of the University of Chicago.

Figure 7.4: Epigraphic Survey Negative 19874. Courtesy of the Institute for the Study of Ancient Cultures of the University of Chicago.

Index

About the Author

Sean Elliott Photography

Kathleen Sheppard is professor of history at Missouri S&T in Rolla, Missouri. Sheppard earned her master's degree and Ph.D. in the history of science at the University of Oklahoma in 2006 and 2010. She earned a master's degree in Egyptian archaeology at University College London in 2002. Sheppard is the author of the scientific biography of Margaret Alice Murray (Lexington, 2013), the correspondence collection between Caroline Ransom Williams and James Henry Breasted from Archaeopress (2018), and most recently *Tea on the Terrace*, a book about the social networks of Egyptologists in the nineteenth century (Manchester, 2022).